GENDER, 'RACE' AND PATRIARCHY

For Martin

Gender, 'Race' and Patriarchy
A Study of South Asian Women

KALWANT BHOPAL
Thomas Coram Research Unit, Institute of Education
University of London

Ashgate

Aldershot • Brookfield USA • Singapore • Sydney

Published by
Ashgate Publishing Limited
Gower House
Croft Road
Aldershot
Hants GU11 3HR
England

Ashgate Publishing Company
Old Post Road
Brookfield
Vermont 05036
USA

British Library Cataloguing in Publication Data
Bhopal, Kalwant
  Gender, 'race' and patriarchy : a study of South Asian
  women. - (Interdisciplinary research series in ethnic,
  gender and class relations)
  1.Women - South Asia - Social conditions 2.South Asians -
  Social conditions
  I.Title
  305.4'8'8914

Library of Congress Catalog Card Number: 97-073610

Typesetting by Bad Seed Productions, London

ISBN 1 84014 139 5

Printed and bound by Athenaeum Press, Ltd.,
Gateshead, Tyne & Wear.

Contents

Figures and tables

Acknowledgements

I would like to thank the 60 women whose lives are represented in the research and for their time and willingness to participate. I would like to thank the Economic and Social Research Council for providing me with financial support to carry out the research. I would sincerely like to thank Sylvia Walby for sharing her expert knowledge and wisdom with me and for her support and encouragement. Thanks to Marie Derby (of Quantime) for her time in producing Labour Force Survey statistics. I would like to thank the following who have all supported me in different ways; Jaswant Bhopal, Rohit Barot, Harriet Bradley, Sarah Neal, Paul Connolly, Annie Phizacklea, Valerie Troop, Toby Brandon, Janet Ramsdale, Kirpal Singh and Doris Otomewo. Finally I would like to thank Martin Myers for the precious time he spent in typesetting and proof reading.

1 Introduction

Feminism and 'race'

Gender and feminism have emerged as important areas of study which have attempted to explain the position of women in society; the limited access of women to economic, social and political power, the nature of the sexual division of labour and those social expectations about the behaviour of women which limit and inhibit their achievements. This has raised the problem of how equality for women is to be achieved, or in feminist terms how the subordination of women is to be ended. Many feminists have attempted to understand, analyse and explain the subordination of women (Barrett 1980, Millett 1977, Mitchell 1971). These feminists have attacked traditional social theory for excluding and marginalising women and have specifically investigated women in order to include their experiences and render them legitimate. There is a growing body of literature on gender which examines women's position within households and families (Finch 1983, 1989, Oakley 1974) women and education (Deem 1978), women's exclusion and segregation from the labour market (Hakim 1979, Walby 1986), women and politics (Currell 1974, Kirkpatrick 1974), sexuality (Dworkin 1981, Mackinnon 1979) and violence (Brownmiller 1976, Pizzey 1974).

However, feminism has always been vulnerable to the accusation that its concerns and priorities reflect those of white, middle class women and conceal the variety and diversity of human experience and subjectivity. Some black[1] feminists (Collins 1990, Davis 1990), are now demanding that the experiences of women who have hitherto been marginalised become a central starting point rather than an optional extra for feminist theory and practice.

Some writers are also beginning to acknowledge their own limitations (Barret and Macintosh 1985). Ramazanoglu (1986) argues that the problem is not simply one of acknowledging that differences exist between black, third world and white women, but challenging the underlying assumptions that white women are the norm and that the experiences of black and third world women are some kind of 'alien' problem. This assumption not only denies the validity and primacy of these 'other' experiences,

1

but can often lead to simplistic generalisations with regard to all women. It can also deny the pain of racism in which white feminists can be the beneficiaries *and* perpetuators of the racism that many black women see as the primary experience of their lives.

For other writers, the solution is to develop a specifically black feminist approach based on black women's own experiences which sees racism as the central issue (Joseph 1981). However, the problem remains, just as the term 'man' marginalised women and the term 'women' marginalised 'non-white' women, so too the term 'black women' can marginalise some groups and ignore the vast economic and cultural differences amongst those the term supposedly encompasses. It can also ignore the class divisions and racism that may exist *within* and *between* 'black groups'. Nevertheless, the whole feminist project does insist that the category 'woman' is a meaningful one and a critical awareness of the problems involved in the use of such terms as 'white women' or 'black women' need not invalidate a use of the terms themselves or a political action based upon them. On a global scale, this means that the differences between women cannot be understood outside the context of colonialism, imperialism and nationalistic struggles for independence.

Other feminists (Davis 1990, King 1988) insist, not only that issues of class, sex and 'race' are inherently connected, but that a black feminist perspective is the most truly radical because:

> ...the necessity of addressing all forms of oppression is one of the hallmarks of black feminist thought (King 1988:43).

The idea of sisterhood which implies an oppression shared by all women, gives way to that of solidarity which is based upon an understanding that the struggles of all women are different, but interconnected. Gender divisions are not the only source of social inequality, for many women 'race' or class may be more important. This means simplistic assertions of the universality of women's experience are incorrect. These may deny the very real differences that exist amongst women and, by invoking a spurious sisterhood that takes white middle class women as the norm, can constitute a form of racism and elitism.

Rather than engaging in a sterile debate as to which is the most important, feminism can develop an analysis that recognises the interaction of different forms of oppression and does not treat women as a unitary category that can be abstracted from all other social relationships. Such an approach allows scope for solidarity to encourage a worldwide feminism based on the understanding that on a global scale, there are both underlying patterns of gender inequality and an enormous diversity of needs and experiences that divide as well as unite women. It is not simply a case of 'adding on' the perspectives of black women, but may involve a reassessment of understanding as a basis of that which feminism demands of male-stream theory.

The black female constituency as an object of political analysis is demarcated by the experience of 'race' and gender oppression. The response of feminists such as

2

Bhavnani and Coulson (1986), Carby (1982) and Parmar (1982), has been to establish the specificity of black women and their experiences. A black female constituency is further demarcated in many black feminist accounts by the experience of oppression (Carby 1982, Parmar 1982). It is this, which it is suggested, unites black women and places them in opposition to white women. The experiences of which black women speak, arise from being both black *and* female in a white society which may be racist. Oppression is organised around 'race' and gender divisions, with racial divisions being accorded a primacy in the establishment of political priorities. Racial oppression is presented as the result of forms of interaction between black women and black men, British society and a range of British social institutions in particular. Racial oppression is something which black women share with black men. Racial disadvantage and racism can be viewed in terms of practices, procedures and actions which have the effect of excluding, providing unequal access, or in some way disadvantaging black people.

Many accounts of 'race' and gender present oppression as an experience (see Feminist Review 1984) in which white women as well as black women experience sexism, but black women will also experience racism. One of the most challenging issues raised has been the need to recognise, debate and explain the extent to which there are differences *between* women. The recognition of difference and diversity, that women are a heterogenous group divided by class, 'race' and ethnicity, by nationality and religion, by age and sexual preference has slowly gained recognition in feminist analysis. Feminists (James and Busia 1993) are now constructing a greater understanding of the differences and diversities between women's lives, in different places and at different times. The term 'woman' is defined and used in various ways in different circumstances and the historical context of gender relations is specified.

In this sense, feminists (Knowles and Mercer 1992) have attempted to include the multiple 'others'. At the political level, the notion of a 'politics of identity', rather than politics based upon gender and class has gained credence. The idea that there is a clear homogeneity of (class and gender) interests is challenged and difference rather than commonality is placed at the centre. Such a politics of difference, also assists in the rejection of a hierarchy of oppressions, that certain oppressions are more salient than others. Rather than the abstract ranking of relations of power inherent in class, 'race', gender and sexual orientation, the focus has shifted to the ways in which each of these relations intertwine, reinforce and contradict each other in historically specific contexts. Thus, a complex view of feminist politics arose in which women from different class positions and ethnic backgrounds may unite on specific issues, but divide on others. It is important to insist continually on differences, as women cannot develop common political strategies while they have contradictory interests in class, 'race' and culture. The development of feminism has shown that the term 'woman' cannot be treated as a unitary category and interrelations of the sources of divisions between women must be identified. The idea of difference posed new problems for feminism, how to analyse theoretically and recognise politically both power *between* women and the way in which all women, *albeit differently*, were

3

implicated in dominant power structures. This provided the impetus to understand and work with commonalities as well as heterogeneity of experience and sensitivity to one another's cultural specificites, whilst at the same time construct common political strategies to confront sexism, racism and class inequality.

Culture itself is a complex term, frequently important to people's sense and identity of self. It is diverse. Communities have different values and ways of life. The definition of culture is not necessarily limited to religious beliefs, communal rituals or shared traditions. These interactions provide a way of life which define a social collectivity. Culture is not necessarily understood as what expresses the identity of a community, but may refer to the processes and categories by which communities are defined as such, how they are specific and different. The diverse bases of cultural differentiation include ethnicity, class, gender, religion, language and dress. Culture and ethnicity are defining and determining features of women's lives. Shared experience reveals diversity, as much as diversity reveals shared experience. There will be certain commonalities of perception shared by black women as a group such as 'race', culture and language but there will also be a variety of differences such as age, sexuality and experience.

The family and households

Feminists (Barrett 1980, Finch 1983, Oakley 1974) have argued that the family is the key site of oppression for women and we need to abolish the family in its existing form to achieve equality. Some black feminists however (Carby 1982, hooks 1984, Spellman 1990) maintain that the black family is a qualitatively different proposition from the family structure in which white women are involved. White feminists have responded to this, by acknowledging that black women in Britain live in different family arrangements. Barrett and Mackintosh (1985) regard this admission as an attempt to deal with what they consider the 'narrow ethnocentrism' of the women's movement. They maintain that the family is still a site for the perpetuation of gender inequalities which many black women may wish to escape.

I would argue that forms of households in contemporary Britain vary between different ethnic groups, not only between white and black, but within ethnic groups themselves. The family may be a source of oppression for black women. Some South Asian women may be oppressed in the family, by the form of marriage they participate in, the giving of dowries, participating in domestic labour and the degree of control they have in domestic finance. The specific cultural norms and standards of South Asian families may be reinforced through different forms of patriarchy experienced by women. Although black feminists (hooks 1984) have argued that the family is less a source of oppression for 'women of colour', this idea has focused specifically on Afro-Caribbean and African-American families. However, the family may be a source of oppression for some South Asian, Afro-Caribbean and African-American women.

4

The term 'family' lends itself to infinite variation, which contains within it choice and flexibility for negotiation between its members over the conditions in which they inhabit a common living space. The position of black women in families is infinitely varied. The family cannot just be divided into black and white. The black family, like the white family, does not take a particular form. There are significant differences in family forms between ethnic groups and the household may have a different place in the experience of women in a racially divided society (Saradamoni 1992).

Patriarchy

In contemporary feminism the concept of patriarchy has received considerable attention and has been analysed as a system which oppresses women. There have been problems with the definition of patriarchy (Barrett 1980) and differences within feminism as to the causes of patriarchy. Some feminists see domestic labour as the main cause of patriarchy (Delphy 1980), others sexuality (Firestone 1974) or violence (Dworkin 1981). Theories of patriarchy have universalised women's experience which may conceal other forms of oppression based upon 'race' and class. Concepts such as patriarchy can conceal divisions in society in much the same way as male perspectives have concealed the oppression of women (Collins 1990, Ramazanoglu 1986). Furthermore, the term 'patriarchy' has been criticised by black feminists (Carby 1982, Spellman 1990) who suggest that because of racism, black men do not benefit from patriarchal social structures in the same way as white men and that benefit from patriarchy does not distinguish black men from black women:

> Black men have been dominated 'patriarchally' in different ways by men of different 'colours' (Carby 1982:80).

This has encouraged white feminists (Barrett and Mackintosh 1985) to be more cautious of their use of the term. However, other feminists (Mies 1986, Walby 1990) argue that patriarchy ultimately unites all women in a common sisterhood as differentially oppressed subjects, all of whom have in common a disadvantaged relation to men and it is precisely this unity which provides the force for resistance. Barrett and Macintosh (1985) see the concept of patriarchy as one with a valuable, but specific purpose, which is descriptive of certain types of social relations:

> ...characterised by the personal, often physical exploitation of a servility whose causes are usually economic and always strictly regulated through a hierarchical order (1985:37).

Barrett and Macintosh (1985) do not examine how and why the concept of the 'patriarchal' helps us to engage with interconnections between gender, class and racism. The substitution of the concept 'patriarchy' by 'patriarchal relations' will not by itself deal with the charges of ahistoricism, universalism or essentialism that have been levelled at patriarchy.

Racial divisions are relegated to secondary importance as the notion of 'race' and ethnicity have been 'added on' to some existing theories of patriarchy. This is highly problematic and in order to examine the situation for South Asian women, we may ask; what are the forms of patriarchy experienced by South Asian women and how are these different to those experienced by white women? I intend to develop the theory of patriarchy (Walby 1990) which argues that there is a continuum between two forms of patriarchy (private and public). I would argue that patriarchy is a concept which can be used to explain women's position within society. However, different ethnic groups may experience different forms of patriarchy. What are the different forms of patriarchy experienced by South Asian women? Do existing theories of patriarchy apply to South Asian communities in Britain? Do private and public forms of patriarchy exist for South Asian women?

South Asian family

Migration has always been a popular feature of human society. People have migrated to seek opportunities, to improve their economic and cultural levels or to escape persecution. In the post-colonial period (1947 onwards), the size and scope of migration increased to unprecedented levels. The study of ethnic minorities and experiences of migration have been well documented (Anwar 1979, Ballard and Ballard 1977), as well as the characteristics of the South Asian family (Ballard 1994a, Gardner and Shukur 1994, Ghuman 1994, Shaw 1988, 1994, Stopes-Roe and Cochrane 1988, 1990, Visram 1986). Economic migration from India and Pakistan to Britain is characterised by young men and subsequently their spouses and possibly children, leaving their home, friends and extended family in order to benefit from higher wages in another country (Anwar 1985, Ballard 1990, Jeffrey 1976).

The causes of immigration for people from one country to another are manifold, but some scholars (Anwar 1979, Watson 1977) have tended to explain them under the categories of 'pull and push factors'. The major 'pull' factor is improvement of the family's financial and social position. Another 'pull' factor is the active encouragement given by the receiving society to the citizens of other countries through the prospect of better jobs, housing and recreational facilities (Bhachu 1988, Green 1990, Khan 1979). The major 'push' factors may include massive upheavals of population through persecution and famine.

Primary immigration to the UK virtually ceased with the passing of the 1971 Immigration Act. This act restricted the entry of dependents and allowed new entrants only to take up specific jobs for a limited period of time (Fryer 1984). Some research examined the spatial patterns of settlement of Punjabis (Ballard and Ballard 1977, Helweg 1979, Kalra 1980) and Pakistanis (Khan 1979, Shaw 1988, 1994, Werbner 1979, 1988) and found that patterns recreated in the UK were very similar to those based on village and kinship networks back home. Others have investigated the 'myth of return' and what it means for immigrant families (Anwar 1979, Robinson 1981, Taylor 1976).

South Asian communities are composed of people from different religions, castes, regional and language groups with a variety of social and cultural characteristics. There are however, certain factors which characterise South Asians as a distinctive group from westerners. First there is the primacy of family over the individual, it is the family rather than the individual which is the basis of social structure (Ghuman 1994). To ensure the continuous, smooth running of a unit including several adults, a hierarchical and authoritarian structure often evolves (Pillai 1976). This in turn produces certain goals and emphasises in child rearing and family interaction patterns for both males and females (Robinson 1986). Family values for women become pronounced (Shan 1985). Important decisions are made by, and for the group, not by the individual (Brah 1978). Familialistic orientation centres around the fulfilment of role obligations and expectations towards kin members. Furthermore, it is women who are entrusted with the burden of carrying the family honour (Wilson 1978).

Secondly the custom of arranged marriages is very much part and parcel of the South Asian social structure. Marriages are supposed to be primarily for the union of families, to promote mutual financial and social interests (Wilson 1978). Thirdly the majority of first generation immigrants were from a rural background (Dahya 1972). A significant number had only attended primary schools and were completely unaware of the language problems they were going to face in Britain. This is also connected to the poorer positions faced by minorities in terms of housing, education and employment (Rex and Tomlinson 1979). Whatever their economic and social position, the first generation were, and are, firmly rooted in their religion and culture and are sure of their personal identities. Their 'belongingness' is not in doubt, they are Sikhs or Muslims, Indians or Pakistanis (Stopes-Roe and Cochrane 1990). However, the children of these immigrants are less sure of their personal and social identities (Ghuman 1994). They have been described as a 'half-way generation' (Taylor 1976), a generation suffering from a 'culture clash' (Khan 1979, Watson 1977) or youngsters who have the best or worst of two worlds (Ghuman 1991, 1994). Rex and Tomlinson (1979) have described the situation as 'from immigrants to ethnies'.

Much discussion has centred around the extent to which, and the means by which newcomers into any society may, or should be incorporated into the host society (Price 1982, Yinger 1985). Various terms are used to refer to this process; adaption, integration, acculturation or assimilation. They are describing a situation in which newcomers change their habits, ways of life, social groups and personal attitudes and identify in response to the patterns they encounter in the host society. The norms of behaviour of the indigenous population may appear to newcomers as being advantageous (Dahya 1974, Robinson 1986). Discussions of adaption and assimilation of first generation newcomers frequently point to the significance of kinship ties with the sending community and make the assumption, either explicitly or implicity, that these will be strongly functional in directing attitudes towards settling in the new community and will influence behaviour (Brooks and Singh 1978, Robinson 1986). However, this has been questioned due to the persistence of distinct ethnic identities (Drury 1991, Robinson 1984).

Many writers have examined the notion of conflict which exists for South Asians and their representation in society (Anwar 1981, Ballard 1978, Ballard and Ballard 1977, Bhachu 1985). Anticipation of difference and friction between the first and subsequent generations of incoming minority groups rests on a rather simplistic model of the process by which different cultures integrate. The underlying assumption is of a monolithic one-way movement, this has been challenged by many authors over the last twenty years (Banton 1983a, Goldlust and Richmond 1974, Hirschman 1982, Price 1982, Putins 1976). The process of assimilation has been shown to be many-faceted (Stopes-Roe and Cochrane 1987), to take place at different times, and to different extents. It is possible that variation between the generations in their experience and interpretation of the factors involved in assimilation may result in differences in the extent to which they pursue or reject it, particularly early on in the settlement of an immigrant group. This neither presupposes a particular or crucial amount of difference between the generations, nor is the occurrence of a difference necessarily to be expected in all areas of activity, nor in those particularly vital to the maintenance of the group's cultural identity (Banton 1983b).

By the mid-1970's two out of every five British South Asian children were born in this country (Fryer 1984). This percentage is now over 95% (Ghuman 1994). Studies which have examined the relationship between South Asian and western values, have found youngsters wishing to retain the core value of their home culture, namely language (Stopes-Roe and Cochrane 1990). As regards the cultural identity of the second generation, the situation is complex, they have been called 'British Asians' (Wade and Souter 1991) or just 'Asians' by the majority of indigenous whites (Ghuman 1994). Some researchers (Bhachu 1988, Stopes-Roe and Cochrane 1990) argue that young South Asians are synthesising British cultural values with traditional values and are developing new cultural patterns. Other research on the identity of South Asians has shown that many South Asian girls are successfully mixing the two traditions of British and South Asian culture and creating their own way of living which they find satisfying (Drury 1991, Ghuman 1994, Gibson 1988).

Hindus, Sikhs and Muslims have all originated in the same continent and share many experiences and expectations (Jha 1978, Wilson 1978), but they speak different languages and their religions which are profoundly important, give them differing systems of practices, beliefs and relationships. Many of these groups tend to be lumped together, which can often be ethnocentric and misleading (Robinson 1981).

Whilst there exists a body of literature on South Asian social relations which has demonstrated the degree of difference that exists between white and ethnic groups, these studies have not specifically examined relations for South Asian women within households. Furthermore, it has been assumed there is no degree of difference between the experiences of South Asian women. What do differences within South Asian communities tell us about the lives of women? What is the position of South

Asian women within the family? What are the different forms of patriarchy experienced by South Asian women in British society? How is patriarchy defined for South Asian women? Such questions will enable us to investigate whether colour, culture and 'race' may make a difference to the forms of patriarchy experienced by South Asian women and concentrate on a specific group of women who have previously been neglected in sociological understanding.

Without a framework for incorporating 'race' and ethnicity into models of the family, feminist reformulations cannot be inclusive. Just as feminist theories have reconceptualised the family along a gender axis of power and control, racial-ethnic family scholarship has reconceptualised the family along the axis of 'race'. Studying racial-ethnic families enables us to examine 'race' and gender as interacting hierarchies of resources and rewards that condition material and subjective experience within families. Acknowledging that beyond universal similarities, there may be vast differences in the experiences of women is called for.

Employment, gender and ethnicity

Women's inferior position in the labour market has been well documented (Beechey 1978, Bruegel 1979, Hakim 1981, Myrdal and Klein 1970, Phillips and Taylor 1980, Walby 1986). Different researchers have given different explanations for women's position in the labour market. Some writers (Mincer and Polanchek 1974) have argued that women get paid less than men because they have less skill and labour market experience and fewer qualifications than men, as a consequence of decisions they make in the household. Others, (Kanter 1977, Myrdal and Klein 1970) stress the dual roles performed by women. Some writers (Beechey 1977, 1978, Braverman 1974, Bruegel 1979) have argued that women constitute a 'reserve army of labour'. Yet others (Mackinnon 1979, Stanko 1988) examine issues such as sexual harassment in the workplace. An attempt has also been made to combine class analysis with the theorisation of patriarchy to explain women's position in the labour market (Cockburn 1983, 1985, Hartmann 1979, 1981a, Walby 1986, 1989, Witz 1987).

It has been argued that most analyses on gender and paid employment treat women as if they were a unitary category which neglect divisions based upon 'race' and ethnicity (Carby 1982, Collins 1990, hooks 1984). There is a considerable body of evidence which points to the importance of racial discrimination in structuring the disadvantages faced by South Asian and Afro-Caribbean groups in the labour market (Brah and Shaw 1992, Dex 1983, Miles and Phizacklea 1980, Phizacklea 1983, 1988, 1990, Phizacklea and Wolkowitz 1995, Rex and Tomlinson 1979, Roberts 1994, Wallace 1982).

Early studies point to the direct and indirect discrimination in terms of access to employment, promotion and training (Brown 1984, Freeman 1982, Smith 1974, 1980). Other research has shown extensive discrimination against South Asian and Afro-Caribbeans. Even when they have equivalent or better qualifications than their white counterparts, their search for jobs is less successful (Drew et al 1991, Hubbuck and Carter 1980, Lee and Wrench 1983, Roberts 1994, Troyna and Smith 1985). There is evidence that a substantial proportion of South Asian women, (especially Muslim women), are involved in homeworking (Phizacklea and Wolkowitz 1995, West 1982) and they are more likely to be unemployed (Afshar 1989, Lutz 1991, Parmar and Mirza 1993, Shaw 1988). Evidence shows that even in industries where female labour predominates, women of South Asian and Afro-Caribbean descent are found to be concentrated in the lowest level jobs (Beechey 1986, Bruegel 1988, 1994). Occupational segregation by gender affects all women, but within specific occupations women of South Asian and Afro-Caribbean origin are at a greater disadvantage than white women (Owen and Green 1992).

Throughout the last four decades, evidence of discrimination against South Asian groups has grown steadily (Owen and Green 1992). More recently Brah and Shaw (1992) have argued that Muslim women's involvement in paid work, (whether inside or outside the home), was not seen by them as unequivocally advantageous. The 'double shift', of combining paid work with domestic responsibilities, mitigated against many of the advantages of having a job. Furthermore, Brah (1993) has stressed the role of multiple determinations in the relation of young Muslim women to the labour market. More recently West and Pilgrim (1995) have recognised the diversity of experience of different groups of South 'Asian' women in the labour market, the impact of migration and the local economy upon women's familial responsibilities. They found that the participation of Bengali women in the labour force was virtually nil and experience for Pakistani women was minimal, but Indian women (Gujeratis) had extensive employment experiences (Owen and Green 1992, Rafiq 1992). However, West and Pilgrim (1995) do not examine the differences between the 'external' and 'internal' labour markets, which indicates that Bengali women are more likely to participate in the 'internal' labour market, working at home.

There are important differences in the economic, political, legal and ideological position of migrant black women when compared to other women. This is no more evident than in the labour market. As migrants, they experience racial subordination which acts to confine them in certain types of work and reinforces their exploitation as waged workers. These forms of exploitation are shaped and experienced in a particular way because they share with all women subordination as a gender.

It has been shown that migrant and female labour force constitute an attractive labour force (Bryan et al 1985, Phizacklea 1983). Both migrant and female labour forces share similar characteristics; they have been 'produced' by the demand for labour in certain low-wage sectors of the economy and they are confined to these sectors, often by specific policies and practices which are partially justified by the assumption of inferior characteristics (Miles and Phizacklea 1980, Phizacklea 1983, Stone 1983). In the case of women, that inferiority stems from the fact that their primary role is not defined as a waged worker, but as an actual or potential wife and mother who is dependent upon a male 'breadwinner' (Parsons and Bales 1956). This definition of their role has far reaching consequences for the conditions under which they sell their labour power (Beechey 1986). As Phillips and Taylor (1980) have commented:

...capital is concerned not just with a logic of surplus extraction but with an assertion of command it is necessarily sensitive to, those social relations which make some workers already more subordinated than others (1980:86).

It is only within this context that we can understand how male organised labour has struggled to exclude women from areas of waged work where women were viewed as competitors (Alexander 1976). Also, how the demand for the family wage was consistent with these exclusionary practices and could be justified as providing the material preconditions for conformity to the bourgeois family form of 'male breadwinner' and 'dependent wife' (Land 1980).

Some researchers (Anwar 1979, Stone 1983) have shown that the economic circumstances of black migrant women are less favourable than those of white women, because the ratio of dependents to working adults is higher in black households than in white households, and minority families frequently have financial obligations to family members in their country of origin. Whilst other researchers (Bruegel 1988, 1994, Jayaweera 1993, Phizacklea 1983, 1988) have argued that minority women in the post-war periods have entered a highly segregated labour market, whereas Phizacklea (1990) states:

...women generally are confined to low pay, low status and gender-specific employment (1990:98).

Research has shown that many ethnic minorities are concentrated in the clothing industry as homeworkers, which is reproducing the traditional class, gender and racial divisions of labour (Cockburn 1985, Phizacklea 1983, 1988, Phizacklea and Wolkowitz 1995). Hakim (1991) has argued that homeworkers have higher job satisfaction because their jobs can be fitted into their own lifestyle as they have more freedom and flexibility. Furthermore, recession, redundancy and racial discrimination in the labour market has forced an increasing number of minority men into entrepreneurship and minority women to work for them, where the ethnic economy is a gendered economy (Morokvasic 1994, Phizacklea 1988, 1990, Ram 1993).

Some researchers have attempted to explain the continuing rise in women's paid employment in the 1980's set against a significant decline in full-time male jobs. Behind this overall tendency, Acker (1992) and Reskin and Padavic (1994) cite four distinct, but related trends affecting the structure of women's employment in all advanced societies:

1. Restructuring of employment occurred initially in manufacturing, leading to a relative decline in the better paid, male dominated sectors of manufacturing production.

2. The authors note a polarisation in skill demands in which women's jobs are increasingly divided between routine low-wage highly controlled work and non-routine, relatively autonomous higher waged jobs.

3. There has been a growth in flexible work organisations. The search for lower labour and related costs is producing an expansion in the contingent labour force where jobs lack the permanence, security or protection previously enjoyed by many or most male industrial workers. Some writers (Jenson et al 1988) have talked about the 'feminisation of the labour force' which not only refers to women constituting an increased proportion of the labour force, but is often used to refer to declining terms and conditions of employment, so that a larger proportion of the labour force has come to experience 'feminised' (poor and insecure), conditions of work (Reskin and Padavik 1994, Woody 1992).

4. There is an increasing 'diversity' within the labour force, as demographic trends project an increasing participation of women and non-white minorities as a proportion of the labour force (although this does seem to be cited more in the US). The emphasis on diversity is marginalising the language of 'equality' and subsequently making it more difficult for women to demand the rights and benefits that male employees previously took for granted (at least in large enterprises). It may also obscure the occupational segregation which continues along racial and gender lines (Liff 1993). The language of 'diversity' can obscure continuing inequalities in the employment situations of black and white men, women and other minority groups, as well as the ways in which they are affected by restructuring.

Recent research has indicated the degree of racialised segregation that continues to exist in British labour markets (Bhavnani 1994, Bruegel 1994, Jones 1994, Owen 1994). Roberts (1994) has shown that even when black and ethnic minority women are skilled and experienced, they are twice as likely to be unemployed and work longer hours, in poorer conditions for lower pay than white women. Furthermore, the figures are considerably lower for Pakistani and Bangladeshi women, who were five times more likely to be unemployed than white women, the gap being greatest in recessionary periods. The Equal Opportunities Commission suggest three reasons for this (Roberts 1994):

1. Ethnic minority women may have less access to informal organisational networks which may help them in gaining access to a wider range of jobs.
2. Some ethnic minority groups are more likely to use 'word of mouth' recruitment methods which distance them from formal job search methods.
3. Employers are more likely to be operating discriminatory practices in a recession.

Another factor which is important in comparing black and white women's job levels, is that ethnic minority women are much more likely to work full-time than white women (70 per cent compared to 50 per cent of white women, Roberts 1994). Even though more ethnic women are now working, they work through financial necessity, caused by higher rates of black male unemployment, larger family size, lower household incomes and the necessity of working longer hours to bring home a living wage (Phizacklea and Wolkowitz 1995).

Women's experiences in the labour market vary considerably by 'race' and gender which may have a significant impact upon women's pay and job levels (Bruegel 1994, Elias and Gregory 1992, Leffler 1992, McGuire and Reskin 1993, West and Pilgrim 1995). An understanding of racist structures must be considered as an essential part of the explanation of gender relations in paid employment, as the interactive impacts of 'race' and gender on labour force experience remain unclear. Although the research has examined non-white women's experiences in the labour market it has not specifically examined in any detail, the labour market experiences of South Asian women and the diversity of South Asian women's experience itself. To what extent have labour market experiences of South Asian women changed in the past decade? Are there significant differences between South Asian groups? How does the labour market act as a patriarchal structure in explaining South Asian women's position within it? How is this in turn related to the household? Such questions will enable us to examine the diversity of experiences which exist for South Asian women and explore the interrelationship of 'race' and gender and its effects upon the position of women.

Education, 'race' and ethnicity

In the UK, the educational achievement of students of ethnic minority background has become a focus of growing concern for members of majority as well as minority communities during the last 30 years. The existence and nature of ethnic or gender differences in attainment in national qualifications, which are of such significance in determining future education and employment prospects, are clearly of particular relevance to the consideration of equality in access to such opportunities.

Measures of low income, unemployment, eligibility for free school meals, large family size, one parent family status and poor housing conditions have been found to be powerful predictors of academic attainment (Essen and Wedge 1982, Mortimore and Blackstone 1982, Rutter and Madge 1976). UK research has focused upon identifying the factors associated with poor educational attainment and laid an emphasis on the concept of educational deprivation (Hutchinson et al 1979, Macintosh et al 1988, Macintosh and Mascie-Taylor 1985, Maughan and Dunn 1988, Sammons et al 1983). High social class, gender, greater level of parental education and qualifications has been found to be associated with greater participation in higher education (Mortimore et al 1988, Nuttall et al 1989, Sammons et al 1985). A recent research review has been provided by Brown and Riddell (1992) concerning the topics of social class (Patterson 1992), gender (Riddell 1992) and ethnicity (Gillborn 1992).

Research has shown that children from Afro-Caribbean backgrounds are more likely to fare worse at school than their white counterparts (Parekh 1988, Rampton 1981, Smith and Tomlinson 1989, Stone 1981, Swann 1985, Verma 1986, Verma and Ashworth 1981). However, very little research has examined the ways in which South Asian pupils have experienced and responded to schooling in this country. Although South Asian pupils appear in studies carried out by Wright (1985, 1987), they are conspicuous by their absence from her qualitative accounts of pupil adaption in multi-ethnic schools. Several writers have commented upon the relatively positive nature of teacher stereotypes of South Asian students when compared with Afro-Caribbean students (Gillborn 1990, Mac an Ghaill 1988, Tomlinson 1983). Research carried out on South Asian students indicates that they behave and achieve more positively than their Afro-Caribbean peers in schools (Brittan 1976, Mac an Ghaill 1988). Research has shown the crucial differences between the experiences of South Asian and Afro-Caribbean pupils (Gillborn 1990, Smith and Tomlinson 1989). Whereas Taylor and Hegarty (1985) stress diversity in the experiences of South Asian children in British schools.

Although South Asians tended to stay in full-time education longer than other pupils, they experienced like West Indians inequalities of opportunity in the job market. There was differential performance across subject areas and across South Asian sub-groups. Other influences were also important; English language competencies, home-school relations, school factors including teachers expectations, the curriculum and ethos of the school, peer interaction, societal discrimination and racial prejudice. Research has shown how Afro-Caribbean students performed worst in schools, South Asians did less well than whites, but better than Afro-Caribbean students (Drew and Gray 1989, Parekh 1986, Roberts 1988). However, Verma (1987) has pointed out:

> ...there are widely differing linguistic, social, religious and cultural traditions and experiences of the Asian sub-groups (1987:19).

Research (Kysel 1988, Nuttall 1990) has shown that South Asians overall were doing well compared with their local peers, but there was a great deal of difference in the performance of different South Asian groups. Smith and Tomlinson (1989) found that among South Asians in the first year of secondary schooling, Bangladeshi children had the lowest level of initial performance, followed by Pakistanis, then by Indians and other South Asians, with African Asians performing the best, although even they achieved just below the average. In inner city schools, South Asian students with the exception of Bangladeshis again have generally performed better than whites (The Independent 8 March 1990).

Many studies have recognised the stereotypical perceptions, ignorance, prejudice and racism on the part of teachers and professionals (Driver 1977, Rutter et al 1979, Tomlinson 1982, Wright 1987). Many of the factors in the literature regarding the underachievement of ethnic minority pupils have been viewed within a pathological perspective in so far as there been a focus on what might be 'wrong with', 'problematic' or 'deviant', about ethnic minority pupils and their backgrounds (Taylor 1988, Taylor and Hegarty 1985, Troyna 1988). Other examples of a pathological perspective have been found by Dawson (1988) and Roberts (1988). Furthermore, many ethnic minority pupils have been over-represented in lower streams and non-examination classes (Figuero 1984, Taylor 1981, Tomlinson 1982).

Research has shown that South Asian parents place high values on education (Ghuman 1994, Khan 1979, Parekh 1986, Penn and Scattergood 1992, Robinson 1986, Tanna 1990) and strict discipline regarding education (Ghuman 1980, 1994, Ghuman and Gallop 1981). Other researchers (Islamia 1992, Shaikh and Kelly 1989) have found that parents are in favour of separate religious schools to reduce distraction for their children. Furthermore, South Asian parents view the speaking of their mother tongue with the utmost concern and would like it to be taught, where possible in the school curriculum (Cohen and Manion 1983, Smith and Tomlinson 1989). It has also been evidenced that many parents have expressed their general satisfaction of the schooling which their youngsters are experiencing (Ghuman 1994, Knight 1988).

Recent research (Ballard, 1994a) has demonstrated that compared with the white majority, a higher proportion of South Asians continue in full-time education. Furthermore, their rate of enrolment on degree courses is double that of the white norm. Yet they still continue to suffer the same forms of discrimination and exclusion as their parents. Gardner and Shukur (1994) have indicated that an increasing number of Bengali women are continuing into higher education and within the next few decades the numbers of Bengali women in the labour market will show a significant increase. One of the reasons for this is that higher education is seen as a route for greater earning potential and upward social mobility.

In order to examine the opportunities which are substantively available to pupils from different ethnic minority groups, researchers have examined students performance in exams at the age of 16 (Byford and Mortimore 1985, Drew and Gray 1989, Kysel 1988, Nuttall et al 1989). Black young people with educational certification fare significantly better than their black peers with fewer qualifications (Clough and Drew 1985). Despite the proven influence of racism within the labour market (Brown 1984, Hubbuck and Carter 1980, Ohri and Faruqi 1988), exam results can still have a major effect upon the life chances of Afro-Caribbean and South Asian school leavers, as possession of higher grade passes is associated with lower levels of employment for all ethnic groups (Clough and Drew 1985, Craft and Craft 1983). However, most analyses of underachievement have been criticised because they make no allowance for possible variation in the social class composition of different ethnic groups (Reeves and Chevannes 1981, Troyna 1981, 1988).

A body of literature already exists on differences in the academic nature of the subjects which pupils 'choose' according to their social class and/or gender (Ball 1981, Gillborn 1990, Pratt, Bloomfield and Seale 1984). However, very few studies have considered the importance of ethnic origin at this crucial point in pupils' school careers. Research (Smith and Tomlinson 1989, Tomlinson 1987) has shown that ethnic minority pupils tend to appear in option subjects of lower academic status, this is more pronounced for Afro-Caribbean pupils (Gillborn 1990, Green 1985, Mac an Ghaill 1988, Wright 1987).

It is clear that in the 1980's some ethnic minority groups were 'over-represented' in higher education and others were 'under-represented' (Ballard and Vellins 1985, Vellins 1982). The first two years (1990/91), that the University Central Council on Admissions (UCCA) and the Polytechnic Central Admissions System (PCAS), asked applicants to state their ethnic origin showed that, only Bangladeshis and black-others were proportionately less represented than whites in PCAS admissions, though they were under-represented in UCCA acceptances (Modood 1993, Taylor 1993). The data from 1992 applicants presented significant diversity in the levels of representation amongst the minority groups even though some continued to speak of a 'black' or ethnic minority under representation (THES Editorial 5 July 1991). Modood and Shiner (1994) argue that academic performance is an important part of the explanation of ethnic differences in access to higher education. In considering ethnic differences in attainment, it should be made clear that ethnicity should not be treated as a disadvantage. Clearly, underachievement of specific groups may be related as much to the school and assessment system as to cultural and individual differences (Tanna 1990). Moreover, recent research suggests that the performance of ethnic minority groups may now exceed that of majority groups, for example for three consecutive years in GCSE, evidence has shown that no ethnic group performs worse than the 'white' classification (Sammons 1994, Thomas et al 1992, 1993, 1994).

Very few studies have examined the educational achievements of South Asians and in these studies gender and ethnicity have been neglected. Examining the relationship between gender, ethnicity and education enables us to explore the issue of difference for South Asian women. How do South Asian women perform in education? How do their performance levels affect their participation in the labour market? To what extent does education affect forms of patriarchy experienced by South Asian women? How has South Asian women's position in education changed in the last ten years? Such questions will enable us to explore the impact of 'race' and gender and its relationship to patriarchy.

Religion

Religion is an area of study which has received considerable attention (Barot 1987, Sahgal and Yuval-Davis 1992). Religion plays a significant part in the lives of South Asian women. Although South Asian communities have vast similarities, they are divided by their religious backgrounds. Religion is a powerful force for South Asian women, groups are both defined and differentiated by their religious backgrounds.

Among the in-comers into the UK of the post-war period, none are more visible than the Sikhs, at least the male sector of the group. They are visible through wearing turbans which cover uncut hair and maintaining full beards, two practices bound up with their faith as Sikhs. The Sikhs are Indian in origin, the members of a minority Indian religion that began as a Hindu sect, part of a religious movement that flourished in the middle ages. The Sikhs are one of three large groups which constitute the bulk of migration during the second half of the twentieth century from the Indian sub-continent (Helweg 1979), the other two groups were the Gujeratis and Muslims. Ballard and Ballard (1977) have identified four phases of Sikh settlement in Britain. Organisations have been formed which are designed to maintain Sikh culture in Britain or to promote Sikh culture in the wider community (Macleod 1976). The Gurdwara (Sikh Temple), is an important focal point for religious and social gatherings. Divisions of caste play an important role in attendance at the Gurdwara (Kalsi 1992).

Knott (1986, 1987, 1991) has argued that the population of Hindus in the UK has grown considerably. Some authors have examined Hindu communities, their characteristics and religions (Burghart 1987, Kantikar and Jackson 1982, Knott 1986, Vertovec 1992). Little attention has been given to British born children in Hindu families, although Logan (1988) has examined Gujerati children in London. The bulk of the Hindu population migrated after the second world war (Burghart 1987). Some were students who intended to practise their professions in Britain (Kantikar 1972). By a process of chain migration, early migrants were joined by male relatives or fellow villagers, the established residents providing accommodation and helping to find work for the new arrivals (Tambs-Lyche 1980). The second wave of migration began in the late 1960's. Vertovec (1992) argues that there are many differences between Punjabis and Gujeratis and different 'levels' of provenance can become important reference points informing particular social identities and networks.

In tracing the pattern of settlement of Gujeratis and Punjabis, it has often been the case that Gujeratis have moved to areas of cities that already had a Gujerati presence, while Punjabis tended to set up homes near other Punjabis, whether Hindu or Sikh by religion (Sims 1981). Logan (1988) and Macdonald (1987) have shown that the presence of women in families has been highly significant in the perpetuation of domestic religious practices. At school, children are not exposed to Hindu religion, but at home they grow up with it. This exposure does not guarantee children's knowledge of the meaning of customary religious practices (Jackson and Killingley 1988, Larson 1988, Williams 1988). Some studies have examined the Hindu religion in the UK (Bigger 1987, Dwyer 1988, Larson 1988, Logan 1988, Thomas 1992, Vertovec 1992). Other research (Williams 1988) has examined South Asian religions in the USA.

Religious practices are an important part of the lives of Hindus and those who have settled in Britain have faced considerable challenges which call for adaption. Some writers (Abramson 1979) have argued that the nature of the Hindu religion indicates that complexities of religion and ethnicity become enmeshed. Studies which have examined temple practice in Britain (Jackson 1981, Knott 1986) note the differences between the way rituals are performed in India and in Britain.

Although large numbers of Muslims did not arrive in Britain until after the second r, smaller scale migration occurred from the nineteenth century onwards as political, cultural and commercial activities. Approximately three quarters lims in Britain originated from the Indian sub-continent (Joly 1988, Nielsen ihab 1989). The process of settlement had significant implications for the development of Islamic observance. When women and children came to Britain, Muslim communities began to make an effort to create the structures to permit the full observance of their religion. The process of developing a religious superstructure naturally relates to the pattern and chronology of settlement, thus by the 1980's it was well advanced among Pakistanis who had been in the country for two decades, but the Bangladeshis who were still arriving in substantial numbers in that decade remained much more in a state of transition (Barton 1986, Nielsen 1987). This resulted in a number of mosques being built in the UK. The acquisition of these prominent and traditionally Islamic buildings have promoted a sense of dignity, stability and coherence during the 1970's and 1980's as well as providing points of symbolic interaction with non-Muslims (Barton 1986, Joly 1988, Nielsen 1988). There is a general injunction to both sexes to observe decency and avoid sexually provocative behaviour, requiring women in particular to dress modestly, generally wearing a head covering and loose unrevealing clothing. This has been linked to the institution of Purdah, the seclusion of women from all men except their husbands and other close relatives.

Relatively improved incomes and living conditions enabled all who wished to maintain a significant degree of Purdah to do so and fear of easy-going western attitudes to sex meant that girls were even more assiduously isolated from male contact (Khan 1979, Knott and Khokher 1993, Mirza 1989). Wolffe (1992) has identified four kinds of relationships between Islam and British society; assimilation, isolation, integration and redefinition. Wolffe (1992) argues that some middle class Muslims have rapidly adopted secularised western lifestyles and culture. Accordingly, they become alienated from working class Muslims who were more tenacious in holding on to their traditions (Modood 1990). The behaviour of young Muslims has indicated a closer approximation to western attitudes than that existing among their parents. Some younger Muslims however, have been shifting away from the standpoints adopted by their parents not in favour of sexuality or westernisation, but in a sense towards what they see as a legitimate articulation of Muslim principles (Mirza 1989, Nielsen 1983). Islam provides a fascinating example of how ethnicity, community and gender can collide in strange and unexpected ways. The maintenance of a static notion of community requires an ideology, particularly in the face of a dominant culture which may at times appear to offer more rewards, than continued and total allegiance to the community. Islam can provide intellectual strength and collusion to that ideology, which Ali (1992) has referred to as 'ethnicism'.

Some writers have used the term 'fundamentalism' to describe certain religious beliefs, such as Islam (Connolly 1991, Sahgal and Yuval-Davis 1992, Siddiqui 1991). Women affect, and are affected by, ethnic and national processes in several major ways. Some of these are central to the project of fundamentalism which attempts to

18

impose its own unitary religious definition on the grouping and its symbolic order. The 'proper' behaviour of women is used to signify the difference between those who belong and those who do not. Women are also seen as the 'cultural carriers' of the group, who transmit group culture to the future generation (Sahgal and Yuval-Davis 1992) and proper control in terms of marriage and divorce (Anthias and Yuval-Davis 1989). Others have argued that women collude, seek comfort and even at times gain a sense of empowerment within the spaces allocated to them by fundamentalist movements (Ali 1992, Foster 1992, Maitland 1992, Yuval-Davis 1992). Being active in a religious movement allows women a legitimate place in a public sphere which otherwise might be blocked to them. For women of racial and ethnic minorities, it can also provide the means by which to defend themselves as well as to defy the hegemonic racist culture.

For women there is an absence of power and status in visible hierarchies in many religions. A cross-cultural historical study of the role and status of women in different religious traditions shows that the less differentiated religion and society is, the greater is the participation of women (Carmody 1979). Traditionally, most religions have excluded women from advanced learning and teaching (King 1987). It has been said that religions are the most important source for shaping and enforcing the image and role of women in culture and society. One must ask, which images of woman a particular religion has created and handed down from generation to generation and how far these are beset with inherent contradictions. The images of women in the religions of classical antiquity have been closely examined (Cameron and Kuhrt 1983, Pomeroy 1984) and an increasing amount of work is being carried out on women in non-western traditions, such as India (Leslie 1988).

There is a marked tendency towards diversification and variety, the religious constituency and complexity of Britain in the last decade of the twentieth century is much more varied and multi-faceted than that of the period following the end of the second world war. Religious life in Britain has become more complicated and Britain has now become a fundamentally plural society (Davie 1990). Women's experience does not show a uniform development or pattern as conditions of life, age, social class, ethnicity, religion and culture vary widely and make the lives of individual women or different groups of women very disparate. Each culture also knows widely differing myths, models and symbols relating to women. Religion has clearly shown to be an influential factor in the lives of women, it helps to shape and structure their lives and may have a powerful effect upon their roles as women. Although the research has examined the meaning of religion and provided an understanding of its practices, it has not specifically investigated how religion can influence women's lives in terms of patriarchy. If women are members of different religious groups, to what extent do they experience different forms of patriarchy? To what extent does religion play a significant part in the lives of South Asian women? Such questions will enable us to examine religious diversity and how it affects and divides women's lives within a patriarchal structure.

The research

The research examines the intersection of gender and ethnicity with specific reference to South Asian women in Britain. It investigates the dynamics of gender relations within households, in order to explore differences that exist amongst South Asian women focusing on; arranged marriages, dowries, domestic labour, domestic finance, education, employment and religion. The precise focus of the study is the South Asian community in East London. The most important area for analysis is the household as it is the site of the greatest differences between white and South Asian groups and is hypothesised to be the most important cause of the nature of other aspects of gender relations. The research asks; what are the different forms of patriarchy that exist in South Asian communities in Britain, in particular East London? What influences forms of patriarchy experienced by South Asian women? Is it religion, education, employment, domestic labour, domestic finance, arranged marriages or dowries? As South Asian women have different cultural experiences to white women, they have arranged marriages and are given dowries, it is assumed forms of patriarchy experienced by South Asian women may be different to those experienced by white women. The research explores; religion (Hindu/Sikh/Moslem), level of education, type of employment, domestic labour (who does what), domestic finance (who controls what and why), arranged marriages (who has them and why) and dowries (who has them and why).

A very specific group of South Asian women in the UK were investigated. South Asian was defined as those whose forefathers and foremothers had originated from the Indian sub-continent; India, Pakistan and Bangladesh. A total of 60 in-depth interviews were carried out with South Asian women living in East London. The ages of the women ranged from 25-30 years and they had all been born in the UK. Three groups were investigated to examine the impact of religious difference, women who defined themselves as Hindu, Sikh and Moslem. Twenty women from each group were interviewed. Ten interviews were conducted in Punjabi and all others in English. The interviews were tape-recorded (with the exception of five) and the data subsequently transcribed. The sampling method used was that of the snowball sample. The quantitative data was analysed using the SPSS software package and the qualitative data was analysed using the traditional paper and paste method. Hence, the study was both quantitative and qualitative.

Outline

This chapter has introduced the subject of study, outlined the aims of the study, investigated the focus of analysis and demonstrated the importance of the research. The following chapter will provide an overview of the literature on gender, 'race' and the household/family. It will provide a critical analysis of the literature as well as a rationale for the present study. It will also introduce the reader to the methodology and how the use of a 'feminist methodology' helped to empower women who participated in the study. It will argue that studies on gender and 'race' have disregarded the position of South Asian women in society, as well as being falsely universalistic and ethnocentric. The second part of the chapter will focus on how the present study will overcome these limitations. It will argue that issues of culture and 'race' play a significant part in the lives of South Asian women and may affect their experiences in society.

Chapter 3 will examine and critically analyse existing theories of patriarchy and feminism. It will aim to include South Asian women in the theoretical analysis of patriarchy. The chapter will begin by reviewing exemplary theoretical positions within the literature concerning the study of feminism (Black feminism, Dual Systems, Liberal Feminism, Marxist Feminism, Radical Feminism and Patriarchy). It will be argued that there is a need to explore and examine the position of South Asian women in society in reference to women's personal experiences. The chapter will finally provide a detailed criticism of the concept of patriarchy and argue for a new theory of patriarchy which indicates that the social structures of patriarchy which disadvantage South Asian women are different to those which disadvantage white women. This will demonstrate the significance of studying 'race' and culture in women's lives and the different forms of patriarchy they experience.

Chapter 4 will examine previous research on arranged marriages (Drury 1991, Kannan 1978, Stopes-Roe and Cochrane 1990) and indicate how previous studies on arranged marriages are both descriptive and dated. It will provide women's views on arranged marriages by examining how they defined an arranged marriage, whether arranged marriages were considered to be important in South Asian communities, if women had arranged marriages and the type of contact they had with their prospective husbands. It will go on to examine whether women would want their own daughters to have arranged marriages and their views towards women who do not have arranged marriages. It will be argued that arranged marriages form part of the household which is a structure which disadvantages women. Those women who participate in arranged marriages are disadvantaged through the system of arranged marriages. These women are defined as 'traditional' women. They experience private patriarchy through arranged marriages. Women who do not have an arranged marriage are defined as 'independent' women. These women are using their high levels of education to leave households and enter the public world.

Chapter 5 will examine previous literature on dowries (Bhachu 1985, Macleod 1976, Wilson 1978) and indicate that there are very few studies on dowries and the research that does exist has not examined how dowries are defined, what dowries consist of and why they are given. The chapter will also explore the relationship of women and the giving of dowries and whether women would give their own daughters dowries. It will be argued that the dowry system is related to the arranged marriage which is part of the structure of the household which disadvantages women. It is through the giving of dowries that private patriarchy operates for 'traditional' women. The chapter will also draw attention to how some 'independent' women are co-habiting and moving away from the practices of arranged marriages and dowries. They are entering the labour market and experiencing public patriarchy.

Chapter 6 will examine research on domestic labour (Oakley 1974, Warde and Hetherington 1993) and discuss how the study of domestic labour has tended to concentrate on the white nuclear family. It will offer an important development from earlier studies both by examining domestic labour as experienced by South Asian women, and also domestic labour as part of the household which is a patriarchal structure which disadvantages women. It argues that 'traditional' women are more likely to perform the majority of domestic labour tasks where they experience a more private form of patriarchy. 'Independent' women are more likely to share domestic labour tasks with their partners. It will be further argued that socialisation processes and cultural practices play a significant part in women's roles as mothers and wives. It is through these practices that patriarchy operates and South Asian women are expected to participate and perform domestic labour tasks for men.

Chapter 7 will explore the domestic financial situation for South Asian women. It will be argued that existing literature on domestic finance (Graham 1985, Gray 1979, Pahl 1989, Vogler 1994, Vogler and Pahl 1993, 1994, Wilson 1987) has only examined the distribution of domestic finance and its relationship to who has power within the household from a white ethnocentric perspective. This chapter aims to redress this balance and examine the effect culture and 'race' may have upon the organisation of domestic finance in South Asian households. It will be argued that culture and 'race' make a significant difference to the organisation of domestic finance and the distribution of power in South Asian households. 'Traditional' South Asian women are more likely to hand their wage packets over to their husbands. Furthermore, in poorer households it is men who are more likely to control the money. The distribution of domestic finance is an indication of the different forms of patriarchy experienced by South Asian women. In traditional households, husbands are more likely to control money and in independent households, money is more likely to be shared by both partners.

Chapter 8 will examine the wider context of the relationship between gender and ethnicity, by analysing recent statistics from the Labour Force Survey on education, employment and marital status for different ethnic groups. It will be argued that marital status has a differential impact upon economic activity and education. There are differences between ethnic groups, as well as differences within the South Asian category. It will demonstrate that rapid social change is taking place for South Asian women, in particular when they reject arranged marriages, obtain a high level of education and enter the labour market. These women are leaving households, (private patriarchy), and entering public patriarchy.

In chapter 9, the main themes and issues raised throughout the book will be drawn together. This chapter will examine how previous chapters combine to form the different experiences of South Asian women's lives and how they experience patriarchy within different structures. The main theoretical position will be examined in relation to the household as the main private patriarchal structure which includes patriarchy within different structures. The main theoretical position will be examined in relation to the household as the main private patriarchal structure which includes the practice of arranged marriages and dowries as well as the performance of domestic labour and the distribution of domestic finance. The influence of women's education and employment statuses will be discussed as the main public structures of patriarchy. The chapter will conclude by examining patriarchy as experienced by South Asian women in relation to Labour Force Survey data which indicates rapid social change is taking place for the younger cohort of South Asian women (ages 25-30).

Note

1   I use the term 'black' to refer to individuals of South Asian and/or Afro Caribbean descent, as a political term.

2 The study of gender and 'race'

Gender, 'race' and ethnicity

Early feminist theory tended to emphasise the commonalities of women's oppression. In order to establish that male domination was systematic and affected all areas of women's lives, feminists offered analyses of women's subordination, exploitation and objectification at all levels of society. This emphasis on commonality however, often resulted in the neglect of differences between women. Differences based on 'race' and ethnic identity, nationality, class and sexuality have become increasingly important within feminist work, leading both to the documentation of experiences (Lorde 1984), and challenges to theories and concepts within feminism based upon limited models of the category 'woman' (Amos and Parmar 1984, Bryan et al 1985, Carby 1982, hooks 1982, Joseph and Lewis 1981, Ngcobo 1988, Parmar 1982, Ramazanoglu 1989, Spellman 1990). These changes within feminist theory have been influenced by changes within the women's movement more generally, where differences between women have gradually come to be seen as one of the strengths of the feminist movement, in terms of a diversity of both national and international politics (Cole 1986). These differences between women, have also called into question the collective 'we' of feminism, who is the 'we' and who does it refer to (hooks 1984, Ramazanoglu 1989)?

In feminism, what has been relevant is questioning the very concept of 'woman' (Amos and Parmar 1984, Brah 1992, Bryan et al 1985, Carby 1982, hooks 1982, Joseph and Lewis 1981, Knowles and Mercer 1992, Tang Nain 1991). Once it is recognised that women are possessors of multiple subjectivities based upon 'race', class, age, sexual orientation and religion, different affiliations may come into prominence in different circumstances, perhaps according to political priorities (Alcoff 1988). Feminism has been challenged for being preoccupied with privileged western white women's concerns (Jayawandera 1986). One strand of this critique argues for the need to understand imperialism and to inject an international perspective into western feminism (Amos and Parmar 1984). Some writers suggest that rather than reject feminism simply as a white ideology, black women should re-

24

define and re-claim the term (Bryan et al 1985, Davis 1990, King 1988).

Furthermore, the project of women's liberation has been challenged by notions of imperialism and racism. In combination with class, racism and imperialism, feminists have questioned the differences between women. Slavery, conquest and colonialism created dominant and subject peoples within global structures of material exploitation and political subordination. Women on different sides of these global processes have significantly different interests (Bhavnani and Coulson 1986, Bulbeck 1988, Lorde 1984, Moraga and Anzaldua 1981). The political context within which the British racism-feminism debate has taken place continues to be one in which racism and imperialism figures strongly. However, black critiques of feminism have been beneficial (Amos and Parmar 1984, Brah 1992, Carby 1982, hooks 1982, 1984, Joseph 1981, Lorde 1981, Moraga and Anzaldua 1981, Spellman 1990). Feminism itself has provided fertile ground for analysis of politics of the 'other' in history and black women have injected a much needed theoretical and political dynamism into feminism.

Much of the black women's critique has highlighted the suppression within feminism of black and white difference. This can happen in one of two ways. The first is the denial of difference which is implicit in the assumption that all women have certain interests in common. The second is through its representation as black 'deviance'. Black women have been marginalised in feminist discourses, when they are depicted it is as the exception. This problematises the ways in which black women differ from white feminism's standard of 'woman', rather than the general applicability of this standard. In their argument, black women have demanded that feminism should abandon the notion that all women automatically have common interests (and that men and women have opposing interests). The underlying logic is that common interests between women, only emerge as a consequence of common appropriation of historical experiences of oppression, subordination and exploitation through the essentially political practices of solidarity, alliance and resistance. In other words, feminism has been challenged to place itself in history and to locate itself in relation to other forms of resistance such as black, third world liberation and class struggles. Many of the issues raised by black women, (marginalisation and 'otherness'), are familiar to white feminists from their own history of resistance. What has not been so easy to come to terms with, is the need to acknowledge the uncomfortable dual position of oppressor and oppressed. Furthermore, the tendency to homogenise the oppression of black people comes from an understandable desire to find common ground and to resist the power of racism to divide black people from one another. It remains the case that perhaps more than half the people who may be labelled 'black' do not identify themselves as such (Brah 1992, Hazareesingh 1986, Modood 1994, Westwood and Bhachu 1988). If we try to emphasise black and white difference, there is also the tendency to deny the complexity of both black and white experience. This may be unavoidable, but unless it is explicitly acknowledged a racial essentialism may emerge from fixed and oppositional identities.

Many writers have examined the neglect of black women and their experiences

(Amos and Parmar 1984, Anthias and Yuval-Davis 1992, Barrett and Macintosh 1985, Brah 1992, Brittan and Maynard 1984, Carby 1982, Davis 1981, hooks 1982, 1984, 1991, Joseph 1981, Knowles and Mercer 1991, 1992, Lorde 1981, Moraga and Anzaldua 1981, Parmar 1982, Tang Nain 1991). The growing body of writing by feminists has explored the ways in which both traditional and feminist theorising and research has either rendered black people invisible or visible only as stereotypes and deviants. Phoenix (1987) has termed this the 'normalised absence/pathologised presence couplet'. Black women (Carby 1982, hooks 1982, Joseph and Lewis 1981, Spellman 1990) have challenged many of the central preoccupations and conceptualisations of feminism. For example, Phoenix (1987) examines theories of gendered identities and finds them lacking with regard to their non-consideration of the different developmental experiences of black and white children. Lewis (1983) finds that the public/private spheres division does not apply to black men and women because of the relationship between blacks and whites in society.

Phoenix (1987) and Carby (1982) argue, that what is needed is not just an 'adding on' of black women to feminist theorising, but a fundamental reconception of these theories as:

> ...the way the gender of black women is constructed differs from the construction of white femininity because it is also subject to racism (Carby 1982:214).

What white feminists have been producing it is argued, are generalisations based only upon white middle class women's experiences, generalisations that do not take account of, or account for, the experiences of working class or black women.

White feminists (Barrett and Macintosh 1985) have begun to take note of the criticisms of their work made by black feminists (Carby 1982, hooks 1982). Phillips (1987) for example, has noted how her work on the way part-time jobs have defined the experience of women in Britain assumes that this is the experience of women as a whole because black women are much more likely to work part-time. She accepts that 'race' and class differences cut across sex similarity to produce different kinds of inequalities. In a more personal way, Barrett and Macintosh (1985) confess that:

> ...privileged white feminists such as ourselves have been too absorbed in playing our own role of oppressed womanhood, too committed to our existing positions, too insistent perhaps that we should only speak from our own experience (1985:23).

Generally, there has been a recognition of social divisions between women and an acceptance that the effects of these divisions are real. Differences among women need to be explored as seriously as we have treated differences between women and men. In this sense, Lawrence (1982:133) remarks upon the tendency of white sociologists to obscure the question of their relationship to the black people they study, a relationship that is structured by racism. Whereas others (Phoenix 1987, 1990, Tizard and Phoenix 1993) have argued that research itself continues to construct white people as the norm and black people as abnormal by comparison. Furthermore, Amos and Parmar (1981) have argued that if we are examining racism and 'race relations', it is not to the black community that our attention should be directed, but to:

...the structures and institutions which function in that racist manner (1981:129).

Braidotti (1992) argues that unless feminists are clear about the national frameworks and cultural differences within which they work, they run the paradoxical risk of becoming implicitly ethnocentric. Indeed, is the term 'feminist' sufficiently receptive to differences, in order to represent the political will that unites many women (Mama 1984)?

More recently, Anthias and Yuval-Davis (1992) have attempted to provide a theoretical account of the category 'race', ways of conceptualising racism and nationalism, issues of 'race' and class, 'race' and gender and the role of the category 'Black' within racialisation processes. They examine the relationship between ethnicity and gender as they interplay with each other, both in terms of their conceptual similarities and differences and in terms of the ways in which they intermesh in concrete social relations. They consider the specific position of ethnic minority and racialised women in contemporary Britain and show how class, sex and 'race' interact, particularly in the areas of state action around nationality and employment. Anthias and Yuval-Davis (1992) argue that racism or racial categorisation involves discourses relating to subordination as well as exclusion. However, gender relations differ according to ethnicity, gender divisions of the dominant ethnic group will also affect ethnic minority women.

This section has examined white feminist claims for its concerns and priorities with white, middle class women which conceals the variety and diversity of human experience and subjectivity. The study of gender can no longer be assumed to be based upon the experiences of white, middle class women, but must examine the influence of colour, culture and 'race' and the implications this has for women and their individual experiences. We can no longer assume the term 'woman' is a unitary category, but need to investigate difference and diversity in women's lives to understand women's experiences. How are South Asian women's lives different to those of white women? What influence does colour, culture and 'race' have upon their position within households? To what extent is patriarchy experienced differently for South Asian women in comparison to how patriarchy is experienced by white, western women? Such questions will enable us to examine the diversity of experience in women's lives.

South Asian households

The household has often been taken as a unit to be approached for obtaining information about individuals in a population. It has also been viewed as the basic entity (the minimal primary group in the system of groupings in society). Whilst it is difficult to arrive at a minimal or universal accepted definition of the household, some comparison across cultures and societies needs to be attempted. Membership of a household is not a simple issue. There are likely to be different categories of membership in a household with different rights in, and access to, resources and varying expectations. The concept of the 'normal' in respect to household compositions differs across communities and cultures. The area occupied for the purpose of carrying out ones daily existence is regarded as a 'household', (residential unit, living arrangements of a family or domestic group). The family itself plays a vital role in households and influences the whole extent of social organisation and culture.

In South Asian communities, both in Britain and in India, there is a wide variation in the type of domestic groups, ranging from husband, wife and children to larger extended families with three or four generations, patrilineal or patrilocal, matrilineal or matrilocal. In some cases, the entire domestic group may not live in the same household, but may be spread out. The problem lies in whether each residential unit should be regarded as a single household or whether the 'cluster of residential units' should be regarded as a single household.

Very little research exists on South Asian 'households', however a vast amount of literature exists on the South Asian family and its workings (Anwar 1985, Ballard and Ballard 1977, Bhachu 1985, Chandan 1986, Ghuman 1980, Kalra 1980, Kannan 1978, Khan 1976, Shaw 1988, Werbner 1979, Wilson 1978). The research that does exist on South Asian households in the UK, has examined the relationship between South Asian households and employment practices (Warrier 1988).

Countering earlier discussions of Indian women which present them as lacking autonomy in their lives (Brown et al 1981, Standing 1985), Bhachu (1988) has shown how waged work empowers Sikh women in Britain and has had definite effects within the domestic sphere. It has given Sikh women more resources with which to negotiate changes in the division of labour within the home and also in the patterns of expenditure which they control. Households since migration, according to Bhachu (1988), have become more egalitarian, with a decrease in sex segregation and increased contact between women and their husbands.

Warrier (1988) however, examines production relations (in employment), which situate women as workers and class members, and relations of production (in households), which situate women as wives and mothers. She states that forms of households in which Gujerati women live are differentiated in relation to three major patterns; a household of parents and children, the general pattern of a three generational household and a joint household formed by brothers with or without parents. Household composition is not fixed, it could be fluid and grow or diminish in relation to a pattern of visiting and staying with relatives in other parts of the country.

The difficulties of 'fixing' and thereby verifying households as a unit of analysis is underlined when treating households as single units in terms of the generation and allocation of resources. To do so, neither allows for the differential access that men and women, adults and children have to household resources, nor does it alert the analysis to the important sources of both support and conflict that exist within and beyond households.

Werbner (1988) states that when Pakistani women work, their wages are their own, unlike those of women in rural Punjab (Sharma 1981). The pivotal role fulfilled by women in the formation of interhousehold networks raises the question, whether these networks may be regarded as part of the 'domestic' or 'public domains' (cf Bujra 1978, Rosaldo 1973, Yanagisako 1979). However, Werbner (1988) regards the networks as constituting the nexus of the public and the domestic, mediating between the more formal context of public activity and the privacy and affectivity of domestic household life.

There is a vast amount of literature which exists on households in South Asia. It was not until the distinction between the 'household' and the 'family' was firmly established by Mayer (1960:182) in South Asia and Bender (1967) and Yanagisako (1979) elsewhere, that ethnographers began to analyse households as distinct social realms with their own characteristics. Early work on households in South Asia examined the relationship between household and kinship structures (Kolenda 1968, Shah 1974). Whilst other writers had sought to provide an understanding of households as domestic realms and their relationship to the encompassing society (Bennett 1983, Frickle 1987, Kumari 1989, Sharma 1981, 1986, Vatuk 1972).

In South Asian communities in India the household is considered to be one of the most significant social groups in people's lives, it is the primary place for socialisation and for the constitution of an individual's identity (Caldwell et al 1984, Hanjal 1982, Wilk and Netting 1984). It is also the location and beneficiary of a majority of the rituals performed by members of South Asian communities (Gray and Mearns 1989).

Writers have provided a critical and analytical issue of households (Gray 1989, Kondo 1989, Mearns 1989), whilst others have shown how the variety and dynamism of domestic forms in South Asia is related to historical, geographical, economic and social conditions in which it is constituted (Kolenda 1989, Shah 1974, Sharma 1989). Some writers have compared households over time and between cultures (Laslett and Carter 1984). Yet others, have examined the variety of forms the domestic realm takes in South Asia (McGilvray 1989, Vatuk 1989, Wilk and Netting 1984). Different writers (Carter 1984, Gray and Mearns 1989, Kolenda 1989, Mearns 1989) give different definitions for 'households'. Some have taken an historical perspective on households (Sanjek 1982, Verdon 1980, Yanagisako 1979). Others have provided methodological contributions to the study of households (Carter 1984, Freed and Freed 1982, 1983). Some research has looked at urban-rural differences in households (Dyson and Moore 1983, Mandelbaum 1970) and gender inequality in households (Bardhan 1980, Das Gupta 1987, Sharma 1981, 1986).

Clearly a concentration on households does not predict a single approach or point of focus for specific analyses of the relationships it encompasses within its social space.

Households have been much debated in the last decade (Smith et al 1984, Wilk and Netting 1984). Much of this debate has been at a general level and has chosen empirical material from an extremely diverse set of societies. Where the debate has focused on functions of households in relation to the processes at work in the larger social system, the conclusions have all too often been rather general and unilluminating, precisely because the forms and functions of households in their particular contexts are highly variable (Gray and Mearns 1989).

To make too quick a judgement on the social and cultural significance of households may be to beg a lot of prior questions as to the very nature of forms of households and whether they are identifiable as a single logical entity (Gray and Mearns 1989). Household relations are the major experiential mediator between the 'individual' and 'society'. They are also the primary context through which both are reproduced. There are many problems associated with conceptualising households. Saradomoni (1992) argues that households cannot be treated as private entities separable from the context in which they are embedded. Yet Kalpagam (1992) has argued that the distinction between the domestic and public spheres and the societal ideas about relating women to the domestic sphere have contributed to the 'invisibility' of women's work and life.

This section has examined the analysis of households in the UK and in India. Households are not static and insulated units, but are constantly shaped by societal changes and processes. The development of capitalism, modernisation and urbanisation each has its impact upon households. The composition of household activities (production/reproduction) is different at different points in history. So, the intra-household arrangements between members of households are expected to change. Change and continuity are likely to affect different households differently which calls for a differential approach to the study of women and households. New methodologies of enquiry need to be developed regarding women and households, so that the characteristics of all adult members will be taken into account and examined within the context of households in which they live. It is important to obtain pertinent information about all women in households and describe the changing roles of women in relation to domestic arrangements and the household economy. There are different definitions of what constitutes a household and who lives in a household. It is crucial to examine the influence of 'race' and how this may affect definitions of households and relations within them. How do definitions of households affect forms of patriarchy experienced by different women? To what extent do households constitute a structure of patriarchy? Such questions will enable us to examine the relevance of household structures and differences in household forms that exist for South Asian women in Britain.

Methods

Sixty in-depth interviews were carried out with South Asian women living in East London, as well as participant observation, which included living with a South Asian community for a period of six months. The field work took place over a year. Each interview ranged from two to four hours and the majority of interviews took place in the respondent's homes. A very specific group of South Asian women were investigated. South Asian was defined as those whose forefathers and foremothers had originated from the Indian sub-continent; India, Pakistan and Bangladesh. The ages of the women ranged from 25-30 years and they had all been born in the UK. I wanted all women to be in the same age range; as these women were second generation women, were born and educated in Britain, would be in a form of employment and may already have had an arranged marriage. Three groups were investigated to examine the impact of religious difference; women who defined themselves as Hindu, Sikh and Moslem. Twenty women from each religious group were interviewed to examine, the impact of religion on forms of patriarchy experienced by South Asian women. A total of 60 in-depth interviews were carried out with South Asian women living in East London. Sixty was a large enough number in order to make generalisations for the quantitative analysis, yet small enough to conduct detailed in-depth interviews and transcribe the data for the qualitative analysis. East London was taken as a specific area to be investigated as it includes a very high population of South Asians from all three religious backgrounds.

Participant observation

As a South Asian woman, I have lived in the South Asian community all of my life. I became a participant observer to gain further information about the realities of South Asian women's lives. This included participating in cultural and community functions, assisting in temple work, (cleaning and cooking in the temple with other South Asian females), and participating in religious and traditional festivals (weddings, Diwali). An overt role was taken in which I negotiated my access and participation with community leaders. Being a participant observer produced interesting data concerning cultural aspects of South Asian society; rituals, traditions and customs which added depth and richness to the study and helped gain a greater understanding of South Asian women's lives. The setting in which the research took place is an immensely varied South Asian community. The large South Asian community has individuals from diverse social and economic backgrounds. Many of the South Asians in East London are owners of different retail and wholesale businesses. Other members of the community are from professional and non-manual occupations. They are a close knit community who feel proud of their identity as South Asians and of belonging to a community where they feel accepted. Family and non-family members meet regularly to maintain support within their community as they feel, 'the outside world can often be hostile and racist to us Asians'.

Sampling frame

South Asian women are a very difficult group to study, based upon their cultural definitions and strong views regarding male and female roles within their communities. They are a very close knit group who have and portray a very strong, cohesive sense of belonging and security. Their cultural identity is reinforced and regarded as essential to the well-being of the community, culture and individuals. Outsiders who do not identify with the group are viewed with suspicion and seen as a threat. Members of the community question what the outsiders want and how they may affect the daily lives of the individuals who live in the culture.

Random door knocking was rejected as this provoked resistance, and was regarded as being highly suspicious and intrusive. This was investigated in the pilot study, many women were not interested in the research and felt their privacy was being invaded. They felt I was 'overstepping the mark' and 'should have known better' than to 'knock on South Asian people's doors and ask them to be interviewed'. Doctor's surgery lists involved going to an area where there was a high population of south Asians and obtaining names and addresses. Actually obtaining the information from the surgery was problematic, trying to identify the religious background of respondents by their names. Some doctors did not want me to use their lists and said they wanted to protect the privacy of their patients. They did not see the study as having a 'medical element' and so refused to cooperate. Names from telephone directories were examined from a specific area where there was a high population of South Asians. However, there was some difficulty in guessing the religious background of respondents from the names and many South Asian families did not appreciate a strange woman telephoning their home and asking to enter their private domain, in order to carry out research. Many women were angry and wondered where I had obtained their telephone numbers from. They felt I was a member of Social Services and did not want to cooperate. Nursery and school registers were also considered, where the names of children were to be used as a basis to conduct the interviews. However, schools were reluctant for a research student to examine their registers and said the research was not 'directly concerned with educational issues'.

There is no obvious sampling frame of South Asian women. The sampling method used was that of the snowball sample. Once I had made the initial contact with a few women, other women were recommended to be interviewed. The respondents were easily accessible as they had already spoken to someone who had participated in the research and I had less chance of being viewed as suspicious. The respondents respected me and felt comfortable, secure and safe that I had entered the homes of other South Asian women they were acquainted with. Other women were contacted through advertisements placed at the local university and in the local student paper to prompt respondents to contact me. Hence, in order to avoid a biased and skewed sample, two starting points of snowball sampling were used.

In snowball sampling the researcher has no control over the nature of the sample. There is always the danger that the sample will be heavily skewed in favour of particular types of women. I tried to overcome this by using different starting points from which to contact my respondents. On the one hand, the sample may be unrepresentative as it is a snowball sample. On the other, the sample can claim to be representative as different starting points were used to encourage women to participate and there was a different spread of contacting respondents.

Feminist methodologies

In carrying out my research, I have been guided by my understanding of feminist methodologies. Whilst most writers on feminist methodological issues agree there is no one method that can be termed *the* feminist methodology, certain characteristics can be drawn out (Cook and Fonow 1990, Harding 1987, Reinharz 1983, Smith 1987, Stanley and Wise 1983). There is not necessarily one feminist methodology, but many different feminist *methodologies*. Feminist critiques point to a male bias within sociology which structure the knowledge base of the discipline and the social relations of production. It is argued that gender bias is introduced through the theoretical frameworks and methods by which empirical investigations are conducted. However, feminist research methodology has certain principles which are considered to be of importance at all stages of research. First, women's lives need to be addressed in their own terms. Second, feminist research should not just be *on* women but *for* women, to provide for women's explanations of their lives which can be used to improve their situation, research should have emancipatory potential. Third, a feminist methodology involves putting the researcher into the process of production, the researchers can make explicit the reasoning procedures they utilised in carrying out the research and be self-reflexive about their own perceptions and biases which they bring to the research.

A non-hierarchial relationship can also be established in the research process. In order to understand the research subject, we can examine the notion of personal and subjective experiences. This involves being reflexive; putting ourselves in the position of the subject and understanding their perspective. We may also examine how we as researchers and feminists are able to represent reality as objectively as possible. It is important that researchers are critical in their own research project, in order to produce a more objective account of what they 'see'. Researchers can aim to locate themselves within a specific critical paradigm, from which to base their judgements and come to their conclusions. Here the participatory model of research is useful, it aims to produce non-hierarchial, non-authoritarian and non-manipulative research relationships (Reinharz 1983).

Acker (1983) argues that we should locate individual experience in society and history, embedded within a set of social relations which produce both the possibilities and limitations of that experience. This is a method for exploration and discovery, a way to begin to search for understandings that may contribute to the goals of liberation, by gender being understood as being the central focus in constructing all social relations and taking individual women's lives as problematic.

Within feminist methodologies the debate between quantitative and qualitative methods includes the claim that; quantitative research techniques, involving the translation of individual's experiences into categories predefined by researchers, may distort women's experiences and result in a silencing of women's own voices. Advocates of qualitative methods have argued that individual women's understandings, emotions and actions in the world can be explored in women's own terms. Jayaratne and Stewart (1990) argue that much of the feminist debate about qualitative and quantitative research has been sterile and based upon a false polarisation and the solutions offered for methodological problems have frequently been either too general or too constraining to be realistically incorporated into research activity.

Feminist methodological considerations do not automatically advocate the use of particular or 'appropriate' methods, but many feminist writers have used qualitative methods, such as in-depth interviews or ethnography in relation to feminist research (Devault 1990, Finch 1984, Oakley 1981). Other feminist writers have reclaimed quantitative methods for feminist research (Jayaratne and Stewart 1990).

'Woman to woman' interviewing - the influence of 'race'

My structural position as a South Asian woman affected my research and has enabled me to examine the many faceted complexities of the dynamics involved in 'woman to woman' interviewing. The feminist approach to interviewing which is exemplified in the work of Oakley (1981) argues that the research process includes statements and discourses about one's own experiences with the phenomena under question. The goal of finding out about people through interviewing is best achieved when:

> ...the relationship of the interviewer and the interviewee is non-hierarchial and when the interviewer is prepared to invest his or her own personal identity in the relationship (1981:41).

This is also supported by Finch (1984) who argues that women more so than men are used to accepting intrusions into the more private parts of their lives. In the setting of the interviewee's own home, an interview conducted in an informal way by another woman can easily take on the character of an intimate conversation.

Devault (1990) has argued that a feminist sociology can open up standard topics from the descriptive, building more from what we share with respondents as women, than from disciplinary categories that we bring to research encounters:

> ...women interviewing women bring to their interaction a tradition of 'woman talk', they help each other develop ideas and are typically better prepared than men to use the interview as a 'search procedure' (1990:101).

I felt women were able to open up, trust and confide in me, which allowed them to reveal very personal and intimate details of their lives, for example the abusive behaviour of their mothers-in-law. The same information may not have been obtained, if the research was carried out by a South Asian male. However, Brah (1992) states:

> No matter how often the concept is exposed as vacuous, 'race' still acts as an apparently ineradicable marker of social difference (1992:126).

Gender may not be enough to create the shared meanings which are necessary to understand the experiences of women's lives. Is it possible a white, middle class woman carrying out research within a black working class community may create a situation where there are barriers to understanding? Each individual woman has different cultural experiences. The lack of shared norms about how an interview is organised and unfamiliar cultural themes in the context of the interview creates barriers to understanding:

> Gender congruity is not enough to overcome ethnic incongruity, the bond between the woman interviewer and the woman interviewee is insufficient to create the shared meanings that could transcend the divisions between them (Riessman 1987:190).

'Race' infuses itself into the research process and into the interview situation in much the same way that it has been argued a feminist methodology should do and shared gender or sex does. 'Race' is a variable that assists both the researcher and the researched to place each other within the social structure and so can have bearings upon the relationship between the researcher and the researched. Amos and Parmar (1981) indicate that the inclusion of black people in white studies:

> ..serves only to add cross-cultural spice to predominantly ethnocentric work (1981:129).

The question is, should we 'encourage' white researchers to carry out research on black communities? Barrett and Macintosh (1985) assert:

> We do still believe that white women are not the best placed to tackle these specific matters (1985:42).

Similarly, Carby (1982) argues that when white researchers carry out research on black people, they operate within white western supremacist assumptions. She states:

> Instead of taking black people as the objects of their research, white feminist researchers should try to uncover the gender-specific mechanisms of racism amongst white women (1982:232).

'Race' is an analytical tool for investigating and understanding the differences among women. 'Race' is a gendered social category (Liu 1991).

Mies (1991) however argues that the concept of 'partial identification' is important, that we proceed from our own contradictory state of being and consciousness. This enables recognition of that which binds us to the 'other women' as well as that which separates us from them. Binding us are the experiences of women all over the world, of repression, sexism and exploitation. 'Partial identification' means that we also recognise that which separates us, such as forms of oppression that might be rooted in such traits as skin colour, language and education. In these appearances, we see a manifestation of the power relations according to which the whole of society is structured. So 'partial identification' which begins with a double consciousness means, that as researchers we are aware of the structures within which we live and work.

South Asian women who welcomed the opportunity to speak to me enabled this 'partial identification' to surface. I was able to see reality through the eyes of other South Asian women and share a sense of belonging and empathy. If a South Asian woman is able to get another South Asian woman to speak about her life, they not only have 'shared experience', 'shared empathy', but also 'shared identity'.

Issues of difference such as sexuality, class, age, caste, linguistic heritage as well as nationality may operate to set up both commonalities and differences (Ribbens 1989, Stanley 1991). Feminist analysis has also showed that women's lives as subjective experiences were also influenced by other competing identities such as 'race', ethnicity and class, (hooks 1982, Phillips 1992). Simple notions of women as a homogenous group who shared a common experience of oppression gave way to an awareness of the complexity of the material reality of women's lived lives. Acceptance of the need to critically engage with meanings of difference and diversity within feminist thinking created the need to question what difference and diversity meant within feminist research (Anthias and Yuval-Davis 1992, Spellman 1990).

Access

One of the most difficult parts of the research was finding women to interview. Some women were highly suspicious of my motives, they regarded me as some kind of 'secret investigator', and wanted to know what I intended doing with my tape-recorded information. One South Asian women regarded me as a 'nosey girl', who had nothing better to do except, 'listen to the private lives of respectable women'. I was told, 'it's none of your business to know what goes on behind closed doors'. Having been brought up in a close extended network and strong cultural background, my experience as a South Asian women prepared me for a certain sense of traditional stereotyping regarding the definition of roles. As I was questioning this 'taken for granted' division, some respondents showed a general lack of respect for me, because they were confronted by a 'young' so-called 'educated' South Asian woman. One woman began mocking me and became highly offensive:

At the end of the day, men do their work and we do ours, including you, even if you are studying for a PhD (41[1]).

My major decision was to avoid any conflict and confrontation between the respondents and myself. I tried not to become involved and voice my opinions, though at times it was very tempting to do so. The majority of women however, were extremely friendly and welcomed me into their homes. They were glad to assist me and have someone take an interest in their lives, who was willing to listen at great length on an aspect of their lives they felt was 'highly trivial and unimportant'. The interview situation made them feel valued. As the women themselves were able to empathise and identify with me, they expected me to automatically understand their situation:

You should know what I mean being an Asian woman (6).

Many women were quite amused I was spending valuable time conducting research on issues they felt were obvious:

That's a funny question to ask...you probably know Asian men don't lift a finger in the kitchen (44).

It was intended interviews would be conducted in private, however on many occasions husbands were frequently interrupting the interview situation. This made me feel uncomfortable, as if I was under constant surveillance. The sole reason for interviewing women alone was to produce data independently, so that women would not be influenced in any answers they gave. Some women had to stop the interview to cook their husbands their evening meal and in some cases mothers-in-law were present. Other women conducted interviews whilst ironing or cooking, as they were too busy to stop, there was also regular interruption from children. In using the interview method, this brings us to questions of 'real research'. Are the respondents telling the 'truth' and can we rely solely on verbal reports? It is possible respondents want to be portrayed in a certain way and hence provide 'socially desirable' answers. As the interview technique allows for flexibility, this may leave room for bias and personal influence in which the lack of standardisation in the data collection process makes interviewees highly vulnerable to the bias of the interviewer. Sometimes, cues may be given which may influence the respondent's answers. Even if verbal cues are avoided, forms of non-verbal communication may exist over which the interviewer may have no control. It is impossible to achieve complete objectivity and it should perhaps be mandatory that researchers state their biases, in order that their work can be better interpreted and understood.

The notion of access was extremely difficult. Problems of access were concerned with the difficulty of the group being studied. Such problems and questions help us to think whether we should be conducting research and understand the reasons why there are so few research projects in this area.

Personal experience

In my own research, my personal experiences were affecting my views of my respondents. As a South Asian woman, I felt their lives mirrored those lives of South Asian women I myself had close contact with; sisters, aunts and my mother. I began to question to what extent the lives of these women were different to the lives of my relatives and how were their lives different to my own? In being too close and familiar with the subject matter, there is a possibility that certain aspects may be overlooked. Alternatively, respondents may be aware of our knowledge of the subject matter and may withhold information they see as too obvious in the light of a 'shared reality'. When the researcher and the researched operate from shared realities, there may be a tendency to take too much for granted. Researchers may overlook certain aspects of participant's realities, because of presumed familiarity with those realities. Familiarity with the phenomena under study therefore risks blindness to certain details that may be important. As researchers, issues of 'over-rapport' are apparent. Striking an adequate balance between rapport and distance may overcome this, by being able to 'manufacture distance' (McCracken 1988), to create a crucial awareness of matters with which we may have blinding familiarity. This has added importance when the issues are highly private and personal.

The notion of establishing a 'pretence awareness context', that portrays a message of not knowing or pretending not to know what the informant is talking about, is one possible strategy. Simmel's (1950) discussion of the 'stranger' accounts for intimate disclosures. Furthermore, playing the role of the 'objective stranger' incorporates a structured balance between 'distance and nearness, indifference and involvement'. The implications of this for insiders is clear; to use the nearness and involvement afforded by shared experiences to gain access and establish trust, but maintain whenever possible the distance and mystery of the 'stranger', in order to encourage a full account of the participant's experience.

Being too close to the subject matter may threaten the objectivity and attachment that typically are thought to be necessary to make research 'good science'. Although the history of qualitative research is filled with examples of researchers examining aspects of the empirical world with which they have personal experience (Becker 1963), little attention has been paid to the methodological implications of this research role. More attention has been directed to problems associated with researchers being outsiders who must maintain marginal positions with those under scrutiny. Is the research we do as social researchers the research that we describe or the research that is experienced by the researched? It is what we see and who we are that contributes to the end product. The researchers own experiences are an integral part of the research and should therefore be described as such.

Questions concerning personal experiences, perceptions and interpretations enter into the data and it is important for the researcher to identify and understand the relationship between the personal agenda and the research agenda. The research agenda may be nourished by the personal agenda in ways that will enhance sensitivity to what is being researched and generate insight into the issues of the research itself. When conducting research into sensitive areas, it is important to focus on the research goal, to understand how participants assign meaning to their realities, rather than to evaluate their realities through our own responses and opinions. Reflection on personal issues such as our own gender socialisation, our cultural and racial identity and expectations we have of our own family members may affect the research, in ways that we are unconsciously aware of. For insiders, past-related experiences are essential parts of the research process and they demand not just acknowledgement, but conscious and deliberate inclusion.

My identity as a South Asian woman enabled me to identify with my respondents, but at the same time emphasised the real differences between us. I was similar to my respondents. I shared their experiences of the culture, I spoke their language, I understood their experiences. Yet, I was different and regarded as privileged being a PhD student, a member of the academic elite. As a social researcher I was viewed as being an 'outsider-inside'. I was part of the 'us'. I understood women's experiences of living as a South Asian woman in a society which values male power and I also understood women's anger of being racially abused in a society which values white power. I was also part of the 'them'. I was educated to a high standard, I was a professional and I was the one writing about *their* lives in articles and books to be published. This made me very different to my respondents. The 'outsider-inside' status made me feel lost in my own research. I did not entirely belong to either group. However, shared experience reveals diversity as much as diversity reveals shared experience, as Du Bois has revealed:

> ...see what is there, not what we've been taught is there, not even what we might wish to find, but what is (1983:108).

The 'presentation of self'

The research situation requires the researcher to reflect upon her/his behaviour, mode of conduct and dress. The 'presentation of self' includes statements and discourses about ones' experiences with the phenomena in question. For example, what type of role should we take in the research project; covert or overt? Should we tell our respondents who we are and what we are doing, or should we aim to distance ourselves from this? The researcher decides how to present her/his motives, how much to participate and how intensely she/he will become involved in participant families' lives. For my own research the following issues were apparent and had to be considered; the traditional mode of South Asian dress (salwar, camise), hair in the traditional appropriate fashion, Indian ornaments (dhikka) and wearing a wedding ring. Although my identity as a South Asian woman enabled me to gain access , I had to dress in order to accepted into the community. It was inappropriate to conduct my research in jeans and a t-shirt, since this would be regarded as insulting. As Shaffir (1980) has argued:

> ...the intensity of the fieldwork process is typically accompanied by a psychological anxiety resulting in a continuos presentation and management of self when in the presence of those studied (1980:4).

As researchers, the 'presentation of self' is a mode of communication to the respondents and affects the responses we may receive.

Educational status

My educational status was a source of difference between myself and my respondents. Because I was a PhD student, I was seen as being privileged, someone who had it easy:

> It's different for people like you, people like you have it easy, you're lucky to get educated (42).

Some women said they were afraid I was going to ask them 'hard', 'intellectual' questions and were quite relieved to find the interview was like a 'conversation'. A few women saw me as 'an Asian girl made good' and said:

> Your parents must be proud of you, having achieved so much (58).

Age was also an indicator of difference. The older women in the sample saw me as being 'deviant' (a single, unmarried woman still studying):

> Aren't you going to get married yet, you'll be too old to have children and you're too old to be still at college (28).

Some of the younger women who had arranged marriages saw me as a threat, a 'know-all':

> Just because you're still studying, doesn't mean you know everything (42).

Others who had not had an arranged marriage or were studying, saw me as being successful and were glad some South Asian women were achieving, despite cultural pressures and racism in society:

It's good to know we can get somewhere, you've done well going against the culture, that must be hard...and trying in this society...one that doesn't like us Asians (56).

Power

Within the research process, what is to be considered of vital importance is the structures of power and the social practices upon which the power is produced in the process of carrying out research. The process becomes a symbolic and social reality through which power is maintained and exercised.

The balance of power in the research shifted. In some cases, it was evident I had the power, as I was able to control the questions that were asked. I had the pen and the clip board and I had access to the tape-recorder. In other instances, it was the women who had the power as they were able to decide what they wanted to tell me by withholding information. They could also decide to leave the research unexpectedly.

In some instances, women defined the relationship as something that existed beyond the limits of the interview situation. Women wanted to establish an intimate relationship, a friendship. There existed a great tension between these relationships and the goals of the research project. I had the power because it was my decision if I wanted to continue a personal relationship with my respondents. I have decided to keep my relationships with my respondents as professional, research relationships.

Because of the familiarity of the researcher with the subject matter and the casual style with which information is shared, the researcher's role may become confused. Informants may perceive researchers as experts who have all the answers. The women began to move beyond the interview questions and the interview situation and, in some cases, began to discuss the more personal and intimate details of their lives. I had to constantly remind myself that I was not a therapist, counsellor or a social worker. In this sense, Reinharz (1983) has argued that research is:

> ...conducted on a rape model, the researchers take, hit and run. They intrude into their subject's privacy, disrupt their perceptions, utilise false pretences, manipulate the relationship and give little or nothing in return. When the needs of the researcher are satisfied, they break off contact with the subject (1983:95).

During the year I conducted the interviews I kept a diary. In many cases, I left the interview situation wondering how I had affected women's lives. What did they feel about the questions I had asked them? My feelings after the interviews varied from enjoyment to sympathy to relief. In some cases I became over-emotional trying to understand and deal with the situation of my respondents and left feeling quite depressed, as many of them clearly showed signs of unhappiness. The interview process became a dialogue, a conversation, a discussion in which there existed a power relationship between two individuals who were discussing an aspect of life they had personal experience of. An effort to explore and clarify the topic under discussion is evident; both are assumed to be individuals who reflect upon their experiences and who communicate these reflections. This is inherent in the situation, neither the subjectivity of the researcher nor the subjectivity of the researched can be eliminated in the research process. As Acker states:

> We found that we had to assume the role of the people with the power to define, the act of looking at interviews, summarising anothers life and placing it within a context is an act of objectification. Indeed, we the researchers took the position that some process of objectification of the self is a necessary part of coming to an awareness of one's own existence; it is not less a part of coming to an understanding of others (1992:142).

The power relationship between the researcher and the researched is two-way. Cotterill (1992) in writing about issues of power and her own feelings of vulnerability in her research, talks of interviews as:

> ...fluid encounters where balances shift between and during different interview situations (1992:604).

Whilst acknowledging the fluidity of the interview situation, which can result in feelings of vulnerability, she also acknowledges that the final balance of power does rest with the researcher who interprets, analyses and writes up the data. The researchers goal is always to gather information and thus the danger of exploitation and manipulation always exists no matter who conducts the research or who interviews whom. Finch (1984) acknowledges the power the researcher holds when she says:

> I have also emerged from interviews with the feeling that my interviewees need to know how to protect themselves from people like me (1984:80).

The relationship of power in the research process can be viewed as a continuum, individuals in the research process are not just passive. The researcher/researched dichotomy is one of power relations. The researcher can be both powerful and powerless in the research process. The more I revealed about my own personal experiences the more vulnerable and powerless I became. The researcher and the participant establish a relationship that is based on a fair exchange, but power relations may never be fully abolished. Self-disclosure involves a removing of defences and leaves the researcher with feelings of powerlessness. Yet sometimes, we have no choice but to conceal our opinions and withhold our power, for to reveal them would be problematic. Power and how it operates in the context of research relationships is an issue to be considered and re-considered.

Issues of power in research are not of course just a question of feminist methodology, but concern all research as a privileged activity. Our status as researchers often gives us the power to initiate research; to define 'others' reality, to translate 'others' social lives and language in terms that may not be their own. In the final analysis, the researcher departs with the data and the researched stay behind, no better off than before. To this extent, the researcher/researched relationship is an inherently unequal one, with the balance of power weighed disproportionately in favour of the researcher. Gender identity between interviewer and interviewee is not always enough to create common understandings or equalise the power relations between the two parties. The researcher, by virtue of having the data has the power as to what to present. At the same time, the interviewee is able to control the interview and dictate data content and form, but Brannen (1988) notes:

> ...groups without power are not in a position to assert power over the research process (1988:590).

'Giving voice'

Most of the women found the interview a welcome experience, because of the opportunity it presented to 'give voice' to their experiences of being a South Asian woman in Britain. Nobody had ever listened to what they had wanted to say and they were pleased that somebody actually cared enough to ask them about their experiences and wanted to 'give voice' to their concerns. Many interviewees found indirect support through knowing that there were other women in the study who shared similar experiences to themselves. To this extent the research could be seen to 'give voice' to a group of women who would otherwise remain silent.

By adopting a participatory research strategy, (non-hierarchical, non-authoritarian, non-manipulative and empowering women), I have attempted to incorporate a feminist methodology. I have sought to prevent the repetition of established methodologies which have served to maintain and reinforce women's subordination. The methodology influenced the selection of methods to a great extent. It necessitated the use of methods which would allow me to investigate the meanings South Asian women gave to their lives. The methods also had to be sensitive enough to allow the categories of analysis to emerge from the data. To this end, I decided to adopt a qualitative and quantitative approach to the research. I intended the interviews to be non-hierarchial, so the interview technique was structured and unstructured. I hoped to give respondents space to speak about an issue or event as a whole, rather than isolated questions. I explained my motives, revealed personal information about myself, explained the purpose of the research and ensured confidentiality. My identity as a *woman* enabled a 'reciprocity', a sharing of knowledge on the basis of gender identity to surface. My identity as a *South Asian woman* enabled me to understand the racism and discrimination my respondents had suffered. My personal experiences and cultural socialisation as a South Asian woman enabled me to understand the experiences of my respondents (arranged marriages and dowries). I was also aware of the differences which existed between myself and my respondents (power, education and age). I was able to account for the power differences between myself and the respondents, by recognising my location in society affected the research relationship. The women themselves also benefited from the research project. They had the opportunity to talk to a 'sympathetic listener' and to tell their story, for most women the interview process acted as a form of therapy. Women confided in me about personal troubles, not all of which related to the research project. In such cases, I was seen to provide 'a shoulder to cry on'. Many women said nobody had ever wanted to listen to what they had to say, now they could be heard. To this extent, the research 'gave voice' to a silent group and helped to empower these women. The subjective experiences of respondents were prioritised since this was the way in which they made sense of their lives. The respondents were given the space to define the issues that were important to them. Where the interpretations of events and issues differed between myself and the respondents, both interpretations were accounted for. Finally, in my aim to incorporate a feminist methodology the reproduction of the report was produced in an accessible form where respondents were able to see the results and the final write up.

However, in incorporating a feminist methodology, I would argue that the notion of 'woman to woman' interviewing as exemplified by Finch (1984) and Oakley (1981), is too simplistic to account for the complexities involved in 'race', power and status differences in the research process. Finch (1984) and Oakley (1981) argue that as both parties share a subordinate virtue of their gender, power relations between interviewer and interviewee are equalised. My experience of interviewing demonstrates that same-sex status is not enough to create shared understandings or eradicate power differentials between women. 'Race' is an added dimension which affects the research process, as are educational differences, age and issues of power.

As researchers we can individually consider which of the many social characteristics at issue are the most important to a particular situation, ('race', class, caste, culture), and locate ourselves within a specific critical paradigm. This will enable us to be aware of all these commonalities and differences which exist in the research and acknowledge the very real differences between women. These commonalities and differences can be incorporated within the research process itself, from which we can base our judgements and come to our conclusions. At the methodological level, an awareness of the double consciousness that arises from being a member of an oppressed class (women) and a privileged class (scholars), enables feminist researchers to explore women's perception of their situation from an experiential base. Feminist researchers can utilise methods and adopt methodologies which best answer the particular research questions confronting them, but to do so in ways which are consistent with feminist values and goals.

If we aim to move beyond an exploitative relationship between the researcher and the researched and gain insight and meaning into the experiences and lives of women, 'identification with' the researched will enable us to move closer to their view of reality. In analysing the research, reporting how events are experienced or perceived from the woman's own sense of reality, this will help us to gain access to the cultural meanings and categories according to which that particular definition constitutes the world, to see the world through the respondent's eyes. Their sense of reality can be entered into. How we do this, depends upon our own background, our own experiences as black/white, working/middle class, homo/heterosexual women/men. Questions about who is conducting the research, is relevant to the research process and can be made explicit in order to better understand the research.

Note

1   These numbers were used to identify respondents to protect their anonymity. See Appendix 1 for detailed information on respondents.

3 Gender and patriarchy

The study of gender

The first wave of feminism began at the end of the eighteenth century and lasted until the 1960's. The second wave of feminism is based upon writings from the 1960's to the 1990's. Since the late eighteenth century, women's position in society had been excluded from sociological theory and understanding. Women had seldom appeared in analyses and discussions of who has power in society. The inequalities that existed between men and women were deemed practically unimportant and theoretically uninteresting. However, gender and feminist thought now sees women and their situation as being central to academic analysis and asks, why is it that men in most societies have power over women and how can this be changed? It seeks to understand society in order to challenge and change it. The study of gender and feminism attempts to understand the relationship between the sexes as one of inequality, subordination, oppression and difference. Rather than talking of gender and feminism as a unified body of thought, it is possible to identify a number of distinct feminist positions. Here, the approaches most commonly identified are those of liberal, Marxist and radical feminism, as well as the dual systems approach and black feminism.

Liberal feminists examine the denial of equal rights to women in education and employment. They argue that women's disadvantaged position in society is related to specific prejudices against women. In relation to this, they also examine sexist attitudes towards women which act to sustain the situation. This approach has examined the lives of women by focusing on domestic labour (Oakley 1974) and women's employment (Martin and Roberts 1984). Liberal feminism has been criticised for failing to deal with the origins of patriarchal attitudes and the relationship between different forms of inequality.

Marxist feminists however, argue that gender inequality derives from capitalism, where men's domination of women is a by-product of capital's domination over labour. Class relations are the most important features of the social structure which determine gender relations. Some Marxist feminists (Seecombe 1974) argue that the family is considered to benefit capital by providing the day to day care of the workers and producing the next generation of workers for capitalism. Other Marxist feminists (Barrett 1980) have argued that there is a need for a less economistic analysis of capitalism and gender relations. Marxist feminists have been criticised for being too narrowly focused on capitalism and being unable to deal with gender relations in non-capitalist societies and for reducing gender inequality to capitalism.

According to radical feminists, both these theories ignore the nature and ubiquity of male power. Radical feminism was first fully articulated in the late 1960's and it argues that men's patriarchal power over women is the primary power relationship in human society. It further argues, that this power is not confined to the public worlds of economic and political activity, but that it characterises all relationships between the sexes including the most intimate. This insistence, that the 'personal is political', involves a re-definition of power and politics. Hence it challenges the assumptions of political theory, which is itself seen as an instrument of male domination that justifies or conceals the reality of male power and its bases in 'private' life. Some radical feminists (Brownmiller 1976, Firestone 1974) see male violence as the cause of women's oppression, whilst others (Rich 1980) state sexuality itself is seen as a major site of male domination. Radical feminists have been criticised for being essentialist, reductionist and for a false universalism which does not examine historical change or the divisions between women based upon ethnicity and class.

Dual systems theory examines the interrelationship of capitalism and patriarchy to explain women's position within the labour market (Cockburn 1983, Hartmann 1981a). Hartmann (1981a) has argued that although they have become bound up with each other, neither of these 'dual systems' can be reduced to the other. Hartmann (1981a) states that job segregation by sex is central to men's control over women in all aspects of society. Men exclude women from the better areas of paid work and so women are exploited.

However, other writers have rejected the dual-systems approach and argue that what we now have is a unified system of capitalist patriarchy (Eisenstein 1981, Jaggar 1983, Vogel 1983, Young 1981). Walby (1990:140) however, does not reject the dual-systems approach, but has criticised Hartmann's (1981a) theory, and argues that there is more tension between the two systems of capital and patriarchy than is suggested, and ethnic variation and inequality need to be taken more fully into account. Westwood (1984) provides a dual-systems account which explores the intersection of gender and 'race' in factory work.

More recently, some researchers have classified feminisms into different types; empirical, standpoint and post-modern (Eichler 1988, Harding 1986, 1987, 1990, Hartsock 1983, Smith 1987, Stanley and Wise 1983, 1993).

Feminist empiricists argue that sexism and androcentrism in scientific enquiry make research biased and so, male-centred. Such biases enter the research process at the stage when scientific problems are identified and defined, and when concepts and hypotheses are formulated. But, they also appear in the design of research and the collection and interpretation of data (Harding 1990). The goal of this perspective is

47

the development of non-sexist research (Eichler 1988).

Standpoint feminists observe that knowledge is supposed to be grounded in experience, but what has counted as knowledge is measured against a certain limited and distorted kind of experience (Harding 1990). They aim to produce research that is both used *by* and useful *for* women. Standpoint feminists argue that their accounts of the social world are less partial and less distorted than those which are malestream. However, standpoint feminists have been criticised for ignoring differences between women, such as 'race', age and sexuality (Collins 1990).

Post-modern feminists argue that knowledge is rooted in the values and interests of particular social groups. They assume a symmetry between truth and falsity. By rejecting all truth claims, they argue that the production of knowledge is always a construction (Harding 1990). Post-modern feminists are concerned with explaining the discursive procedures whereby human beings gain an understanding of their world. They argue that standpoint feminism does not challenge the idea of a universal truth or the concept of multiple realities. More recently, some researchers (Smart 1995) have used such feminist classifications in reference to criminology.

A contested area of gender and feminism is its alleged racism and ethnocentrism, (Amos and Parmar 1984, Anthias and Yuval-Davis 1992, Barrett and Macintosh 1985, Brah 1992, Brittan and Maynard 1984, Carby 1982, Davis 1981, hooks 1982, 1984, 1991, Knowles and Mercer 1991, 1992, Moraga and Anzaldua 1981, Parmar 1982, Tang Nain 1991), this perspective has come to be known as 'Black Feminism'.

Much as feminists have attacked traditional political theory for excluding or marginalising women, feminism itself has been accused of universalising the assumptions and needs of white women in Europe and America, and largely ignoring the very different perspectives of black and third world women. Indeed, its very use of such terms suggests that white first world women are seen as the norm to which other groups may be added, as well as concealing the vast differences amongst the women so labelled. Some of the practices of mainstream feminisms demonstrate an insensitivity to the experiences of black women and the entire black population (Amos and Parmar 1984, Bryan et al 1985). The concepts of 'patriarchy' and the 'family' were singled out as problematic in their application to black women, as were 'reproduction', 'abortion' and 'male violence' (Tang Nain 1991). Some women (Joseph 1981, Lorde 1981) are now demanding that the experiences of women who have hitherto been marginalised become a central starting point, rather than an optional extra, for feminist theory and practice and that existing approaches can be discarded along with male theory. Others (Davis 1990, King 1988) argue that the limitations of present theories can be overcome, and there is in general a greater sensitivity to such issues than amongst Western feminists in the past.

Many feminists (Bergmann 1980a, 1980b, Brah and Shaw 1992, Dex 1983, Mama 1984, Miles and Phizacklea 1980, Phizacklea 1983, 1988, Phizacklea and Wolkowitz 1995, Wallace 1982, Warrier 1988, Westwood 1988) have argued that the labour market experiences of black women are different to those of white women due to the racist structures which exist in paid work. Hence, there are significant differences between black and white women which need to be taken into account. As a result of their ethnic identity, the chief sites of oppression for black women may be different to those for white women (hooks 1984, Parmar 1982). For example, hooks (1984) has argued that the family is not a site of oppression for black women, rather it is seen as a site of resistance and solidarity against racism. This is also supported by other writers (Amos and Parmar 1984, Carby 1982, Flax 1982, Lees 1986). Furthermore, the intersection of ethnicity and gender may alter ethnic and gender relations themselves, by the particular ways in which ethnic and gender relations have interacted historically (Walby 1990). For black feminist writings, racism is considered to be of significant political concern in which the inequalities between men and women may take different forms.

Patriarchy

In contemporary feminism the concept of patriarchy has received considerable attention and has been analysed as a system which oppresses women. There have been problems with the definition of patriarchy (Barrett 1980) and differences as to the causes of patriarchy. Radical feminists have argued that men's patriarchal power over women is the primary power relationship in human society. This power is not just confined to the public worlds of economic and political activity, but characterises all relationships between the sexes.

Some socialist feminists agree with radical feminists insistence upon the ubiquity of male power, but seek to give patriarchal power a history and to understand its relationship with other forms of domination, they try to explore the ways in which class and sex oppression interact in capitalist society. Radical feminists see the oppression of women as the most fundamental and universal form of domination where patriarchy is a key term. They argue, that male power is everywhere in the public world of politics and paid employment and in the private world of the family and sexuality.

Millett (1977) argues that in all known societies the relationship between the sexes is based upon power relationships and so therefore, are political relationships. Patriarchy also rests upon economic exploitation and the use or threat of force, for example foot binding, suttee and clitorectomy. However, radical feminists have been criticised for their theory of patriarchy on four points. The theory is said to be descriptive rather than analytical, unable to explain the origins of male power and therefore unable to provide an adequate strategy for ending it. The theory is based upon a false idea of 'man as the enemy', and is said to be ahistorical and 'falsely universalistic'. It reflects only the experiences of white, middle class women and obscures the very different problems faced by black, working class and third world women. It sees women only in terms of being passive victims rather than co-makers of history and agents of change. Walby (1990) has claimed that these criticisms are merely contingent.

Radical feminists see patriarchy as autonomous or itself the cause of other forms of oppression, whereas Marxist feminists see the origins of patriarchy as inextricably bound up with class society. Either way, it is agreed that patriarchy is not a mere derivative of economic power or class society and cannot be reduced to other forms of domination. It must be understood in its own terms.

Different writers give different reasons for the origins and causes of patriarchy (Delphy 1980; domestic labour, Dworkin 1981; violence, Firestone 1974; sexuality). For some radical feminists (Firestone 1974) the original shift to patriarchy was simply a consequence of men's greater strength stemming from women's weakness during pregnancy, childbirth and lactation. For others, it is men's ability to rape that enables them to dominate women (Brownmiller 1976). Some say it was the discovery of the male role in reproduction that first led men to seek control over women (Rich 1977). Yet others, see the development of patriarchy as rooted in the early development of hunting by men, which gave them both a new source of power and led to a development of a value system based upon violent conquest (Collard 1988). However, Spender (1985) argues that identifying origins of patriarchy is not important, but rather to identify the structures and institutions that maintain patriarchy, in order that these may be overthrown. An important aspect of patriarchy theory however, is that it enables us to distinguish between the different structures of male domination on the one hand and individual men on the other (Walby 1990).

Another problem with patriarchy is that in insisting on women's universal and shared oppression, it does not examine the changes that have taken place throughout history, the differences between one society and another and the importance of class and 'race' (Anthias and Yuval-Davis 1992, Collins 1990, King 1988, Ramazanoglu 1986, Spellman 1990). Women do have experiences in common involving sexual exploitation, but these experiences are qualitatively different due to class, 'race', age, sexuality, religion and language. Concepts such as patriarchy can conceal divisions in society in much the same way as male perspectives have concealed the oppression of women (Collins 1990, Ramazanoglu 1986). Black feminists (Amos and Parmar 1984, Carby 1982) suggest that because of racism, black men do not benefit from patriarchal social structures in the same way as white men and that benefit from patriarchy does not distinguish black men from black women. Joseph (1981) states that the term patriarchy can only be applicable to white male dominance, since:

...all white women have ultimate power over black men on account of the racist nature of the executive, legislative and judicial systems (1981:100).

Indeed, part of the problem lies in confusing different levels of analysis in terms of patriarchy (Chhachhi 1986). Westwood and Bhachu (1988) have pointed out that patriarchal relations are neither monolithic or static, but contexted by cultural elements within which they interact, including the means available to minority women to contest and negotiate patriarchal relations. This has encouraged white feminists (Barrett and Macintosh 1985) to be more cautious of their use of the term patriarchy as indicative of the female condition and a commonality among women. However, other feminists (Mies 1986, Walby 1990) argue that patriarchy ultimately unites all women in a common sisterhood as undifferentially oppressed subjects.

Some writers (Dahlerup 1987, Walby 1990) have attempted to produce a more sophisticated theory of patriarchy which argues that far from being unchanging, patriarchal domination takes a number of different forms which are the product of particular historical situations. Walby (1990) has argued that in western societies, there has been a general shift away from private patriarchy based upon individual control within the household to a more public form of patriarchy based upon structures outside the household. Walby states, this is based upon a:

...continuum rather than a rigid dichotomy (1990:180).

She states that different groups have been affected in different ways. Domination by men is not only experienced in the public worlds of politics and employment, but also in the family and personal relationships. A satisfactory understanding of patriarchy cannot be reduced to examination of any one structure, but must explore their interrelationships. Walby (1990) mentions religion as a cultural influence of patriarchy but does not provide a detailed account of this. What influence do religion and culture have on shaping forms of patriarchy? Furthermore, how do 'race' and ethnicity affect forms of patriarchy experienced by women? Does 'race' make a difference to forms of patriarchy experienced by women? Does culture make a difference to this? Racial divisions in theories of patriarchy are relegated to secondary importance as the notion of 'race' and ethnicity have been 'added on' to some existing theories of patriarchy. This is highly problematic and in order to examine the situation for South Asian women, we may ask, what are the different forms of patriarchy experienced by South Asian women and how are these different to those experienced by white women? Do South Asian women experience different forms of patriarchy from the private and public forms identified by Walby (1990)? I would argue that patriarchy is a concept which can be used to explain different women's position within society. New theories and analyses of patriarchy are necessary in order to incorporate difference and diversity to examine South Asian women's position within households and what patriarchy means for them.

Patriarchy and the family

Definitions of the family are problematic (Barrett 1980). The term family is used in contemporary western society to refer to either a group of people who live together and have some degree of shared housekeeping, (which is strictly speaking a household), or to those who are seen as being related by marriage or descent from common ancestors. The family most commonly however, and as a social ideal refers to a combination of the two meanings, to a group which lives together and is related by marriage and close kinship and specifically a domestic group made up of a man and his wife and their children. Some theorists (Delphy and Leonard 1992) refer to domestic groups as households. However, domestic groups are not necessarily composed of people related to each other by kinship and marriage. Also, some adults may live alone or with friends or in homosexual couples. This indicates not all members of a family may share a common household and not all members of a household are members of the same family. Other writers have reinterpreted the notion of the family as a discourse and have attempted to explore the various meanings of the term in western society (Bernades 1986, Gubrium 1988). Whilst others (Chester 1986, Segal 1983) have used the distinction between household and family as a means to downplay the significance of family relationships, (and their gender and generational hierarchies), in structuring people's lives in contemporary western societies. Millett (1977) argues that the family is a central part of society's power structure, it both sustains patriarchal power in the public world and is itself a source of women's oppression.

Radical feminists (Delphy 1980) argue that men benefit from domestic comfort more than women and their refusal to change and participate in domestic labour demonstrates the power men have over women. Delphy (1980) argues that marriage is a labour contract through which men exploit women's labour and because most women perform this unpaid labour, the position of all women in the employment market is depressed and marriage continues to appear to be their only viable option.

However, Delphy (1980) has been accused of not attempting to explore changes in marriage over time and between classes, and whether it is at the level of domestic exploitation rather than paid work or ideology that women should be struggling against (Barrett and Macintosh 1985). Is it possible to universalise from a particular historical moment and say domestic labour is the sole or even the prime source of women's oppression? Exploitation of women's labour in the home is connected to other aspects of economic and social life, it is not an unchanging source of oppression. Even though household tasks are not shared equally, some slight increased involvement in the home by men may mean it is less important than it was thought.

For other radical feminists, it is sexual rather than domestic exploitation that is seen to be important (Firestone 1974). Increased awareness of domestic violence and the sexual abuse of both women and children within the home, mean that for many feminists the family is seen as the cutting edge of patriarchal oppression (Firestone 1974). The connection between individual acts of violence and wider patriarchal power is underlined by the reluctance of authorities to interfere in 'private' domestic affairs (Hanmer and Saunders 1984) and that in some places marital rape is still not considered a crime (Russell 1984).

Firestone (1974) argues that reproduction is the basis of women's subordination by men, it is their role as producers that has disadvantaged women and so men have been able to dominate them. It is women's role as childbearer and childrearer (their biological role) that disadvantages women, rather than the economic structures that forms the material basis for the most fundamental division in society between men

and women. However, Firestone has been criticised
biologist, as well as universalistic and ahistoric (Barrett 19
change or offer any suggestions as to how the change should ta
from reproduction. O'Brien (1981) states that Firestone's
framework is confused and simplistic. The issues of reproduction n
other areas of patriarchal control and the struggle over reproductive
fought in this context, rather than isolated as a simple cause of oppressio
  Dinnerstein (1987) argues that it is women's participation in childcare whi
root of women's subordination. Whereas Chodorow (1978) states it is women'
in mothering which is the basis of their exploitation. Rich (1977) however, states th
it is not the biological fact of giving birth, but the fact that women reproduce in a
patriarchal society. However, many of these ideas have been criticised for a biological
determinism which contradicts current scientific thinking. As Bacchi (1990) has
argued that insistence on, or denial of significant sexual difference may also be based
upon a false dichotomy that distracts our attention from the need to challenge the
dominant values of women *and* men.

  Radical feminists have been criticised for having a reductionist, biologistic,
universalistic and ahistoric analysis (Barrett 1980) as well as being essentialist (Segal
1987). However, radical feminists analysis of the household does examine the
relationship of power and inequality between the sexes. It does not however, examine
the relationship between issues of gender and 'race' in the family.

  Some black feminists (Carby 1982, hooks 1984, Spellman 1990) have argued, both
that there are significant differences in family forms between ethnic groups and that
the family is less a source of oppression for black women than it is for white women.
Hence, previous feminist theory has made a serious error in attempting to develop a
general theory of women's oppression on the basis of white women's experiences
alone. However, forms of households in contemporary Britain vary between different
ethnic groups, not only between white and black but between the ethnic groups
themselves. For example, forms of households for South Asian women may be
different to forms of households for Afro-Caribbean women. The family itself may
have a different place for these two groups. In order to examine women's diverse
experiences of the family, it is important to analyse this difference and its contribution
to explanations of patriarchal theory. For example, to what extent does racial identity
affect women's position in the family? What difference does culture make to
definitions of the family and women's position within it? Such questions will enable
us to examine the impact of 'race', colour and culture upon South Asian women's
experiences within the family.

Culture

The concept of culture is significant when investigating the position of South Asian
women within households. Each South Asian group may be differentiated by their

spects of culture indicate a significance of
an groups. We need to examine the concept of
n the lives of South Asian women. The term
different ways, by many different writers and
ion of the term. Early research on the concept
nition of the term. Parsons and Shils (1951)
interaction and culture. They argued that
lopment of culture on the human level and it
he determination of action. Culture is also part
h we respond, because of the expectations of
luchkohn (1952) state:

ing their perceptions of events, other persons
ys not wholly determined by biology and by
environmental pressure (1952:186).

Other researchers however, have emphasised the symbiotic and transmitive aspects of culture (White 1947), the physical and material aspects of culture (Sorokin 1947), the learned quality of culture (Coon 1954) or the intellectual quality (Bidney 1953). Murdock (1946) classified the qualities or characteristics of culture as; the learned, the transmitive, the social, the ideational, the gratifying, the adaptive and the integrative. People must be able to feed, clothe and house themselves by adapting to their surroundings (Meggers 1954). Culture must also adapt to itself, in the sense that its different aspects are continually changing (Ogburn 1959). Linton (1968) incorporated the concept of culture to include the overt (materials and behaviour) and the covert (psychological aspects). It is the overt aspect of culture which is the principal agent in culture transmission. Kannan (1978) has used this definition in reference to immigrant communities.

Other research (Kroeber 1952) has emphasised the importance of the 'trait' in defining culture. Cultures also consist of social values. These are not static, they differ from one society to another and within the same society at different times (Linton 1968). Brown and Selznick (1955) suggest that the socialisation process involves the basic disciplines of society, which includes learning social values and appropriate roles. However, later research (Taylor 1971) defined culture as including folkways, mores and laws which emerge from social interaction and carry a normative content. Williams (1981) has defined culture as a social collectivity, which refers to the processes, categories and knowledge through which communities are defined as such, how they are rendered specific and differentiated. Further research (Clifford and Marcus 1986, Geertz 1973, 1983) has examined the influence of culture on shaping individual's lives.

In the study of 'race relations', the relationship between 'race' and culture became an important issue, where black cultures were regarded as being deviant and judged in comparison to the white norm. Hall (1978) stressed the role of racist representations of social problems such as crime in the emergence of a 'law and order' society in Britain in the early 1970's. The Empire Strikes Back (CCCS 1982) criticised the pathologisation of 'race' within 'race relations', sociology and the racism of some white feminist analyses (Carby 1982, Parmar 1982). It also explored the importance of racist ideologies in both shaping aspects of state regulation in Britain, such as immigration law and the construction of notions of Britishness and citizenship, informing contemporary definitions of national identity (Hall 1978, Lawrence 1982).

Work carried out by the Centre for Contemporary Cultural Studies has taken a dynamic, structural view of culture by theorising it as lived experience, inextricably linked with 'race', sex and class and only having meaning in the context of the society in which it occurs. Hence, everyday features of society and behaviour, such as the media, styles of dress and music, as well as what these mean to and for the groups under study, are closely examined. Gilroy (1987) has referred to these as 'black expressive cultures'. Culture is broadened to include the ideas of 'cultures of resistance' rather than being narrow versions of cultural influence (CCCS 1982, Hall and Jefferson 1976, McRobbie 1994). Earlier modes of subculture were transformed and challenged to include an acknowledgement of both the history of ethnic inequality and racism, and the struggles for collective self-representations for black people (Gilroy 1987).

However, recently there is emerging a new cultural politics of difference which overlays the older ethnic differences (Donald and Rattansi 1992, Hall 1992), which Hall (1992) has referred to as 'new ethnicities'. Hall (1992) has argued that in the discourses of black cultural production, we are beginning to see constructions of a new conception of identity, a new cultural politics which engages rather than suppresses difference and which depends upon the cultural construction of new identities. Furthermore, Rattansi (1992) has argued that in order to move forward in terms of 'race' and culture, we need to acknowledge the political significance of questions of national culture and ethnic identity and to grasp how these interact with questions of 'race' and racism. Other researchers have examined the concept of culture with reference to multiculturalism and education (Donald and Rattansi 1992, Troyna and Carrington 1987).

Many researchers (Brah 1992, Phoenix 1988, Warrier 1988, Westwood and Bhachu 1988) felt studies on black people used a narrow definition of cultural influence to explain their behaviour (Ineichen 1984, Skinner 1986). Such explanations are unsatisfactory because they oversimplify cultural influence and in doing so, serve to reinforce the social construction of black people as deviant from the norms of white British behaviour. The concentration on cultural differences between black people and white people has frequently obscured the fact that cultural beliefs, ideas and practices, necessarily embody the structural forces that affect people's lives and that culture itself is dynamic rather than static (Phoenix 1988). Although it is generally thought that 'race' only influences black women (and black men), what it means to be white can only be understood in contradistinction from what it means to be black. White women's lives are thus racially structured as are black women's lives (Frankenberg

1993). Furthermore, Westwood and Bhachu (1988) have argued that cultures are understood to be composite entities, generated and sustained by collectivities which promote dynamism and contradictions within the overall social formation. Culture is not viewed as fixed or static, but as multi-faceted, embracing most simply a way of life with specific symbols that define membership and resonate with the lived experiences of people (Khan 1982, Phoenix 1988, Westwood 1984). Rituals add to this, confirming and underlining cultural elements in the common sense world (Westwood 1988).

Phoenix (1988) states that complex (rather than simple) representations of culture need to be used. Such complex definitions encompass structural influences of class, gender and 'race'. This approach allows the representation of differences in style among black and white women. It also takes account of the common experiences that black and white women share as the result of being the same sex and similar class positions (Brah 1992, Phoenix 1988). More recent research (Donald and Rattansi 1992) has pointed out, that the rethinking of culture in the light of theoretical advances and political experience over recent years, has undermined the claims of community understood in terms of a normative identity and tradition; whether that of nation, religion, ethnicity, or the 'black experience'. Some researchers (Donald and Rattansi 1992, Lynch 1990, Parekh 1989, Verma 1989) state that definitions of culture are either not provided at all or conflate distinct conceptions such as symbolisation, ethnicity and lifestyle. Anthias and Yuval-Davis (1992) have examined the concept of culture in relation to citizenship, religion and origin and how these can become racialised as a structuring principle for national processes, by defining both the boundaries of the nation and the constituents of national identity. Much of ethnic culture is organised around rules relating to sexuality, marriage and the family and a true member will perform these roles properly. Communal and cultural boundaries often use differences in the way women are socially constructed as markers. They further argue that there has occurred an increasing ethnicisation of groups, where traditional cultural divisions are often displaced by the growth of more unifying identities.

Culture is a dynamic and multi-textured entity, it is not a fixed set of characteristics which are used to distinguish the normal from the abnormal. In early research, cultures were dissected and pieces of them offered as a means of understanding minority peoples and their lives. Once we dispense with this, and present a material and dynamic account of cultures and ethnicities, we can see the ways in which cultures and ideologies are embedded one with another. It is also possible to move beyond simple unitary views of culture and see differences and complexities that exist *within* and *between* ethnic groups. Since all societies have a plurality of socioeconomic groupings it is inaccurate to describe a country as having one culture. For example, the non-unitary nature of culture is particularly relevant for India, which is composed of a variety of languages, religions and traditions. To speak of 'Asian' culture is therefore, inaccurate.

There is a need to examine the differences which exist between white and black people's lives and cultures. Furthermore, there is a need to examine the differences which exist within black communities themselves. Individuals from South Asian groups are a diverse group of people. What are the different cultural experiences of South Asian women? How is culture related to forms of patriarchy? Such questions will enable us to examine the impact of cultural influence for South Asian women and analyse the differences and diversities which exist within South Asian communities.

4 Arranged marriages

The phenomenon of the arranged marriage in India has received a great deal of attention (Caplan 1985, Hershman 1981, Jyoti 1983, Trautman 1981). Early research on arranged marriages examined the relationship between age at marriage (Gupta 1972, Vatuk 1972), whilst other researchers demonstrated the endogamous and exogamous rules associated with caste, kinship and village (Karve 1965, Madan 1965). The early research (Fox 1975, Prabhu 1963) found no significant departure from the traditional methods of mate selection, in which the Indian family system was maintaining its basic character and adhering to traditional patterns of marriage. However, later research (Goldstein 1972, Gupta 1972, Rao and Rao 1982, Vatuk 1972) demonstrated that marriage patterns in India reflected changes in social customs, attitudes and values. With the effects of modernisation, the young wanted more freedom and choice in the marriage process. Other researchers (Mitter 1990, Papanek 1990, Sharma 1981) have demonstrated the position of women in the conjugal realm and their value in the wider society, the purity of women at marriage (Yalman 1963) and status differences between parents of the bride and groom (Trautmann 1981). The arranged marriage in India has been shown to reveal the following characteristics; it helps to maintain the social stratification system in the society (caste), it gives parents control over the family members, it enhances the chances to preserve and continue the ancestral line, it provides opportunity to strengthen the kinship group, it allows the consolidation and extension of family property and enables the elders to preserve the principle of endogamy (Rao and Rao 1982).

To what extent are arranged marriages in Indian society similar to those in the UK? Does culture make a significant difference to the prevalence of arranged marriages? Is the system of arranged marriages changing in the UK? Bhachu (1985) has argued that the traditional criteria of spouse selection and kinship organisation in the UK of South Asians, follows much the same pattern as that of North India (Pocock 1972, r Veen 1972, Vatuk 1972). Arranged marriages take place within one's own d inter-caste marriage is uncommon (Macleod 1976, Vatuk 1972). Caste y is a basic criterion of marriage arrangement in the UK, as it was back home

(Lannoy 1971, Michaelson 1983, Pocock 1972). Marriage is based upon the rule of exogamy (Karve 1965, Madan 1965), including the rule of village exogamy (Inden 1977, Madan 1965, Mayer 1960, Van der Veen 1972). In the arranged marriage system, ascribed and achieved status is important (Pocock 1972). Residence after marriage is predominantly with the joint family of the groom, in which the daughters in law have subordinate positions in the family (Van der Veen 1972, Vatuk 1972). In marriage selection, education, status and personal moral qualities of both the patrilineal and matrilineal kin are important (Kannan 1978). However, Bhachu (1985) has argued that increased attention is being paid to the individual assets of the spouses as opposed to general family background which has lost prominence since migration, this has also been found in India (Vatuk 1972). There has been a shift from viewing marriage as a match between two families, (the traditional view), to the more individualistic 'western' notion of marriage between two people (Bhachu 1985, Drury 1991, Gardner and Shukur 1994, Stopes-Roe and Cochrane 1990, Van der Veen 1972). Others (Ballard 1994a, Shaw 1994) have indicated that few young South Asians experience any difficulty in conforming to their parent's values and expectations of marriage.

There are profound differences between arranged marriages and the western notions of 'free' marriage (Khan 1979, Lannoy 1971, Michaelson 1983). The most significant being, in the West individuals retain the right to autonomy and personal responsibility for their lives. For South Asians, a lower age of marriage is desirable and customary since individuals have no need of courtship patterns. Furthermore, young South Asians are not socialised into rituals and mechanisms of finding a marriage partner for themselves (Anwar 1979, Ballard 1978, Brah 1978, Kalra 1980).

Within South Asian traditions, Hindu, Sikhs and Moslems differ critically in some precepts and customs concerning marriage. The groups from which a partner is drawn may differ (Bharanti 1972, Werbner 1979, Westwood 1988). Moslems marry within the kin group, Hindus and Sikhs may not, but may marry within caste or occupational groups (Anwar 1981). For Hindus and Sikhs, the importance of marriage is primarily sacramental, whereas for Muslims it is primarily contractual, which means that attitudes to re-marriage and divorce may be different (Ballard 1978, Brah 1978, Stopes-Roe and Cochrane 1990). However, the similarities between the three groups in terms of the relationship of the individual to the family, the social and economic importance attached to marriage, the family structure and the possibilities for mate selection are all important concerns (Wilson 1978).

Arranged marriages in the UK are seen as an 'alien' problem. A large amount of media attention has been given to the stereotypes of arranged marriages being forced and performed against the wishes of the young (Anwar 1979, Kalra 1980, Taylor 1976). Young South Asian women become visible as a stigmatised group when it is thought that they will experience an arranged marriage (Brah and Minhas 1985). Researchers (Ballard 1978, 1994a, 1994b, Bhachu 1985, Gardner and Shukur 1994, Stopes-Roe and Cochrane 1988, 1990), have identified the complexity of the arranged marriage where internal cultural values have evolved in response to external forces, potential conflict has been reduced and cohesion increased. The arranged marriage must be understood in the context of South Asian traditions, culture, religion and family structure of which it is a part.

The research which exists on arranged marriages, (both in India and in the UK), has provided a greater understanding of the dynamics involved within the South Asian family. However, much of the research is dated and does not specifically examine the arranged marriage and its relationship to patriarchy. What difference does participation in an arranged marriage make to forms of patriarchy experienced by South Asian women? How are arranged marriages defined? Why do some South Asian women have arranged marriages and others not? What is the relationship between arranged marriages and other structures of patriarchy? Such questions will enable us to explore the differences and diversities which exist in South Asian women's lives.

Marital status

The marital status of respondents varied considerably, half of the respondents in the study (50 per cent) had an arranged marriage, 38 per cent of respondents were living with their partners, (but were not married to them) and 12 per cent of respondents defined themselves as single women. However, there were no respondents who were married by a non-arranged marriage.

Table 4.1
Marital status

Status	n	%
Arranged marriage	30	50
Married, not arranged	0	0
Living with partner (Not married)	23	38
Single	7	12
Total (N)	60	100

The definition of an arranged marriage

In South Asian communities, arranged marriages are usually defined as parents and relatives choosing partners for their sons and daughters to marry. All respondents defined the arranged marriage as a process whereby a partner was chosen *for* them *by* another individual, this could be a member of the extended family, or a 'middleperson'.

Table 4.2
Definition of an arranged marriage

Definition	n	%
Parents	30	50
Parents & relatives	22	37
'Middleperson'	5	8
Father only	3	5
Total (N)	60	100

Half of the respondents in the study (50 per cent) defined an arranged marriage as parents finding a partner for their daughter to marry.

... when the parents tell you that you have to marry someone and you don't have any choice in who it is and you have to do it...because they make you do it (11).

...it's when the parents tell you of a boy they think will be alright for you and then you might see him at a wedding and then you get married to him (9).

Other respondents (37 per cent) defined an arranged marriage as parents *and* *relatives* choosing a partner for their daughter to marry.

...all the parents and the aunts and uncles get together and they start looking for someone and then they get you married (7).

...your mum and dad and then all the other people in the big family, all sit down and discuss your life, then they start to look for someone for you...they all do it together... (15).

A small number of respondents said it was a 'middleperson' (8 per cent) or the father (5 per cent) who chose a partner for the daughter to marry.

They go and ask someone who knows lots of people in the community...they get

61

someone who we call a 'middleperson' to do it...that person isn't related to you, they just know you in the community (35).

We're very strict in our families and we all leave things like that to the head of the family...our dad's are the ones who go and find someone for us to get married to...he's the head of the family and so he chooses who he wants us to marry (44).

Arranged marriages were defined as an agreement, a contract, a business arrangement between two families rather than between two individuals. Parents had the ultimate control over arranged marriages, as well as relatives who were able to influence the parent's decision. The families control who they choose for their daughter to marry. They are the ones who tell the parents which people they think are suitable, the parents then making the final choice. The pressure of the extended family indicates parents too, must conform to behaviour that is expected of them, by their family and the community. The importance, influence and opinions of family members, (both nuclear and extended), are fundamental to the arranged marriage. The social and economic importance attached to marriage is based upon the structure of the South Asian family. Duty towards and respect for the family is firmly laid down, and daughters have to rely on their parent's wisdom and authority in selecting a suitable boy.

The importance of an arranged marriage

Respondents were asked why they felt arranged marriages were important. Arranged marriages were considered to be very important in South Asian communities, they were part of the identity of South Asian people.

Table 4.3
The importance of an arranged marriage

Important	n	%
Culture	15	25
Respect	10	17
Work	4	6
Family bond	3	5
Religion	1	2
Sub-total	33	55
Not important		
Community pressure	19	32
No choice	3	5
Unhappiness	3	5
Degrade women	2	3
Sub-total	27	45
Total (N)	60	100

A total of 55 per cent of respondents said arranged marriages were important in South Asian communities. Different responses were given for the importance of arranged marriages, 25 per cent of respondents said arranged marriages were important due to the cultural expectations and traditions which existed in South Asian communities, these were linked to South Asian identity. The cultural identity of South Asian people was a very important part of individual's lives which were influenced and reinforced by having an arranged marriage.

...they are part of the culture and the people believe in them and it's the people who want to stick to the culture, it's like it's their identity to have an arranged marriage (16).

...the arranged marriage exists in our culture and we follow it, because it's part of our Asian identity and it's part of what we believe in, it's our tradition...mostly it's our whole identity...(23).

Participating in an arranged marriage demonstrated the respect daughters had for their parents, 17 per cent of respondents said this.

...if you have an arranged marriage, it shows you really do respect your parents and you respect what they think and so you do what they tell you to do, the best thing you can do is show that respect by doing what they tell you to do (29).

...respect is very important to us, you show you care about what they (parents) think and so you do what they tell you to do...(7).

A minority of respondents (7 per cent) said arranged marriages were important because they worked or they demonstrated the strength of the family bond (5 per cent).

I think they work...the divorce rate is low for us Asians, because we make our marriages work, it just shows what a good thing the arranged marriage is...all my family have had arranged marriages and they have all worked (42).

...if you have an arranged marriage it just means you have a strong link with your family and you are very close to them, it shows you care about them...and it's because we're all very close knit....(28).

However, a total of 45 per cent of respondents said arranged marriages were not important in South Asian communities. Different reasons were given for this, 32 per cent of respondents said it was the pressure from the community which made individuals feel arranged marriages were important.

...people make you think the arranged marriages are very important...because they come with the culture and so everyone has to have them...they don't want to be the ones who'll be talked about....(14).

...it's Asian people, they make us think they are (important)...they make us think that's the only thing we have in our life to aim for and if we don't have an arranged marriage we are nothing...and we've done nothing with our lives...people just make you think you have to have an arranged marriage and so you have to make sure you please them...like people in the community (37).

The pressure from the community was immense and South Asian parents felt they had to conform in order to be accepted and in order to preserve their 'izzat'. 'Izzat' is based upon family pride, honour and reputation in the community which is primarily related to male members of the family. However, it is women who are able to alter, destroy or enhance the 'izzat'.

> ...you have to make sure you have a good clean reputation and a good 'izzat' and so you want all your children, especially your daughters to have an arranged marriage...and you do what has to be done to make sure this happens (4).

A minority of respondents (5 per cent) said arranged marriages did not bring happiness to women, degraded women (3 per cent), or gave women no choice in their lives (5 per cent).

> ...lots of Asian people do think that they're (arranged marriages) important, because they want their children to have them...but that doesn't mean the girls will be happy...they (parents) just want to get them married, so they will be happy themselves (15).

> I think they (arranged marriages) degrade women, they make women look worse than men, and it's always the men who have the choice and not the women...men are the ones who benefit from the arranged marriages, women don't...it's the worse thing for women (17).

As young women grow into adulthood, there is great pressure towards conformity, obedience and support of the family. Hence, a daughter's reputation must be guarded at all costs. If a daughter steps out of line, she not only jeopardises her own chances of marriage and respect from the community, but also the chances of her siblings and the standing of her parents. Not only are women the guardians of the family honour ('izzat'), but they are also the transmitters of the religion and culture and if they deviate, they will be unable to adequately fulfil this task. South Asian women are entrusted with a large part of the burden for carrying the family honour. Their personal reputation should be spotless and the spirit of the family tradition is passed on from mother to daughter from the beginning of the child's life. South Asian families generally give greater protection to girls and encourage them to be a good wife and mother. Traditionally, she is protected by her family, (father and brothers), and then her husband.

The idea of parents emphasising the arranged marriage, was based upon the need for a separate South Asian identity. If women rejected arranged marriages, they were not only rejecting their traditions, but their identity. The whole notion of arranged marriages being part of South Asian identity was seen to be more important for women than for men. Women were the ones who felt they had to hold onto their identity, because the arranged marriage was part of their whole life. Part of being a woman was to have an arranged marriage and this was part of being identified as a *South Asian* woman who participated in her traditions. The families and parents themselves emphasise the importance of arranged marriages and see arranged marriages as an acceptance of traditional standards. The importance of adhering to traditional standards of behaviour indicates the ways in which individuals feel the need to retain their South Asian identity, at all costs. The hierarchial and authoritarian structure of the South Asian family produces certain goals and emphasises in child-rearing practices and family interaction patterns. Family well-being and success are not seen to be advanced by concentration on the development of personal characteristics, abilities or ambitions of individual members. Self-definition is based upon social roles and relationships. Esteem is more dependent upon properly fulfilling these roles.

Obedience to family and authority indicates a concern with family values rather than individualistic ones. Getting the young person married is seen to be the main responsibility of parents. Family reputation is also considered to be of utmost concern. The rebellion of older siblings, even if successful, might inhibit rather than facilitate the possibility of such action by younger siblings. Marriages of future siblings can also be taken as pointers to a satisfactory future rather than as threatening or inhibiting. Many accept the arranged marriage, because they believe in the principles from which it is based. They have grown up with the values of respect, obedience, filial duty and parental obligation; with a knowledge of the supreme importance of the family, its position and honour within the community; with a strong sense of tradition and a self-definition in terms of role rather than personal individuality. In addition, as the family is the primary support system, individuals must expect to give support to all family members, particularly parents and siblings. Since the family is the essential social and economic unit, they should also expect to consider its interests before their own. The prime responsibility is towards family welfare rather than personal development, this together with concern for the family's reputation and proper attention to what is due to elders and those in authority, are the superordinate requirements.

Type of contact

Respondents who had an arranged marriage (50 per cent) were asked the type of contact they had with their prospective partners before marriage. During the process of selecting a suitable boy for their daughter, parents allowed little or no prior contact between the prospective partners, this was considered breaking the rules of South Asian traditions.

Table 4.4

Type of contact for respondents who had an arranged marriage

Type of contact	n	%
Met once	13	43
Telephone	10	33
Letters	5	17
Dated	2	7
Total (N)	30	100

Of those respondents who had an arranged marriage, 43 per cent said they met their prospective partner on one occasion, before they were married.

> I only met my husband once for about 20 minutes...we talked and then he said yes and we got married about 6 months later and I didn't see him until then (6).

> I was only allowed to meet my husband once, and even then I wasn't even going to be allowed to do that...then we met once at a family function, but I wasn't allowed to talk to him and after that we got married (44).

Others (33 per cent of respondents who had an arranged marriage) were allowed to telephone their prospective partners.

> ...we were allowed to phone each other...that was considered safe because I lived in Bradford and he lived in London and when we chatted my parents were in the same room....(48).

> ...my husband would phone me, but I was never allowed to phone him...and they (parents) didn't mind really, we needed to get to know each other...(29).

Some respondents (17 per cent of those who had an arranged marriage) wrote to their prospective partners and a small minority (7 per cent of those who had an arranged marriage) dated their prospective partners.

> I was living in Pakistan then and so we wrote to each other all the time, that was allowed, because it was so far and they knew it was only letters...we couldn't meet, it was too far away (41).

I went out with my husband before I got married to him, but nobody knew about that, if they did they would have gone mad and things would have got nasty...but we just made sure nobody saw us and we went to places that were safe, where we wouldn't see people we knew...it was fun then (4).

Love was something which came after the marriage relationship and not before. Minimum contact with husbands before marriage was the norm. Parents did not allow much contact, because if the female were to change her mind, this would reflect badly upon their 'izzat' and bring 'sharam' upon their whole family. Arranged marriages are linked to strict moral codes, premarital celibacy is considered a great virtue especially for girls. Parents look to education, economic status and reputation of the family and the partner before they make a decision. There is great pressure upon women, more so than men to follow the tradition of arranged marriages. If women wanted to rebel, their non-conformist behaviour was not tolerated, because it would result in gossip, scandal and humiliation for the parents, who would be subject to social criticism, which would jeopardise their relationship with the kinship group and the community in general. Women are constantly under pressure to please others; their parents, the extended family and the community. If they marry, their parents achieve respect and status in the community.

Own children and arranged marriages

All respondents were asked whether they would want their own children to have arranged marriages.

Table 4.5
Own children and arranged marriages

Arranged marriage	n	%
Continue traditions	24	40
Demonstrate love	3	5
Obedience	3	5
Sub-total	30	50
Non arranged marriage		
Choice	10	17
Degrading	14	23
Disagree	4	7
Don't know	2	3
Sub-total	30	50
Total (N)	60	100

A total of 50 per cent of respondents said they would like their children to have arranged marriages. Different reasons were given for the continuation of arranged marriages, 40 per cent of respondents said they wanted to continue the tradition in South Asian communities, which for them, meant participating in an arranged marriage.

I believe in my culture and in keeping it the way it is, that's why I want my children to have arranged marriages, they will know where they're coming from and who they are (4).

I want the traditions of the arranged marriage to stay in my family, all the people before us did it and I hope all the people after us do it...I want my children to carry on that tradition (22).

A minority of respondents (5 per cent) said they wanted to demonstrate the love they had for their children and so wanted to continue the custom of arranged marriages. Others (5 per cent) said they wanted their children to obey them and so their children would have to have arranged marriages.

...it's a way of showing you care for them when you choose someone for them to marry...you have their best interests at heart...(29).

I want my children to do what they are told...I don't want them to do what the white people do, roam free, they have to do what we tell them...it's the only way they will be happy (48).

However, 50 per cent of respondents said they would not want their children to have arranged marriages. All these respondents had not had an arranged marriage. Different reasons were given for not continuing the arranged marriage, 23 per cent of these respondents said arranged marriages were degrading to women.

I don't want my daughters to have an arranged marriage...they just make women look inferior and they humiliate women, because women don't have a choice and women are the ones who are worse off than men...I think they degrade women in a bad way (37).

...if women have arranged marriages, they are the ones who are seen to be inferior to men and men are the ones who have the power over women, they (arranged marriages) put women down and make them look cheap...like pieces of meat...(20).

Other respondents who had not had an arranged marriage (17 per cent) said they wanted their children to have their own choice in life.

I want them to make their own decisions and they can choose who they want to marry...they should be able to do that, it's their life, let them live it how they want to live it...nobody should decide who you're going to marry, that should be one decision you should be able to make by yourself (11).

The strong force of the arranged marriage and South Asian traditions co-exist. Both are seen to be part of the identity of South Asian people, more so for South Asian women. If South Asian women pass the 'marriageable age', they are stigmatised. Not only do women have to have an arranged marriage, they must be a certain age when they marry and they must be able to cook, clean and sew. These are all lessons learnt in childhood, where the female from a very early age is prepared for the arranged marriage; prepared to perform specific duties as the wife, to be the perfect wife and mother.

Arranged marriages do not necessarily create a new and independent family, but are an expansion of an already existing family. The arranged marriage, its customs and traditions demands parents of male children to see that their sons are married and have male children, to continue and preserve the ancestral line for generations to come. Since the family continuity and preservation for generations to come is highly valued, parents are mainly concerned with their sons early marriage to please their ancestors as well as the future members of the family line, so the continuation of arranged marriages is considered to be fundamental in South Asian communities.

Single, independent women

Respondents were asked their views on single women, who lived their lives independently. Single, independent women in South Asian communities were considered as 'deviant' women. They had broken the rules as they had not participated in an arranged marriage.

Table 4.6
Single, independent women

Single women	n	%
Strong/independent	16	27
Risk losing family	12	20
Sexually promiscuous	15	25
Ruin family name	17	28
Total (N)	60	100

Respondents who said single women were strong and independent (27 per cent) were more likely to be independent and single themselves.

> ...they are very brave and strong and I think they stay single because they want to be independent and they are making a stand...I think they must really want it because it's so hard for Asian women if they want to do what they want.... (36).

Other respondents (20 per cent) said single women took a very big risk if they wanted to remain single, they risked loosing their family. These women were also more likely to be independent and single.

> ...we are made to know the great importance of the family from an early age...if

we don't obey, we have nothing...because of the way we're brought up we're made to believe we can't do anything for ourselves...so when we leave it's very hard for us, it's like you have no-one to rely on anymore...it's scary, but it's worth it, because you have your freedom...and then you learn to live with it...it becomes part of your normal life...(18).

Respondents who said single women were sexually promiscuous (25 per cent), were more likely to have had an arranged marriage.

...they have a problem...they just want to be single, so that they can sleep around, they want to be like the white women so they give us all a bad name...they're just selfish women...just slags really...(50).

Other respondents said single women ruined the family name (28 per cent), they were also more likely to have had an arranged marriage.

...they just put us all to shame...we can't walk down the street without people talking about us...we can't look people in the face...they just make us feel as though we wish we were dead...we may as well be...it's the worst thing seeing an Asian girl with a white man, and you know the whole community suffers...she gets what she wants, but everyone else has to pay for what she's done...I hate them, they make me sick...(6).

South Asian women felt because the arranged marriage was part of their entire socialisation, they were unable to reject it and were afraid of rejecting it, as they in turn would be rejected by the community. As the arranged marriage is part of the socialisation process for South Asian women, it is something that is embedded into their lives and is seen as being 'natural'. The idea of keeping things as they were was important. South Asian people wanted their society to remain static and did not see change as being part of their lives. Change was considered to be a bad thing, this was based upon fear. Change indicated men would no longer have control over women. Men want to maintain this control as it preserves the traditions and holds on to South Asian identity. For South Asian people, the arranged marriage is part of their childhood socialisation and is something they grow up to expect, it is instilled into them from an early age and is reflected in the different gender role socialisation that exists for males and females in South Asian communities.

If women reject arranged marriages, they are punished for having broken the rules in South Asian communities and having rejected its values. They are regarded as sexually promiscuous. It is their parents, and in turn their family members who are punished. If a woman decides she does not want to have an arranged marriage, her whole family is affected by her actions. When women break the rules of their communities, their behaviour affects other members of the family and community. The extended family and the community punish the family, by criticising the lack of control they have over the women in their family. Parents through fear, then place stronger demands upon their daughters. The effect of a woman rebelling enforces a chain reaction to take place.

Cultural view of single, independent women

Respondents were asked their opinions on the cultural view of single, independent women. Single, independent women in South Asian communities were regarded as being sexually promiscuous and selfish.

Table 4.7
Cultural view of single, independent women

Cultural view	n	%
Broken rules	15	25
Ruined 'Izzat'	25	43
Should be punished	10	16
Sexually loose	10	16
Total (N)	60	100

Respondents who said single, independent women would be seen as having ruined the 'izzat' of family members (43 per cent) were more likely to have had an arranged marriage, 15 out of 25 respondents who said this were married women.

...they are not respected...they have committed the worst crime, they have ruined the 'izzat' and it would be never be able to returned...they are never respected again...(25).

...they are just selfish, they ruin everything for everyone, they ruin the family's name and then people don't want to marry the other women in your family, because they think they're all like that...(48).

However, other respondents who said this had not had an arranged marriage (10 out of 25).

...if women want to do what they want, they are not seen as being strong women, but they are seen as having ruined the family name...everything depends on other people...the Asian culture is very selfish, it doesn't allow people to be themselves, they have to please their parents first and they have to satisfy the 'izzat'...(20).

Other respondents (25 per cent) said single, independent women would be seen as having broken the rules which exist in South Asian culture. These women were more likely to be single (12 out of 15).

...if you're taught to do certain things when you're young, these things are expected of you...and then if you decide to do what you want to do, that's a different story then...you've broken all the precious rules of what they (parents) and the culture wants you to do...(16).

However, a small minority of respondents who said this, were married (3 out of 15).

...these women have broken all the important rules of the culture...they have gone against everything they were taught not to do...and so once they have broken the rules, nobody cares about them...it's too late, too much is damaged...(7).

Other respondents (16 per cent) said the culture would want single, independent women to be punished. All respondents who said this had an arranged marriage.

....they should be punished badly, so that other girls can see what they're doing is wrong and so they won't want to do it...they'd be better off dead for the pain they've caused their parents...they should be punished...(49).

Yet other respondents (16 per cent) said the culture would regard single, independent women as being sexually loose. These respondents were more likely to be single (8 out of 10).

When Asian women decide they don't want to follow the culture, the culture just punishes them...instead of trying to understand the reasons for living alone and being independent, they immediately think you want to sleep around...they don't understand and they will never understand...they make too many assumptions and don't bother to try and understand what's going on (20).

A small minority who said this were married (2 out of 10).

If they don't do what they are told, what do they expect? They are just women who want to sleep with different men and they want the culture to approve...that will never happen and all the men will see them like they see prostitutes and they will just get used (21).

In South Asian communities, women who rebel are regarded as having ruined the 'izzat' of the whole family. Furthermore, they are seen as being sexually promiscuous and selfish, putting their own needs before those of the family. Respect in the community is regarded as a strong force of social control, which is directed towards women, their behaviour influences it and they are the ones who may suffer because of it. Achieving status in South Asian communities is gained by conforming to acceptable standards of behaviour. Once this happens, respect is achieved and status is enhanced. If women rebel, they break the family bonds. A breaking of family values is breaking a fundamental rule in South Asian communities. Arranged marriages, (the processes and methods of selection), are considered to be specific and unique to South Asian people. It is from arranged marriages that South Asian women maintain their identity of being *South Asian*. If they do not participate in arranged marriages, their whole South Asian identity is at stake. Arranged marriages were seen as part of South Asian identity, they were historical, traditional and generational.

The significance of religion, education and employment

Religion affected whether South Asian women had an arranged marriage. Moslem women were more likely to have had an arranged marriage, followed by Sikh and Hindu women. However, religion did not affect women's attitudes to arranged marriages. Level of education affected women's attitudes on whether they felt arranged marriages were a good thing. Respondents who said arranged marriages were important as they indicated the respect individuals had for their parents and the communities had low levels of education (those who had no qualifications or 'O' levels). Respondents who felt arranged marriages were not important as arranged marriages indicated the pressure of the community, gave women no choice in life or degraded women were highly educated (those who had a BA or MA). Highly educated respondents (those who had a BA or MA) said arranged marriages were negative for women and were less likely to have had an arranged marriage. Respondents who had a lower level of education (those who had 'O' levels or no qualifications), said arranged marriages were positive for women and had an arranged marriage. Women's position in the labour market affected their attitudes to arranged marriages. Those who said single, independent women were strong, were in high positions in the labour market (semi-professional and students). Those who said single, independent women were sexually promiscuous were in low positions in the labour market (skilled manual and semi-skilled). (See Appendix 3 for chi square tables on education and employment.)

'Traditional' and 'independent' women

Respondents who had a low level of education (those who had 'O' levels or no qualifications), were in low positions in the labour market (skilled manual) and were defined as 'traditional' women. They portrayed conformist, traditional attitudes towards arranged marriages. They saw arranged marriages as being positive for women, had an arranged marriage and experienced private patriarchy inside the household through the system of arranged marriages. Highly educated respondents (those who had a BA or MA), were in high positions in the labour market (semi-professional) and were defined as 'independent' women. They portrayed non-conformist attitudes towards arranged marriages and saw arranged marriages as being negative for women. They were living with their partners and did not intend to have an arranged marriage. They experienced public patriarchy outside the household through paid employment.

Conclusion

Different forms of patriarchy exist in South Asian households. One of the ways private patriarchy manifests itself is through the system of arranged marriages. Arranged marriages are customary practices which have existed for generations in South Asian communities. Opinions and practices on arranged marriages are divided. Some respondents felt arranged marriages were positive for women, whilst others felt arranged marriages degraded women.

Religion influenced whether South Asian women had an arranged marriage, but did not influence women's attitudes to arranged marriages. Level of education and position in the labour market affected women's attitudes to arranged marriages. Highly educated women were in high positions in the labour market, these women decided not to have an arranged marriage. They saw arranged marriages as being disadvantageous for women and held liberal attitudes to arranged marriages. These women become educated, decide they do not want to have an arranged marriage and become employed which results in them being self-sufficient. These women ('independent') experience a public form of patriarchy through forces external to the household, such as paid employment.

'Traditional' South Asian women who participate in arranged marriages have limited resources and access to power. They are economically dependent upon the men in the family and do not share in access to new economic opportunities with men. These women also *want to* continue in the traditions of their ancestors. They feel to do so enables them to maintain their own identity, belonging and security within their communities. Women with different attitudes are more likely to stay in the education system longer. These women decide *not to* participate in arranged marriages and so a process of assimilation is taking place. Some women reject practices they do not agree with and develop a new identity. They assimilate into British society, rejecting some aspects of their traditional South Asian practices in favour of others. 'Independent' women are moving away from the marriage relationship, as they want more freedom of choice to choose their own partners and see arranged marriages and dowries as being disadvantageous for women.

Previous research (Ballard 1994a), has argued that a process of 'code-switching' takes place in which the younger generation of South Asians are able to switch from one set of norms (such as at school) to another (such as at home). Ballard (1994a) argues that this involves a process of 'cultural navigation', the means by which individuals manoeuvre their way inside and outside the ethnic colony to their own advantage. So to say that some South Asians are in the process of 'culture conflict' is incorrect. I would argue that my research does not demonstrates that 'code-switching' takes place, rather, some women are openly rejecting aspects of South Asian traditions in favour of other, British ones. These women define their own sense of being, they accept their British born identity and feel they *have the choice* to reject the traditions of their ancestors. They recognise the status and opportunities that educational advancement brings. They also recognise that change is an inevitable process for British born South Asian women. For these women, the process of assimilation is one which includes shifting identities. Their lives are different to those of their mothers and they do not want their own daughters to engage in traditional practices. 'Independent' women see themselves as British based, some of whom have never travelled to the homes of their ancestors. As these women reject arranged marriages, some enter into relationships with non-Asian men to cohabit, moving away from the traditional stereotype of South Asian women in British society.

However, Shaw's research (1994) demonstrates that some Pakistani girls had gained higher educational qualifications, but had stayed within the organisation of the family in which they found few problems in combining careers with arranged marriages. My research did not demonstrate this, rather 'independent' women indicated that entering into an arranged marriage would hinder their chances of participating in higher education and having a professional career. These women saw marriage as a disadvantage. Many 'independent' women did not want to leave their place of residence to move to a strange town and live with their in-laws, something which happens often in the process of arranged marriages. There was an emphasis amongst 'independent' women that the British born and British educated second generation South Asian women will find it hard to resist the temptation to assimilate. Yet they were aware the difficulties assimilation may bring. On the one hand, these women were openly rejecting traditional South Asian practices, yet they still recognised their *difference* in a predominantly white British society. For them, racial exclusion was something they felt they would always encounter. Ballard's research (1994a) has also demonstrated that although a high proportion of South Asians are in higher education, they still encounter similar forms of racism and exclusion as their parents. Despite these prejudices however, the younger generation have made a substantial shift towards professionalism, with many British South Asians becoming more middle class. Ballard (1994b) indicates that these individuals sustain a sense of their own distinctive identity, in complex and varied ways, but few have turned away from their traditions. This is also demonstrated by Gardner and Shukur (1994) who explore how some British South Asians have constructed new and varied lifestyles of their own. They have adapted and re-adapted their identities to interpret their values and lifestyles in their new settings. Yet Gardner and Shukur (1994) argue that young British South Asians continue in the tradition of arranged marriages, but at the same time have compromised between the traditional arranged form to western style relationships. My research demonstrates that although South Asian 'independent' women have adapted their lifestyles in British society, they *do not* continue with the practice of arranged marriages. For 'independent' British born South Asian women a process of re-definition is taking place, their identities are shifting and complex. They want greater freedom of choice than their mothers, indicating a move towards the majority society in which they live.

The present study indicates that there are significant changes taking place for South Asian women in contemporary British society. Those women who continue to participate in arranged marriages emphasise the importance of women's value in South Asian communities and the purity of women at marriage. This has also been shown in previous research (Mitter 1990, Yalman 1963). Previous research has also indicated that the traditional criteria of spouse selection in the UK follows much the same pattern as North India (Bhachu 1985) as well as residence after marriage being with the groom's family (Vatuk 1972). The present research also found similar findings; the importance of caste in marriage as well as daughters-in law moving to residence with the groom's family.

Previous research (Drury 1991, Stopes-Roe and Cochrane 1990) has argued that the arranged marriage system has moved from being a match between two families to a more individualistic notion between two people. However, this was not found in the present research. Those who participated in arranged marriages saw arranged marriages as being an arrangement between *two families* in which families played a fundamental part in *all* decision making processes. Families continue to play an important part in the selection and arrangement of arranged marriages.

Previous research (Ballard 1994a, Gardner and Shukur 1994, Shaw 1994) has indicated that significant numbers of South Asians are in higher education and within the next few decades the numbers will continue to increase. However despite this, most young South Asians still continue to stay within their community and participate in traditional practices such as arranged marriages. My research did not demonstrate that women with high levels of education were committed to upholding their community traditions. These women were moving away from such traditions to create an identity of their own. I would argue that the present research has revealed new empirical data on the lives of South Asian women in British society. It has argued that women's participation in education affects their attitudes towards traditional South Asian practices. These women begin to question their own identity as South Asian women in British society. They reject traditional South Asian practices in favour of others. This behaviour indicates that a process of cultural re-definition is taking place as well as a process of assimilation into wider British society.

5 Dowries

The arranged marriage is related to the dowry. The dowry is considered to be a very important part of the arranged marriage. A great deal of research exists on dowry in India (Bennett 1983, Camaroff 1980, Fruzzetti 1990). Dowry is essentially a gift given to the bride or the couple by the girl's parents for the setting up of their new conjugal estate.

Different researchers have used different definitions to describe the dowry. The term dowry, as commonly understood in the South Asian context, conflates several different gifts that are given by the bride's parents at the time of her marriage and usually in forfeit of claims by her on the immoveable property of the parental estate (Miller 1980, Sharma 1994, Uberoi 1994). These are gifts of clothes and jewellery to the bride herself, which largely remain her personal property, household items which may or may not be successfully reclaimed if, and when, the bride and groom set up an independent household (Hooja 1969), gifts of clothes, jewellery and luxury items, (watches, cars, bikes) to the groom and his near kin, substantial sums of cash and consumer goods to the groom's parents to be used at their discretion (Uberoi 1994). Other research (Caplan 1994) has defined the dowry as consumer goods and cash which are laterally transferred from the bride's family to that of the groom. They are in no sense, the girl's own property, for they are very much under the control of senior male and female members of the groom's household and may be used by them towards the future marriages of the groom's sisters. On the other hand, Vatuk (1975) has defined dowry as a 'bridegroom price', it is one of the long series of asymmetrical gift-giving transactions that mark the relations between 'bride-giving' and 'bride-taking' households. Some researchers have argued that the daughter is seen as a gift, (the 'gift of the virgin'), (Schlegel 1991, Sharma 1986). Others (Chekki 1968, Rao and Rao 1982) have demonstrated the dowry as a cash payment. However, the generally used definition of dowry is a more restricted one, referring to the wealth given along with the daughter at marriage (Pocock 1972, Tambiah 1972, Van der Veen 1972). The bond between the daughter and her parents never ceases and is reaffirmed at every ceremony, through the presentation of gifts to her and her husband's kin. The groom and his family are recognised as endless receivers of gifts, even long after the marriage (Tambiah 1972, Vatuk 1972).

In North India, dowry marriage is considered to be the most prestigious form of marriage (Madan 1965). Dowry acts as an indicator and enhancer of family and caste status (Pocock 1972, Van der Veen 1972, Vatuk 1972). Tambiah (1972) states that dowries enable families of low status and high wealth to acquire prestige by arranging marriages with higher status families. On the other hand, dowry may be seen as a 'compensation' to the groom's parents for taking on a non-productive family member, as a 'pre-mortem inheritance', so called in those societies where women have recognised, though severely limited rights in parental property (Goody and Tambiah 1973). Alternatively the dowry may be seen as a response to a situation where there are too few eligible grooms in the marriage 'market' (Uberoi 1994). It is clear that dowry has the effect of controlling competition among women for the most desirable husbands in a hypergamous marriage market, whilst expanding the pool of desirable wives in the case of men (Murickan 1975, Vatuk 1975).

Much research has looked at dowry in India and women's rights in property and roles in production (Agarwal 1988, Miller 1989, Sharma 1989, Uberoi 1994). Despite anti-dowry legislation, the quantum of dowry *given* and *expected* in India has sharply increased over recent years, and is increasingly felt to be extortionate. In Northern India, unmet dowry demands have been associated with extremes of domestic violence, including the notorious phenomenon of 'dowry deaths' (Ghadially et al 1988, Kishwar 1986, Kumari 1989, Stein 1988, van Willigen and Channa 1991). Dowry giving has gained popularity amongst non-Hindu groups (Christians), whose religious ethos gives it no explicit approval (Caplan 1994, Visvanathan 1989). Social scientists have been concerned to find out to what extent the increase in dowry-giving can be related to other social indicators such as, the decline in the sex-ratio of females vis-a-vis males, the changes in women's relations to production, particularly the declining female workforce participation rate in areas that have experienced agricultural and industrial development, the expansion of the cash economy and the growth in education and literacy (Matthews 1990, Milner 1988, Sharma 1981, Srinvas 1984).

One feature of dowry systems in general, which applies strongly to India, is the concerns of kin groups with maintaining or enhancing social status through marriage (Goody 1973). Kishwar (1986) however, has provided a competing explanation to this and argues that the dowry functions to disinherit women and promote their economic dependency upon men. Schlegel (1991) more recently, has confirmed a strong association between dowry transactions and cultural concerns with premarital virginity, which she argues help to prevent lower class males from claiming wealth through impregnating higher class females. The whole complex of cultural values centering on female 'purity' and the notion that the honour of male kin groups rests upon the seclusion and sexual purity of its women, is related to the institution of dowry as an instrument in preserving and perpetuating socioeconomic classes (Mandelbaum 1988).

The expense of providing dowry for daughters is one reason for the relatively intense preference for sons and the relative neglect of female children (Miller 1989). Early research in India suggested that attitudes towards dowries were changing (Prabhu 1963, Vatuk 1972). Yet parents continue to give dowry as they may feel that a lavish dowry will help to secure their daughter's favourable treatment in her in-law's home (Bordewich 1986, Stein 1988). Recent research (Stone and James 1995) has shown that dowry, (and dowry exploitation), occur in India because women do not have shared access to new economic opportunities with men and their one traditional source of leverage, their fertility, has possibly diminished in value.

There is little research which has examined the phenomenon of dowries in the UK. Researchers (Bhachu 1985, Kalra 1980, Kannan 1978, Lannoy 1971, Macleod 1976, Robinson 1984, Wilson 1978) have explained the phenomenon of dowry in relation to arranged marriages and characteristics of the South Asian family structure. Different researchers have given different reasons for the importance of the dowry. Some have indicated the inferiority of bride givers to bride takers (Macleod 1976, Wilson 1978), whilst others (Bhachu 1985, Westwood 1988) have indicated the weak position of the bride in her marital home. However, some research (Bhachu 1985, Westwood 1988) has demonstrated a change in the dowry system, where the control of dowry has shifted from the mother-in-law to the daughter-in-law, which is based upon the increasing earning potential of brides. More recently, Bhachu (1991) has described how the elaboration of dowry among Sikh women draws upon and reproduces their class locations.

The research which exists on dowries in the UK is both descriptive and dated. It has not attempted to examine the dowry system and its relationship to patriarchy. Dowry giving and dowry taking needs to be explained and analysed in the context of patriarchy within South Asian households. The giving of dowries is considered a ritual in marriage alliances in South Asian communities. Although the amount may vary from one caste to another, one status group to another, one region to another, the practice of dowry *giving and taking* has become part and parcel of the marriage system. To what extent is this true for South Asian communities in the UK? Are dowries still common? What do dowries consist of? Such questions will enable us to examine the system of dowries and provide a greater understanding of South Asian women's position within the dowry system and its relationship to other structures of patriarchy.

Were women given a dowry?

All respondents in the study were asked if they were given a dowry. Half of the respondents in the study (50 per cent) were given a dowry. All respondents who were given a dowry also had an arranged marriage.

Table 5.1
Table 5.1
Whether women were given a dowry

	n	%
Given a dowry (Had an arranged marriage)	30	50
Not given a dowry (Not married)	30	50
Total (N)	60	100

Definition of a dowry

Respondents were asked to define the dowry. A range of responses were given for the definition of the dowry. Some respondents felt dowries were given to the bride by her family, others felt dowries were given to the groom by the bride's family, yet others felt dowries were given to the couple. But, on all occasions the dowry was given *by* the bride's family.

Table 5.2
Definition of a dowry

Definition	n	%
Gifts given to the bride by her parents	29	48
Gifts given to the bride by her parents and her relatives	16	27
Gifts given to the groom by the bride's parents	2	3
Gifts given to the couple by the bride's parents	7	12
Gifts given to the groom's family by the bride's parents	4	7
Gifts given to the groom's family by the bride's parents and relatives	2	3
Total (N)	60	100

Most respondents (48 per cent) defined the dowry as gifts that were given to the bride, by her *parents*.

...that's the giving of very expensive gifts to the bride on her wedding day...they're given to her by her parents...(32).

...the giving of gifts to the girl when she gets married...they are given for the wedding from her mum and dad...(7).

A dowry was linked to the ritual of getting married, it was part of the arranged marriage.

A dowry is when the girl gets married, the parents have to buy her lots of things for the house...and they give her lots of other things she needs for when she will be married...she gets it on the day she gets married...it comes with the wedding (54).

The dowry itself is part of the arranged marriage...you wouldn't have the arranged marriage without the dowry and you wouldn't have the dowry without the arranged marriage...they both go together...it's always been like that for us (25).

Some respondents (27 per cent) defined the dowry as gifts that were given to the bride by her parents *and her relatives.*

The whole family wants to give you away properly and so they all get together with all the uncles and aunts you never see and then they give you this large dowry...it's huge and costs them so much...they all get together and discuss it, it's done as a family thing (22).

Other respondents (12 per cent) defined dowries as gifts given to the *couple*, by the bride's parents.

...the giving of gifts to the couple, by your parents...they give you these things to help you in your married life...they want you to have all the things you need, so you don't have to worry about buying anything...so the couple can be happy (49).

A small number of respondents (7 per cent) defined the dowry as gifts given to the *groom's family*, by the bride's parents.

The girl's parents have to give the dowry to the boy's family, to make sure they are satisfied, it's given to them, lots of gifts for their house and for all the people...so they will be happy with the marriage and not complain (53).

A minority of respondents (3 per cent) defined the dowry as gifts given to the groom by the bride's parents, or as gifts given to the groom's family by the bride's parents *and relatives* (3 per cent).

When parents have daughters they feel like they have to sell them and so they give the boy (groom) lots of expensive gold, money and maybe even a car when he gets married...they think it will make a difference to how he will treat their daughter...and so they sell her to him (18).

...the groom is the one who has to be made happy and who has to be kept happy and so the parents give him the dowry...so he might respect them...(34).

Data from participant observation also indicated the ways in which it was parents and in many cases the relatives, who were in control of the dowry. On the eve of a wedding, there was a small celebration at the home of the bride. The mother of the bride displayed a vast number of silk suits, saris, 'western' clothes with matching handbags and shoes as well as jewellery, which included three 24 carat gold sets, a watch and three rings. These were on display for all the elder members of the family to see. The mother of the bride began talking through the items, describing which were to be given to her daughter and which to her future son-in-law and his immediate family. She also included the extent of the 'other' items of the dowry, which would be 'too large' to fit into the room. Later on she told me:

All this, it's for Seeta, she's my daughter and we've done it all for her...the silk suits and saris are for her to wear and all the furniture is for her, so that she never goes without (M398[1]).

There was great emphasis placed upon the dowry being given to her daughter to start her new married life. This was also confirmed by other mothers I spoke to.

If we give our daughters all these things, we feel good about it, we feel we have helped them...and being the mothers of daughters we have to do it (M376).

On the wedding day, just before the daughter was to leave the home of her parents and start her new life with her 'new family' in Bradford, a very large van was being loaded with large quantities of gifts and furniture. This I was told was the dowry, which had to leave at the same time as the bride and groom, as it was a symbol of the start of their new life together. Some objects had already been ensconced inside the van, however those I witnessed included; a tv, video, stereo system, microwave, dressing table and a large silver trunk, which I was told, was always traditionally included in the dowry. Inside the trunk was the bride's clothes (all new), shoes and handbags. There also other items in the van such as pots and pans, dishes, ornaments, kettle and toaster. I asked whether this was considered to be an extravagant dowry.

No, it's not really, it's just average it's what most people get...things like a tv and video they're normal everyone gets them and the furniture, the extravagant things are if you get a car or a house...but this sort of things is just normal (M230).

The idea of materialism was apparent, not only in the value of the dowry, but in women's appearances at weddings. All women, (especially the married women), were dressed lavishly and flamboyantly. They wore expensive saris and heavy gold. It seemed every married woman appeared to be wealthy.

> ...weddings are important...it's the only time we can show people what we've got...all our gold and expensive clothes...I do it because it makes me feel good...I like it when people look at me and think she must be rich...none of us are poor, we've all got a gold set, it just depends how big it is...when people see what you're wearing then they might want to marry into your family...and so it's important for us if we do have money (M683).

This was obvious with the women who appeared most wealthy, they were wearing extravagant gold sets and some were wearing two or three. Men too were wearing gold bracelets, rings, necklaces, expensive watches and expensive suits. They also drove very expensive cars, such as Mercedes or BMW's. Wealth and materialism in South Asian communities is related to respect and status. Those who have greater wealth are those who gain a superordinate status. These higher groups have control and power over lower groups who have less wealth and status. The real measure of wealth is demonstrated by the display of dowries which can increase or decrease the status of 'bride-givers'. The dowry itself is seen as an avenue for families to enhance and display their social status and economic worth. Parents of brides are able to boost their self esteem through feasts and displays of material objects. The public display of dowries serves as a statement of one's financial position.

Description of dowry

Respondents were asked to describe the dowry. Different responses were given for the description of the dowry. Dowries generally consisted of different types of gifts such as clothes, furniture, jewellery and sometimes maybe even cash payments or larger material items such as a car or a house.

Table 5.3
Description of dowry

Description	n	%
Furniture & money	30	50
Furniture & clothes	23	38
Jewellery & money	4	7
Money	3	5
Total (N)	60	100

Half of the respondents in the study (50 per cent) described the dowry as *furniture and money*.

The dowry itself consists of a lot of different things, but mainly it's quite a lot of furniture and money that is given...the furniture is things like a fridge, microwave, washing machine, video, bed, tv and all that...it costs a lot of money...then they give cash money as well to the girl...it's a very expensive business (13).

Other respondents (38 per cent) described the dowry as *furniture and clothes*.

It's lots of different clothes, very expensive saris and suits for the man as well...as well as that, they have to furnish a house for the bride...and that means all the furniture that you need when you buy a new house...like a sofa set, kitchen things, a bed, tv, video, microwave and much more (25).

However, a minority of respondents (7 per cent) described the dowry as *jewellery and money* or as just *money* (5 per cent).

...they just give the bride and groom money, so then they can spend it on what they want to spend it on...and it's their choice...but it's a lot of money though...(29).

Although 50 per cent of respondents were given a dowry, which they all said was very expensive and worth a lot of money, few were prepared to admit the total cost of the dowry. It is possible the dowry can cost thousands of pounds, ranging from £5,000 to as much as £15,000.

I don't want to say how much the dowry cost...I don't think you need to know that...anyway, my parents gave me the best things, so it would probably be a lot of money to you...and you might think my parents are really wealthy, but they're not...they had to give the dowry because they had no choice and they had to make sure I got married properly and in the traditional way us Asian people get married (7).

Dowries are large gifts, which range from furniture for a whole house (such as a tv, video, bed, wardrobe, washing machine) to gold and cash for the groom and his family. The dowry is not necessarily given exclusively to the bride, but is given to her for her husband and his family when she is married. It is for their use as much as it is for hers. Being married, qualifies South Asian women to partake of the dowry, in some cases women felt it was their right to partake of the dowry. Men have much to gain from an arranged marriage. They gain a wife as well as a large dowry. The dowry is taken with the wife as she leaves her parents home, to go to her in-laws home. This is significant and indicates the movement of property, (which also includes the bride herself).

The amount of dowry parents give, determines to a very large extent their status in the community. To give a large dowry will increase the prestige of the family, not just by attracting an influential son-in-law, but by determining the family's capacity to give freely without expectation of immediate return. Women are therefore important instruments in the competition for prestige. Indeed, dowry property is not women's wealth, but the wealth that goes with women. Women are the vehicles by which it is transmitted, rather than its owners. Dowry functions to disinherit women and promote their economic dependency upon men. A bride does not have, (and historically never had), genuine control over the use and distribution of her dowry. As a result, 'traditional' women when they marry, may suffer considerable harassment and even physical abuse in connection with their roles as bringers of dowry. Furthermore, the expense of providing dowry for daughters is one reason for the relatively intense preference for sons. In some cases, 'bride-takers' may have an expectation of a rising lifestyle they themselves cannot on their own earning power quite afford, hence the dowry is an attractive source of status-seeking.

Why dowries are given

Respondents were asked why they felt dowries were given in South Asian communities. Dowries were given in South Asian communities as they were a recognised custom and tradition that had existed for generations with the arranged marriage.

Table 5.4
Why dowries are given

Why given	n	%
Custom/tradition	16	27
Separate identity	2	3
Demonstrate love	10	17
Demonstrate wealth	8	13
Parental control	3	5
Achieve respect	11	18
Women inferior	5	8
Fear of change	1	2
Keep men happy	1	2
Sold to men	3	5
Total (N)	60	100

Many respondents (27 per cent) said dowries were given as they were part of the custom and tradition in South Asian culture, they were part of the arranged marriage.

It's the culture and it's expected...like the arranged marriage is expected and you don't question it...you know you're going to have an arranged marriage and you know the dowry comes with the arranged marriage...if you didn't have a dowry it would be like getting married without the wedding ring...that's how important it is to us in the culture (25).

Some respondents (18 per cent) said parents gave dowries as this enabled them to achieve respect in the community, the larger the dowry, the more respect they would gain.

In our culture, people only respect you if you have money, they think you are a good person...if you don't have money then they don't want to know you...everyone in the community knows how much dowry you give, and so all the parents want to give a large dowry, then other people talk to them and sort of look up to them (4).

Other respondents (17 per cent) said dowries were given as parents were able to demonstrate the love they had for their daughters.

...parents want to show people that they care about their daughters and they love them...and so they give them the dowry...lots of large gifts and expensive presents so that she has what she needs when she leaves her parent's house...if they (parents) didn't care about her, they wouldn't give her the dowry would they? (28).

Yet other respondents (13 per cent) said dowries were given to enable parents to display their wealth to the community.

...just to show who has the most money, so they can then show this to all other members of the community and so they think other people will like them, because they have lots of money...rich parents enjoy it all because they can really show people they are rich, and then they are seen as the most important people in the community (37).

However, other respondents (8 per cent) said dowries were given as women were regarded as being inferior to men or women were sold to men for marriage (5 per cent) or parents wanted to keep the groom happy (2 per cent).

The dowries are only given for women and not for men because the women are seen as second class citizens compared to the men...men are seen as the kings in our culture...the dowry is just one way of reminding us we're not the same as the men are...and that we have to be sold to men, so that they can keep us (18).

...it's degrading really, women have to be sold to men otherwise they won't marry them...all the men want to do is marry a woman who has a large dowry and then they will be happy...it's alright for them, they get a wife and they get lots of gifts and money and they don't have to move away from their house to a strange town...parents sell their daughters to men, and the one with the highest price gets the best husband (14).

A small percentage of respondents said dowries were given as South Asian people wanted a separate identity (3 per cent), were afraid of any change taking place (2 per cent) or parents wanted to demonstrate the control they had over their daughters (5 per cent).

Asian people want to be different from other people and so they keep giving the dowry, because it separates us out...we have arranged marriages and we give dowries and people know that and that's how they identify us (41).

Parents have to give dowries regardless of their financial situation. Those who do not, are heavily stigmatised and those who have little money are left with unmarried daughters. Unmarried daughters are seen as a burden, and their parents are seen as having failed, not only themselves, but also the community. Women are constantly being judged on their performance as women. They must behave in accordance with community rules and so must become marketable (marriageable). They must be trained to be the dutiful wife, so that men will want to marry them. Parents are prepared to spend great amounts on the dowry, as they cannot have an unmarried daughter on their hands. The bigger the dowry, the more offers of marriage the daughter will receive. Unmarried daughters are considered to be failures and parents become stigmatised as they have been unsuccessful in finding a partner for their daughter.

Dowry itself is moveable property made to the husband's family at the wedding day. There are two main principles of authority which underlie the structure of authority in traditional South Asian households, those of seniority and gender. Juniors of either sex are expected to defer to elders and women are expected to defer to men. So, brides as women have little control over the way in which dowry is given and received. The very concept of the bride as a 'gift', implies the idea that she herself can be represented as a kind of property, to be transferred from one family to another. The passivity of the bride in her wedding ritual supports this inference. She is led by her father, brother and the female members of her family. Dowry favours and is favoured by a cultural ethos in which brides can be viewed as objects to be passed from one social group to another, both as a means for the procreation of children and as vehicles for aspirations to social prestige. So, brides are more controlled by, than controllers of property. There is a traditional lack of female control over family property and marriage arrangements. This is also linked to the association of dowries with the concern of kin groups with maintaining or enhancing social status through marriage. It is important to ensure that control over property remains with 'bride-givers' before marriage and is passed on to the hands of 'bride-takers' after marriage. Individual women themselves have limited control over their own dowry. However, women identify themselves in some situations as mothers (dowry-givers), and in others as mothers-in-law (dowry-takers).

The relationship of women and the giving of dowries

In South Asian communities, it is women who are given dowries and not men. A number of reasons were given for the relationship of women to the giving of dowries.

Table 5.5
The relationship of women and the giving of dowries

Relationship	n	%
Burden/disrespected	13	22
Sold to men	25	42
Have to be looked after	10	17
Cultural/historical	5	8
Parents demonstrate love/duty	7	11
Total (N)	60	100

Most respondents (42 per cent) said the relationship of women and the giving of dowries was based upon women being sold to men for marriage.

> The reason why Asian women are always treated badly is because of the dowry...they are like property and they get sold to men, it's only men who are allowed to buy them...let's face it, men have more power than women, they always have...otherwise why don't we give dowries for Asian men...they wouldn't put up with that (20).

When respondents were asked why dowries were given, only 5 per cent said women were sold to men for marriage (table 5.4), yet when respondents were asked about the relationship of women to the giving of dowries, 42 per cent said women were sold to men for marriage (table 5.5). When respondents were asked to think about the reasons why dowries were given *for women* and not for men, they were able to make a connection with the relationship between gender and the giving of dowries. However, when asked why dowries were given, respondents were more likely to say dowries were given as they were the custom and tradition in South Asian communities.

Some respondents (22 per cent) said the relationship of women and the giving of dowries was based upon women being seen as a burden and not being respected.

> Women are seen differently to the way men are...they are not respected...and nobody wants to have girls because they see them as a burden, because they haveto pay them the dowry and keep on giving gifts to the husbands family for the whole marriage lifetime (18).

Other respondents (17 per cent) said the relationship of women and the giving of dowries was based upon women having to be looked after.

> When a girl lives with her mum and dad, she is looked after by them and then when she gets married, she is looked after by her husband...so everyone feels they have to look after women, that's why they give them dowries...women are seen to be in need of being looked after, they are weaker than men (50).

Yet other respondents (11 per cent) said the relationship of women and the giving of dowries was based upon parents showing they cared about their daughters and it was their duty to give the dowry.

> The reasons why parents give the dowry is because they think it's their duty to give it...if they didn't give it, people would think they don't care about their daughters and other people would think they were bad parents (4).

A minority of respondents (8 per cent) said the relationship of women and the giving of dowries was based upon dowries being part of the historical customs in South Asian communities.

> People want to keep on giving the dowries, because that's the way it's always been for us...they don't know any different...and so they want to give them, it's all part of our culture (53).

Data from participant observation (wedding ceremonies), demonstrated that South Asian women themselves were seen as objects of beauty. They were dressed flamboyantly in bright, sparkling colours and were adorned in gold. Women's inferior status was evident. I asked why it was women and not men who received the dowry.

> Men don't get dowries, don't be stupid...women get them because they (men) don't need them, if he's a half decent man someone will want to marry him, if a girl's dark or ugly no man will want to marry her, unless she's got a big dowry (M452).

Hence, appearance, colour of skin and looks were considered to be important, more so for women than for men.

> ...if a boy's dark, it doesn't *really* matter (respondent's emphasis)...but he has to be educated and maybe have so much money...but he'll get married...looks for men aren't that important...but if a girl's dark, everyone will comment and she won't get any proposals...who wants to marry a dark girl, and if she's poor that's worse (M586).

Although it did appear that many South Asian women at the wedding were beautiful, not all were fair skinned however. I was told they were able to be married as they presented a large dowry.

> When a girl's dark, the parents just give lots and lots of money and a huge dowry...that's what happened for lots of women here (M489).

During the marriage ceremony itself, the bride and groom had to walk four times around a holy altar. Each time this happened, the bride was led by the groom and was not allowed to walk or stand alone. She was also helped up by her female relatives who were sitting beside her, then as she walked, it was as if she was being passed around, by the male members of her family (brothers and male first cousins), as each had to lead her to the next person. I was told:

> She (bride) isn't allowed to walk by herself anywhere, it would just be seen as being really bad, people would talk about her and it would just seem really degrading...and then people would say things to her parents and they would loose their 'sharam'...and everyone would think she was too free (M908).

The force of shame ('sharam') is powerful for South Asian parents as they have to conform to the standards of South Asian communities. If they break the rules, they will be punished and the price they have to pay is high. Dowry continues, (and will continue in future generations), because 'bride-givers' continue to give them. This may be due to concerns that a daughter may not be married at all or that the family could not secure an appropriate match. Also, parents of the bride may continue to believe that a lavish dowry will help to secure their daughter's favourable treatment in her in-laws home. They may also feel dowry can be used to overcome disadvantages in the marriage market (such as dark skin colour). It is evident, materialist values lie behind dowry harassment. The issue of the bride's reputation and female purity serves as a link between the institution of dowry, family concerns with status and the perpetuation of socioeconomic classes. Dowries themselves can only be understood in reference to South Asian communities, which are characterised by patrilineal descent, patrilocality, the joint family and strongly prescribed subservience of wives to husbands and in-laws.

Dowry goes hand in hand with a class system and with maintenance of the superiority of higher groups over lower ones. Superior groups are those who are able to place demands upon 'bride-givers', for they have the sons and they are the ones who have greater choice. 'Bride-givers' are in an inferior position as they must get their daughter married at all costs. Hence, they are more likely to present a lavish dowry as an attraction. There is a strong association between dowry transactions and traditional concerns with premarital virginity. Ultimately, the whole complex notion of traditional values centres upon female purity and the notion that the honour of male kin groups, rests upon the seclusion and sexual purity of its women. Women come to be regarded as 'vehicles of property' and lack control over this property. They are also seen as the 'cultural carriers' of the group whose behaviour is closely monitored. Individuals who marry without a dowry would be in a very weak position in their marital home. A marriage without a dowry would reflect badly upon the 'izzat' of the bride's parents.

Whether respondents would give their own children dowries

Respondents were asked whether they would give their own children dowries.

Table 5.6
Whether respondents would give their own children dowries

Would give	n	%
Continue traditions	24	40
Demonstrate love	3	5
Want daughters to be obedient	3	5
Sub-total	30	50
Would not give		
Own choice	10	17
Inferior to men	14	23
Disagree	4	7
Sub-total	28	47
Don't know		
Unsure	2	3
Total (N)	60	100

Half of the respondents in the study (50 per cent) said they would give their own children a dowry, all of whom had an arranged marriage and were given a dowry.

Most of these respondents (40 per cent) said they would give their own children a dowry as they wanted to continue the traditions and customs of South Asian culture.

> If we keep giving dowries and having arranged marriages, that's the only way we can keep our culture and be proud of our customs...I have a daughter and I will give her a good dowry...but I also have a son and will want to get a dowry for him...it's my right...it works both ways (43).

A small number of respondents (5 per cent) who had an arranged marriage and were given a dowry said they would give their own children dowries as they wanted their daughters to obey them or the dowry would enable them to demonstrate the love they have for their children (5 per cent).

> I want my daughter to do what she is told and that means she will be told who she will marry and she will have a dowry, that's why I feel parents should give the dowry...if you have a son, you get it back when he gets married...it's what you're entitled to, by rights you should give the dowry and you should receive it (7).

However, 47 per cent of respondents said they would not give their own children dowries, these respondents had not had an arranged marriage. Most of these respondents (23 per cent) said dowries portrayed women as being inferior to men.

> ...no, I think it's like a payoff...it's an insult to women and they are the ones who suffer in the end and are seen as being worse than men...because people carry on giving dowries, women keep being seen as lower than men and people continue to treat them like that (39).

Other respondents (17 per cent) who had not had an arranged marriage said they would not give their children dowries, as they wanted their children to have their own choices in life.

> I don't want to give my daughters dowries...when I have children, I want them to have their own choices in life and make their own decisions...it's their life and they should be allowed to make their own choices (35).

Data from participant observation (wedding ceremonies) indicated, parents' of unmarried daughters were collecting ideas about their own daughter's weddings.

> I never thought of having a waiter service, that would be a very good idea on Anita's wedding (daughter)...then we can all relax and enjoy the wedding...and it would be a good idea to give her money towards a house, so she doesn't have to stay with her mother-in-law for long (M981).

By attending a wedding and watching the lavish display of dowry and other items, this reinforced parents' ideas of encouraging their own children to have an arranged marriage and present them with a dowry. Parents go to great extremes to present a large dowry, the importance of materialism and displaying the dowry is fundamental, for this will bring with it acceptance. South Asian parents seek approval, status and respect and feel they deserve it, but they do so at the expense of their daughters. Those who had attended the wedding were very interested to see what the dowry itself consisted of and what other women were wearing. Attendance at weddings reinforced the giving and taking of dowries and the prevalence of the arranged marriage and its relationship to the dowry. Mothers who attended weddings were able to get ideas about their own daughters' weddings and the sorts of things they too would give to their daughter, which they felt would please other people and earn them respect, status and approval in the community.

Dowries for many people were a 'natural' ritual attached to the arranged marriage. They had been in existence for generations and were part of the identity of South Asian people. They were historical and unlikely to be questioned. To continue giving dowries was a sign of acceptance. The dowry was seen to be unique to South Asian communities, as separating South Asian people from others, the practice of dowries was part of their identity and enabled them to have a secure sense of belonging and security.

The significance of religion, education and employment

Religion affected whether South Asian women were given a dowry and had an arranged marriage. Moslem women were more likely to have been given a dowry and have an arranged marriage (43 per cent, 13 out of 30), followed by Sikh (30 per cent, 9 out of 30) and Hindu women (27 per cent, 8 out of 30). However, religion did not affect women's attitudes to dowries. Level of education affected women's attitudes to dowries and whether they had an arranged marriage and were given a dowry. Respondents who were highly educated, (those who had a BA or MA), saw dowries as being negative and degrading for women. Respondents who had a low level of education, (those who had 'O' levels or no qualifications), saw dowries as being positive for women and wanted to continue the tradition of giving dowries. Women's position in the labour market affected their attitudes to dowries and whether they had an arranged marriage and were given a dowry. Respondents who were in low positions in the labour market, (unemployed housewives, skilled manual), saw dowries as being positive and would continue the tradition of giving dowries. Those who were in high positions in the labour market, (semi-professional, students), saw dowries as being degrading for women and did not want to continue the tradition of giving dowries. (See Appendix 3 for chi square tables on education and employment).

Conclusion

Through the giving and taking of dowries, private patriarchy manifests itself within South Asian households. Dowries are part of the arranged marriage. When women participate in arranged marriages, the giving of dowries is presumed and expected. Dowries are defined as gifts that are given by the bride's parents to the groom and his family. Sometimes it is possible the groom's family may ask for certain gifts, but on the majority of occasions the bride's family simply provide a large dowry. The dowry is something which comes with the bride. Dowries are important as they are regarded as part of the custom and tradition of South Asian communities. South Asian people see the dowry as being part of their unique South Asian identity. Respect is achieved for the bride's parents, as they will be judged upon the size of dowry they present to the groom and his family. Parents feel they must give the dowry as they must conform, to refuse to give a dowry would result in a disapproval from the community and being stigmatised, something South Asian parents would be unable to live with. Male pride ('izzat') cannot be destroyed. The shame ('sharam') would be too great to bear and so parents go to great lengths to give a dowry. On the one hand they have to get their daughter married and on the other, they have to satisfy the community.

Traditionally, dowry marriage seeks to be an ideological denial of reciprocity, because it is the duty of the 'bride-givers' to do this without expecting a return and it is the 'bride-takers' right to be constant recipients. The marriage system is characterised by the existence of an asymmetrical relationship between 'bride-takers' and 'bride-givers'. The former, despite being presented with lavish gifts from the latter, do not face any form of subordination because of their superior status accorded to them within this context. This type of ideology recognises their status of endless receivers of gifts, even long after the marriage process. The bond between the daughter and her parents never ceases and is reaffirmed at every ceremony through the presentation of gifts to her and her husband's kin. The acceptance of such gifts by the 'bride-takers', reflects that of superordinate status, hence dowry marriage is considered to be the most prestigious form of marriage for 'bride-takers'. Dowry acts as an indicator and enhancer of family status. Dowries are excellent vehicles for pursuing greater levels of status. Families of lower status but superior wealth, can attempt to acquire prestige by arranging marriages with higher status families. By doing so, 'bride-givers' are able to convert material wealth into higher status through the presentation of dowries for superior 'bride-takers'.

The dowry may also be seen as a 'compensation' to the groom's parents for taking on a family member with little or no earning capacity. When the bride takes her dowry to her new home, that of her husband, his parents and family, the dowry itself is in no sense the bride's property, but is under the control of the senior male and female members of the household. The norms regarding relationships within the household, (the ideology of seniority, of male competence, of the distinction between daughters and daughters-in-law), suggests that dowry property will not be under the control of the woman in whose name it is given. This does not mean that it will not be controlled by other women, such as the mother-in-law. The dowry situation is also compounded by the religious and social inferiority of the bride's family to that of the groom. The inferior and subservient position of a wife to her husband is on another level shared by the family who gives her. The subordination and frequently disadvantaged position of the daughter-in-law is exacerbated by the exclusion and deference of her own kin. As 'bride-takers' this gives them the right to humiliate the bride into accepting an inferior position in the home of her in-laws. The bride however must aim to please her husband and her mother-in-law. With the birth of her own sons, her position will improve. For sons are valued to continue the patrilineage, serve as heirs, perform important rituals for parents and family and to provide security in old age.

Previous research on dowries (Macleod 1976, Wilson 1978) has demonstrated the inferiority of 'bride-givers' to that of 'bride-takers'. This was also shown in the present research, where the parents of the groom were accorded a higher status during, before and after the marriage ceremony. They were not asked or expected to present gifts, those they did present were few and for the bride and select members of her family. They were the ones who were waited upon and pleased. If the groom's family were to complain, this would be disgraceful and damage the 'izzat' of the bride's family. Hence, 'bride-takers' had a higher status than 'bride-givers'. Other research (Bhachu 1985, Westwood 1988), has argued that there has been a change in the dowry system with control of the dowry now being in the hands of the daughter-in-law rather than the mother-in-law. However, this was not shown in the present research. It seemed that although in name the dowry was for the daughter, it was controlled by her mother-in-law and other senior members of the groom's family. Hence, women had little or no control over their own dowry.

Previous research has shown that the dowry is a phenomenon which is related to the arranged marriage and has to be examined within the context of the South Asian family structure (Bennett 1983, Camaroff 1980, Tambiah 1972), also that dowry marriage is considered to be the most prestigious form of marriage (Karve 1965, Madan 1965). This was also demonstrated in the present research where arranged marriages without dowries were uncommon. When dowries were given, this helped to increase the status of 'bride-givers' to that of 'bride-takers' and dowry was associated with the concerns of kinship groups with maintaining or enhancing social status through marriage (Goody 1971, Schlegel 1991).

Early research suggested that attitudes towards dowries were changing (Bhachu 1985, Vatuk 1972), however the present research indicates parents continue to give dowries, as much as grooms and their families expect to receive them. Women themselves feel a dowry may help to enhance their status in their in-laws home (Bordewich 1986, Stein 1988), dowry itself is a compensation for their gender. Dowry transactions continue to disadvantage women, especially those who have little or no wealth. Dowry serves to perpetuate different status groups to gain and achieve respect, which for South Asian people is the ultimate reward.

An alternative view of dowries is a demonstration of gender inequality which exists within South Asian households, it links material conditions with traditional norms and prescriptions. Women are sold to men for marriage as property, as arranged marriages include a financial contract in which money and/or material possessions are exchanged. Dowry links the family with status, the perpetuation of socioeconomic classes and 'izzat' where the bride's sexual purity and reputation are important. So great is the pressure to marry the daughter, that a woman's parents remain in a weak and vulnerable position with respect to dowry harassment. Marriage of the daughter and presentation of a large dowry are matters of status and family honour. 'Traditional' South Asian women who participate in arranged marriages and are given dowries have limited resources and access to power. They are economically dependent upon the men in the family and do not share in access to new economic opportunities with men. Regrettably, South Asian women are valued for the dowry they will bring and their valuation rests primarily in their being vehicles of property transmission. However, as 'traditional' South Asian women give birth to sons, it is through their female fertility that their position within marriage may improve, being mothers of sons, they too will one day hold a position of power and may demand large dowries.

Note

1   These references are based upon women I spoke to during participant observation in the research.

6 Domestic labour

In the literature on housework there is a consensus as to its essential economic characteristics; it is work, it is unpaid and it is carried out mainly by women. However, there are many differences in studying domestic labour. Some studies have focused on the usefulness of housework for capitalism (Malos 1980, Sargent 1981), which resulted in the 'domestic labour debate' (James 1980, Molyneux 1979, Seecombe 1974). There has also been a debate as to whether housework is 'productive' and whether or not it is unpaid because of the specific nature of the work (Adamson 1976, Gardiner 1975). There have been various attempts to assess the monetary value of housework to the family or society (Glazer-Malbin 1976). Some authors have stressed the aspect of 'work' in the sense of 'tasks', looking at changes in the nature and the component parts of housework and the history of domestic technology (Bose 1979, Cowan 1983, Davidson 1982, Hartmann 1974, Oakley 1974, Pahl 1984, Young and Willmott 1973). Others have looked at time-budget studies, (Gershuny et al 1986, Meissner et al 1975), how the time spent on housework and the type of commercial products used as substitutes vary with whether or not wives have paid employment (Morris 1990), also at changes over the life course (Berk 1980, Lopata 1971, Pleck 1977, Robinson 1977). Yet others have looked primarily at how the work is experienced by those who do it, what 'being a housewife' means to women's self-identity, what satisfactions and frustrations are to be found in domestic labour (Allan 1985, Oakley 1974, Rogers 1980) and studies which include the issue of responsibility for household tasks (Hochschild 1989, Morris 1985). Some writers have looked at the ideologies of men's and women's separate spheres, examining the changing representations of the private sphere of the home and the public sphere outside the home (Davidoff 1976, Davidoff and Hall 1987). Whilst others have stressed the changing marital roles in the marriage relationship (Berk 1985, Bott 1975, Edgell 1980, Geerken and Gove 1983, Gershuny 1983, Gershuny et al 1986, Harris 1983, Pahl 1984, Rapoport and Rapoport 1971, 1976). Economists have looked at time-allocation in terms of domestic labour (Leibowitz 1975).

Some writers (Allan and Crow 1989, Berk and Shih 1980, Coltrane 1989, Daniels 1987, Henwood 1987, Vanek 1980, Warde and Hetherington 1993) indicate that it is women who perform domestic labour and hence the role of the homemaker has become a low-status job which is bound up with sex roles which are considered to be appropriate for women. This is further demonstrated in feeding and caring for the family, where the relations of power which characterise the family are reproduced through the provision and consumption of the meal (Charles and Kerr 1988, Devault 1991). Yet other writers have looked at 'emotional labour' in the household (Abel and Newson 1990, Duncombe and Marsden 1993, Hochschild 1983, James 1989, Ungerson 1987), childcare and parenting (Rothman 1989, Thompson and Walker 1989) and family relationships (Finch and Mason 1993).

The definition of housework is problematic and is taken as what scholars define it to be. Some writers (Warde and Hetherington 1993, Williams 1988) have argued that there are many problems involved in adopting a framework for analysing the various ways of thinking about domestic labour. The terms 'housework' and 'domestic labour' are used interchangeably. Different writers have included various different tasks under the heading of housework or domestic labour (Eichler 1981). In the same vein, Bose (1979) states that little is known about the housework role and the occupational privilege attributed to it. Whereas, Jackson (1992) argues that it is important to examine the concept of domestic labour under capitalism and patriarchy. More recent research (West and Pilgrim 1995) has examined the pressures of domestic labour in terms of struggle and isolation for South Asian women. Many South Asian women in the study were likely to show signs of depression (Fenton and Sadiq 1993), and to be living in poor housing conditions (Pilgrim et al 1993).

However, many of the studies on domestic labour have tended to be ethnocentric and falsely universalistic and have underestimated the significance of ethnic diversity. The research on households has rarely examined South Asian households and women's position within it. Does ethnicity make a difference to who performs domestic labour? How does this affect forms of patriarchy experienced by South Asian women? Are domestic labour tasks sharply divided by gender in South Asian households? Such questions will help us to examine South Asian women's experience of domestic labour within households and how it may be related to different forms of patriarchy they experience.

Domestic labour can be defined as work activities in households which consist of three components; the general maintenance of the household which includes activities such as cooking and cleaning; childbearing and childrearing which includes the socialisation of children; and finally, looking after the partner. Domestic labour is the web of activities that take place inside households, in which people and households have to be maintained (Oakley 1974).

Who does what?

Generally speaking, it is women who perform most, if not all aspects of domestic labour, men are less likely to participate and will only do so when it is convenient for them. Respondents were asked three questions concerning domestic labour tasks. Who carries out the domestic labour activity? How often is the activity carried out? Who carried out the activity on the last occasion? These questions were asked to examine whether a discrepancy existed between female reports of who carried out domestic labour and who actually did so on the last occasion.

Table 6.1
Domestic labour tasks

Task	Male (%)	Female (%)	Both (%)
Cooking	-	90	10
Last occasion	8	92	-
Washing dishes	-	75	25
Last occasion	17	83	-
Vacuuming	8	57	35
Last occasion	8	72	20
Dusting	8	57	35
Last occasion	8	80	12
Cleaning oven	8	62	30
Last occasion	2	90	8
Cleaning toilet	8	79	13
Last occasion	-	92	8
Washing clothes	-	62	38
Last occasion	23	77	-
Taking out rubbish	47	8	40
Last occasion	60	8	32

Three different families were shown to exist in the study. The 'traditional' family consisted of women who had an arranged marriage and were given a dowry. The 'cohabiting' family consisted of women who were living with their partners, (but were not married to them). There was also the 'single' family, which consisted of women who were single (not married), some of whom were without partners and others who were with partners, but were not living with them. 'Traditional' women were in 'traditional' families and independent women were in 'co-habiting' or 'single' families. Most activities were carried out exclusively by females, (regardless of family type). The majority of women (92 per cent) cooked the breakfast, lunch and dinner and performed this activity on the last occasion. The majority of women also did the cleaning, washing and vacuuming and did so on the last occasion. Activities such as cleaning the oven and toilet were carried out exclusively by the female, all women performed these activities regularly and did so on the last occasion. However, a small minority of men (9 per cent) who were in 'co-habiting' or 'single' families participated in washing clothes. Childcare was also an activity that was female. All married women with children in the study carried out childcare activities (47 per cent). However, changing the plugs (36 per cent), gardening (36 per cent) and taking out the rubbish (60 per cent) were all regularly performed by men.

Men and women participated in different domestic labour tasks. Women referred to male participation as 'helping' behaviour and their own behaviour was one of responsibility. Domestic labour is regarded as a female activity where men *'help'* the woman with what is considered to be *her* role. Furthermore, men were more likely to participate in the 'clean' tasks of domestic labour, such as playing with children, drying dishes, dusting and vacuuming and did so only when it was convenient for them. Women were more likely to perform the 'dirtier' tasks of domestic labour, such as cleaning the bathroom, toilet and changing the nappies. There exists a segregation of 'his' and 'her' tasks. Men perform tasks they can typically perform whenever they choose, whereas the tasks women perform are more immediate. This has also been found in previous research (Oakley 1974).

How much?

How much time did men and women actually spend performing domestic labour tasks?

Table 6.2
Number of hours spent on housework per day

Number of hours	Male (%)	Female (%)
None	54	-
Under 1 hour	24	-
1-2 hours	18	8
3-4 hours	4	42
5-6 hours	-	40
7-8 hours	-	7
Don't know	-	3
Total	100	100

There was a significant difference in the number of hours spent on domestic labour by men and women. Women spent more time performing domestic labour tasks than men. A minority of women (7 per cent) spent between seven and eight hours a day performing domestic labour tasks. These women were from 'traditional' families.

...it's what I do all day...it's really what my job in life is, what else can I do? I have to make sure the house is clean, the food is cooked and my husband and children are looked after...that all takes a long time and I can spend up to eight hours doing all the housework, sometimes I do more...but what else would I do...it's what I have to do...I don't mind, I want to look after my family (42).

Some women (40 per cent) spent between five and six hours a day performing domestic labour tasks.

I think when you start to clean up, you don't realise how much time you've spent on it and then you realise that five hours have gone by and it's midnight...it's difficult having two jobs, it makes it harder, because it all gets left to me and I know if I don't do it, then the house would just be a pigsty...it has to be done...housework is one thing you just can't ignore and get away from (28).

Most women however (42 per cent), spent between three and four hours a day on domestic labour tasks. These respondents did not think three or four hours of their time was a great amount, even though many of them went to work everyday.

> I try and get it all done in about four hours if I can, and that isn't that long...when you start cleaning up, the time goes by very quickly...I think I should spend more time on it, but I think I cut corners to get it done...housework is not something that I enjoy very much...it's a chore that has to get done...it can't be left alone and forgotten about (9).

A minority of women (8 per cent) spent between one and two hours a day performing domestic labour tasks. These women were from 'single' families.

> We share the housework and we both do a bit...I do about one hour and that's all...sometimes it varies and I do more...but I don't do that much...I know some women spend all night doing the housework, I just think they must get so tired and so I do the least I need to do (13).

Women were also asked how much time their husbands/partners spent on domestic labour tasks. A minority of women (4 per cent) reported that their husbands/partners spent between three and four hours a day performing domestic labour tasks. These women were from 'co-habiting' families.

> I feel very fortunate that my partner is like a 'new man' because he realises that men have to do more round the house, because he can't rely on me all time...and I want him to be independent and not have to wait for me to come home before he can eat something...he's an adult and should behave like one, instead of wanting to be looked after all the time (32).

Some women (18 per cent) reported that their husbands/partners spent between one and two hours a day performing domestic labour tasks. These women were from 'single' families.

> ...to tell you the truth, he doesn't like doing the housework and I know he only does it to please me, because if he didn't, I would just give him a very hard time and he would hate that...he just wants a quiet life and doesn't want me to nag him...and so he does it...but then if I didn't nag him, I would be the servant around here (14).

Other women (24 per cent) reported that their husbands/partners spent under one hour per day performing domestic labour tasks. These women were from different family types.

> ...men get away with as much as they can...they are so lazy and don't want to do

the housework, they don't think they should...when he does about an hour, which is the most he will ever do, he thinks he's done so much and goes on and on about it, he forgets about the fact that I do much more than him...and I'm never allowed to complain, and when I do, he thinks I'm just moaning about nothing (57).

However, the majority of women (54 per cent) reported that their husbands/partners did not spend any time performing domestic labour tasks. These women were from 'traditional' families.

I think that's a funny question...and you should know the answer to it...my husband doesn't do anything...and he never would...our men don't do that kind of thing, they'd be laughed at...anyway, it's women's work, it's what we do best isn't it? I don't think I want my husband to do it anyway...he'd be seen as a bit of a sissy if he did it, I want my husband to be a real man...don't you? (44).

Even though some respondents reported that their husbands/partners participated in domestic labour tasks, this was not to a significant extent. In comparison to female participation (up to eight hours per day), male participation was considerably low (up to four hours per day). Yet the women felt this was enough, it was something that was 'better than nothing'. Married women who had an arranged marriage, performed all domestic labour tasks ('traditional' families). They emphasised two separate roles for men and women; homemaker and breadwinner. The division of roles was considered to be part of South Asian traditions and 'natural' behaviour for men and women.

Who should do the housework?

Respondents were asked who they felt should do the housework. It was women who performed the majority of domestic labour tasks in South Asian households. Men did not participate to a significant extent.

Table 6.3
Who should do the housework

Who	n	%
Women		
Female role	9	15
Female more capable	6	10
If female at home	4	7
Total	19	32
Both		
Equal sharing	41	68
Total (N)	60	100

A total of 32 per cent of respondents said it was women who should do the housework in South Asian communities. These respondents were from 'traditional' families. A number of reasons were given for this. Most respondents (15 per cent) said women should do the housework because being the housewife was the female's role.

> I think I should do the housework and I know this and so I just get on with it...at the end of the day it has to be done and it's me that has to do it...it's my role in life and so I have to do it...women everywhere in the world do the housework, it's our role that we have to do...men do one thing and we do the other (28).

> I do it, because I have to do it...we have different things we do...my husband is the one who goes out to work and I am the one who stays at home to do the housework...it would be stupid if he had to worry about doing the housework, wouldn't it? (48).

Other respondents (10 per cent) said women were more capable of performing this role.

> We have to do it, we're better at it than they (men) are and we know what we're doing...my husband doesn't know what to do, he can't cook, as a woman I know what to do in the kitchen...it's like it's inbred in us, we know what to do in the kitchen (24).

A minority of respondents (7 per cent) said if women stayed at home, they should do the housework.

> ...if men work and women stay at home, they can't expect the men to come home and do the housework for them...one should do one job...if the women are at home and are housewives, I don't think there's anything wrong with her doing the housework and looking after the family...that's why she's at home isn't she? (47).

However, the majority of respondents (68 per cent) said both partners should do the housework and there should be an equal sharing of roles. Most of these women were from 'co-habiting' or 'single' families.

> I think we should both do it, because we both live in the house and so we should both make an effort...but it never works like that...if I ask him to help me, he just says I'm nagging him...it would be good if I came home one day and the food was cooked for me...but it's not just the cooking it's all the other stuff I have to do that makes me tired...like the washing up and the hoovering (32).

Many women from 'traditional' families did not want their husbands to participate in domestic labour, they saw it as an 'unnatural' and 'unmanly' thing to do. It was regarded as obscene for men to participate. This was seen as breaking the traditional rules which existed for men and women in South Asian communities. The kitchen is the female's domain, men do not need to participate in the kitchen and see the world of work as their domain. In these respondents' minds there existed a clear division of roles, one for the wife and one for the husband. If men participated in domestic labour, they were regarded as losing power and lacking male authority. Although some women from 'traditional' families felt men and women should *both* participate in domestic labour, their own situation did not reveal this, as they were the primary domestic labourers. There existed a discrepancy between what women wanted in their ideal situation and what existed in reality. The perfect situation would include men taking on a more participatory role, 'helping' with the cooking and cleaning, yet it was a role they knew traditional South Asian men would not want to take on.

Why women do the housework in South Asian communities

Respondents were asked why it is women who do the housework in South Asian communities. Women performed domestic labour in South Asian communities, as it was a role that was expected of them. It was considered to be a female role based upon women's 'natural' attributes. Women are expected to be the homemakers and men the breadwinners.

Table 6.4
Why women do the housework in South Asian communities

Reason	n	%
Maternal training	11	18
Socialisation/culture	25	42
Natural/instinctive	23	38
Religious influence	1	2
Total (N)	60	100

Most respondents (42 per cent) said women did the housework in South Asian communities due to the socialisation and cultural influence they received.

...it's the way the culture makes them and it's the way they've been brought up...they are the ones who are taught how to cook all the foods and the boys just go out to play and enjoy themselves...later on this is reinforced and women are expected to be really good cooks and good at everything in the home...and if they're not, nobody wants to marry you...because you have to be good in the home (23).

Some respondents (38 per cent) however, said women did the housework as it was a natural and instinctive role for them.

I think it's because we're made to believe that it's instinctive and that it's natural for us to do it and because it's what is expected of us...and because we're women we have to be good cooks and good mothers (55).

Other respondents (18 per cent) said women did the housework as it was the maternal training they received.

...being a woman you want to be like your mother and she brings you up to be like her...she wants you to be good at cooking and keeping house...and she makes sure you know how to do these things...but that's related to getting married...you learn all the skills of your mother and she's learnt them from her mother...and when you have a daughter you'll pass them on to her (1).

Gender norms in South Asian communities assign female behaviours and attributes that are of low social esteem and more importantly, those that function to reinforce the gender divisions of labour and male dominance. Masculine norms in South Asian communities stress traits that are defined as socially valued and those associated with dominance. Male power in South Asian communities results in social definitions that support the gender division of labour and reinforce their power and prestige, hence it is considered 'unmanly' for South Asian men to participate in domestic labour.

Is a woman's place in the home?

Respondents were asked whether they felt a woman's place was in the home. In South Asian communities women were expected to stay at home, perform domestic labour tasks and look after the children and their husband. They were expected to be the primary caregivers and homemakers. This was a role that was not expected of men, they were expected to be the main breadwinners. If women did not take on the role of caregiver and homemaker, they were considered to be 'bad mothers' and 'bad women'.

Table 6.5
Is a woman's place in the home?

In the home	n	%
Yes		
To look after home/children	19	32
Cultural expectation	4	7
Sub-total	23	39
No		
Choice/independence	21	35
Traps/imprisons women	5	8
Career/job satisfaction	11	18
Sub-total	37	61
Total (N)	60	100

A total of 61 per cent of respondents said a woman's place was not in the home. A number of reasons were given for this. Most respondents (35 per cent) said women should have a choice in their lives if they wanted to be independent.

I think women should have a choice in their lives and be allowed to do what they want to do, and not what the culture or other people want her to do...if she wants to be independent she should be allowed to (56).

Other respondents (18 per cent) said women should have a career and achieve job satisfaction.

...why should women stay at home? Because men want them to, women should go out and get a job and get some kind of job satisfaction from their lives...then they will realise there is more they can do, than be just a housewife (32).

A minority of respondents (8 per cent) said the home trapped and imprisoned women.

...the home makes women become confined, because they feel they can no longer get out and it's all a vicious circle for them...once they stay in the home, they end up staying like that forever...it just traps women (39).

However, 39 per cent of respondents said a woman's place was in the home. These respondents were from 'traditional' families. A number of reasons were given for this. Most respondents (32 per cent) said women's role in society was to look after the home and children.

It is and it should be...she's the one who has the children and she's the one who has to breast feed them, and so she should stay at home and be the housewife and look after all the things in the house that need to be looked after (7).

A minority of respondents (7 per cent) said a woman's place was in the home due to cultural expectations.

Men are expected to be one way and women are expected to be another...Asian people want their daughters to be good at cooking and want them to be able to look after the children...it's a cultural thing for us...men would never be seen to be doing these things (47).

Domestic labour is considered as 'women's work' and one that men do not want to participate in, they see it as infringing upon their roles as 'men'. Married women in 'traditional' families said having these different roles for the sexes worked best, men were not expected to participate in domestic labour, it was not their role. Even though some men offered 'help' in households, the household was still considered to be the 'woman's sphere'.

The cultural influence of women being housewives

Respondents were asked their views on the cultural influence of women being housewives. In South Asian communities, women were expected to look after the home and the family, this was their primary role in life. Women were socialised to learn to accept and perform this role adequately. Such behaviour was then passed on to daughters who were expected to be 'happy homemakers'. Men were not expected to perform this role.

Table 6.6
The cultural influence of women being housewives

Cultural influence	n	%
Cultural expectations	16	27
Natural/best role for women	37	62
Maternal influence	7	11
Total (N)	60	100

The majority of respondents (62 per cent) said the cultural influence of women being housewives was based upon this role being considered natural and the best role for South Asian women.

...women's role as housewives is just seen as a natural role for Asian women to take...just because they are women, they are seen as being naturally good with children and naturally good cooks, and if you're not that way, then you're not seen as a real woman...(11).

Other respondents (27 per cent) said it was cultural expectations which encouraged women to take on the role of housewife.

...to be a good woman in our culture, you have to be a good housewife and you have to be a good mother... that's how people judge you and that's if they decide you are a nice person or not...it's what the culture expects of you as a woman...this is something you should know...(40).

112

A minority of respondents (12 per cent) said it was the maternal influence women received which encouraged them to take on the role of housewife.

> Women are influenced by the women in their lives and their mothers want them to be good at the things they're good at, this is because they want them to be married, and so when men know women can cook and keep house they will want to marry them...(12).

Domestic labour is reinforced for women as it is considered to be a feminine, 'natural' role. Mothers train their daughters and bring them up to be a specific way. They must be able to cook, clean and perform housewifely duties, it is in this role they are judged. Men are not expected to participate in domestic labour, it is a role that is not expected of them and one which is considered to be 'unmanly'. Men are free from the socialisation mothers provide for their daughters and so are able to work outside the home and escape the expectations imposed upon women. Maternal influence was regarded to be a powerful force and influenced women becoming and taking on the feminine role of the housewife. Some respondents saw mothers as strong figures who had power. This power however, was limited. It only existed in the domains of the home. Mothers were able to take complete control of their daughters and strongly influenced their roles. The mother's role was taken to be an example and mothers wanted daughters to follow and obey them. They were trained to be 'good housewives', which in turn would prepare them to become 'good wives and mothers'. Mothers trained their daughters to follow specific traditional standards, these would prepare them for housewifely and maternal duties.

The significance of religion, education and employment

Religion did not affect respondent's views on domestic labour. Domestic labour was considered to be a female activity and was related to traditional practices in South Asian communities. Level of education affected respondent's views on domestic labour. Respondents who said women should be the domestic labourers in South Asian communities had low levels of education (those who had no qualifications or 'O' levels). Respondents who said there should be an equal sharing of roles were highly educated (those who had a BA or MA). Women's position in the labour market affected their views on domestic labour. Respondents who said women should do the housework in South Asian communities were in low positions in the labour market (non-employed housewife, skilled manual). Those who said there should be an equal sharing of roles were in high positions in the labour market (semi-professional, students). (See Appendix 3 for chi square tables on education and employment).

Conclusion

In South Asian communities, it is women who perform the majority of domestic labour tasks, men do not participate to a significant extent. The home and the kitchen are the 'traditional' woman's domain. The female must participate in domestic labour as a career, men do not participate in domestic labour to a significant extent.

The three questions asked on domestic labour were useful. Who carried out the activity? How often? Who did so on the last occasion? In some cases, there were discrepancies between who was said to regularly carry out the domestic labour activity and who did so on the last occasion. There were some contradictions in responses. When asked who should do the housework, most respondents felt *both* partners should do so, yet their own situation revealed it was *women* who carried out the majority of domestic labour tasks. When asked whether they felt a woman's place was in the home, many respondents said a woman should have a career, yet their own situation did not reveal this. Most women expressed their views on the way things *should* be in the home, for them both partners participating in domestic labour was an ideal situation, but one they felt would never be achieved. There existed a contradiction between what respondents wanted and what happened in reality.

In the study there existed three different families. The 'traditional' family consisted of those who had an arranged marriage and were given a dowry. These women lived with their husbands and children, (and in some cases with their extended family). In this family, domestic labour was considered to be the female's role, she was the one who performed it and there existed a segregation of roles; one for the male (breadwinner) and one for the female (homemaker). If women worked, they were expected to perform 'dual roles'. The 'co-habiting' family consisted of women who were not married, but were living with their partners. In this family, the partner participated in some aspects of domestic labour and both partners were more likely to work full-time. The 'single' family consisted of women who were either single without partners, or single with partners, (but not living with them). Single women carried out their own domestic labour activities and single women with partners, said their partners 'helped' them some of the time. These families consisted of 'independent' women. There is a degree of difference in domestic labour between 'independent' and 'traditional' women. 'Traditional' women perform most, (if not all), domestic labour tasks and experience private patriarchy inside the household. 'Independent' women indicate a movement towards a sharing of domestic labour tasks and experience a more public form of patriarchy outside the household.

7 Domestic finance

The study of domestic finance has investigated the extent to which financial organisation acts as a powerful determinant of who has power and how it is distributed in the household (Blumberg 1991, Brannen and Wilson 1987, Edwards 1981, Graham 1985, Gray 1979, Pahl 1989, Wilson 1987). Some writers have approached the study of household finance by the identification of distinctive patterns which can be used to classify households (Morris 1984, Pahl 1989). From this research four basic classification of finance types have emerged (Morris 1990, Pahl 1989).

The whole-wage system; one partner is responsible for managing all household expenditure, usually the woman. This association between women and the domestic sphere has led to a particular pattern of finance management in the case of low-income households. The man handing over his full wage to the woman, occurs where income is low, position in the labour market weak or in areas of traditional working class culture (Dennis et al 1956, Edwards 1981, Graham 1985, Gray 1979, Land 1976, Pahl 1989, Wilson 1987). Some researchers have identified a whole wage system in which husbands have sole responsibility for managing all household finances. This system has been found in studies of abused women (Evason 1982, Pahl 1989).

The allowance system; individuals have different spheres of responsibility, with the woman generally given a housekeeping allowance. This system is adopted at higher income levels than the whole wage system in which the husband is the only earner (Dennis et al 1956, Edwards 1981, Gray 1979, Pahl 1989). In this system, the woman may not see the unopened wage packet and may not even know how much her husband earns (Gray 1979, Marsh 1979).

The joint management system; both partners have access to household income and are jointly responsible for expenditure from a common pool. This system is found across all income levels especially where wives are in employment (Edwards 1981, Pahl 1989, Wilson 1987). More recently, some researchers have attempted to sub-divide this system into a 'male controlled pool', 'female controlled pool' and 'joint pool' (Laurie and Rose 1994, Vogler 1994, Vogler and Pahl 1993, 1994). This recent research suggests that it is misleading to place all joint management systems in the same category as there may be significant differences between the different types of pooling.

The independent management system; both partners keep their incomes separate and each is responsible for different spheres of expenditure. The connection between separate accounting systems, independence and equal authority within marriage has been made by Hertz's (1986) study of professional dual earners.

The domestic financial system indicates the relationship between a woman's earnings and her power (Pahl, 1989). Some researchers (McDonald 1980, Scanzoni 1979), in attempting to measure the concept of power have used information about which partner makes specific decisions in households. Other researchers have investigated the relationship between women's earnings and their power in households (Morris 1984, 1990, Pahl 1989). The argument that women's earnings increase their power in households is not convincing in all cases (Jephcott et al 1962, Morris 1984). In some cases, the woman's earnings clearly do enhance her status and this is most likely where there is a strong career attachment on the part of the woman, where finances are handled jointly and where the woman's wage covers clearly visible items of collective expenditure, for example mortgage repayments or payments of bills. However, the lower the woman's earnings, the more critical they are for household survival (Edwards 1981, Graham 1985, Gray 1979, Pahl 1989, Wilson 1987). Pahl (1989) has identified a hierarchy of financial responsibility. This includes the 'control', 'management' and 'budgeting' of income. However Morris (1984, 1990) has made a distinction between 'household' and 'domestic' income.

More recently some researchers have examined the impact of the labour market on patterns of financial management (Vogler 1994, Vogler and Pahl 1993,1994). Vogler and Pahl (1993:93) argue that changes in labour market participation do not lead to greater equality in household financial arrangements in any deterministic way. Elsewhere they (Vogler and Pahl 1993) and others (Morris 1984) indicate that it is full-time work which may give women power financially, part-time work does little to increase women's power within the home. This is also supported by Laurie and Rose (1994) who indicate that women in full-time employment, dual earner couples or couples where the woman is the main breadwinner are more likely to employ a shared system of financial management. Others (Laurie 1992, Ritchie and Thomas 1990) have pointed out that the organisation of domestic finance in households is not necessarily static and is open to change.

To examine which characteristics determine the type of financial systems couples use, some researchers point to level of income (Wilson 1987), employment status (Pahl 1989, Vogler and Pahl 1993) or the source of the income, especially if the income is derived from state benefits (Hunt 1980, Morris 1988). More recently Vogler and Pahl (1993) indicate that it is a combination of factors such as income, employment and social class as well as education, age and attitudes towards work both inside and outside the home.

Although the research on domestic finance has provided a sophisticated understanding of the management of household income, it has not examined the situation in non-white households. There is little research on 'race' differences of domestic finance which exist within households. We cannot generalise about findings from studies that have concentrated on white families. Male involvement in household organisation and collective expenditure can vary by class, culture, 'race' and personal orientation. Hence, the need to examine if the same types of financial arrangements are found in non-white households. Is it possible that the distribution of power within South Asian households may be related to male earning and control over domestic finance and women's *lack of power and control* may be related to their non-earning capacity within households? There is very little research on South Asian households and domestic finance. Bhachu (1988) has shown how waged work empowers Sikh women in Britain and has had definite effects within the domestic sphere. It has given Sikh women more resources with which to negotiate changes in the division of labour within the home and also in the patterns of expenditure which they control. Werbner (1988) has also found that when Pakistani women in the UK work, their wages are their own, unlike those of women in rural Punjab (Sharma 1981). Although research on domestic finance has increased our understanding of the relationship between domestic finance and control, it is still an important area to be explored. Examining the financial organisation of South Asian women will enable us to investigate the influence of 'race' and culture upon domestic financial control and distribution. Domestic finance is an indication of one of the ways power is distributed in households and reflects the relationship between a woman's earnings and her control. Wives and husbands/partners incomes are significant influences of who has control over domestic finance and who is able to make decisions on how money is spent.

Type of account

Respondents were asked whether they had a bank account to examine if they had access to money and how this affected domestic financial organisation within households.

Table 7.1
Type of account

Account	n	%
Own	36	60
Joint	3	5
None	21	35
Total (N)	60	100

The majority of respondents had their own bank accounts (60 per cent).

> I need my own bank account, I don't want to have to keep on asking him (partner) for money, that would mean I rely on him, and he would love that, because he would decide what I spend...that's not a good thing to do (20).

> I have my own bank account and I don't believe in a joint account, why should I have a joint account...he can spend what he wants and it's better for me, I can control my own money and I can spend my own money (17).

Other respondents did not have a bank account (35 per cent).

> I don't need an account, what do I want a bank account for? That's just another headache, I've got enough things to worry about...anyway, I ask my husband for it (money) and he gives me what I need, and then I can spend it on whatever I want to spend it on...and I know he looks after it and I can spend without worrying about it (4).

A minority of respondents had a joint account (5 per cent).

> We do everything together, and we believe in sharing our money...even though he does earn more money than me...at least I still have access to it...although a lot of the money goes into the house, and that's both of ours (37).

Women who had their own bank accounts felt they had some control over their own money and wanted this control as they felt it gave them some power and independence, which they valued. Others did not have a bank account as all finance was handled by their husbands. These women did not feel they needed any direct access to money and were content with asking their husbands for it. However, respondents who had a joint account, wanted their own money to be shared with that of their partner and felt it was something they did together as a couple, it was not controlled by one or the other, but was a joint venture. However, in some cases where women worked, they handed their wage packets over to their husbands and it was the males who decided how money was spent. This was generally found in poorer households.

> When I get paid I just give the money to my husband and he looks after it, he decides how we spend it. We don't have much money and so I give it to him and he knows the best way how to spend it (26).

In the present research, in lower income households it was *men* who were more likely to control finances. Furthermore, these women were more likely to hand their wage packets over to their husbands. This was further linked to the educational

118

background of respondents. Highly educated women were less likely to hand over their wage packets, but demanded negotiation and sharing with *both* wage packets. Male readiness to cooperate with negotiation, was also related to how significant the woman's earnings were judged to be for the household's standard of living. If they were considered to be very significant because of low income, men were more likely to control, if not, men were more likely to negotiate. Previous research has indicated that in poorer households, it is *women* who are more likely to be in control of finances (Edwards 1981, Graham 1985, Gray 1979, Pahl 1989, Wilson 1987). Even though some women earned an income they did not necessarily control it. Women in poorer households who earned an income did not have access to control that income. Men's control over women's income increased their access to power within households.

Money for personal items

How much direct access to money did respondents have? Did they have complete access all the time or did they have to ask their husband/partner for money? Asking respondents where they would obtain money to purchase personal items indicates the extent to which women have the freedom to spend when they want and how they want.

Table 7.2
Money for personal items

Where from	n	%
Self/own earnings	39	65
Husband	20	33
Mother-in-law	1	2
Total (N)	60	100

The majority of respondents said they obtained money for personal items from their own earnings (65 per cent).

> I take it out of my account and spend it on what I want to spend it on...that's the whole point of having my own account, so that I can spend it on what I want to spend it on, not what someone else tells me to do (35).

> ...at the end of the day, it's my money and I want to spend it and that for me means, being able to get what I want and so I just take it out and spend it on

119

myself, or sometimes I buy things for the house (13).

Other respondents said they obtained money for personal items from their husbands (33 per cent).

> When I ask him for it...sometimes he asks me what it's for and other times he just gives it to me...and I think it depends on the mood he's in...but I don't mind if he asks me, he's the one who earns the money and so he has a right to ask me what *I'm* spending *his* money on (respondent's emphasis) (48).

> I would ask my husband for it and he just wants to know what it's for...but he never questions me...he will always give it to me, he just wants to know where it's going, he knows what I like to spend money on, and he likes me spending money on the children (26).

Respondents who used their own earnings for personal items felt they had the right to spend them as they pleased. Those who asked their husbands for money were unlikely to have their own income and felt it was up to their husbands to decide how much they were allowed to spend. Since they did not earn it, they felt they did not have the power to decide how much they were able to spend. Similarly in poorer households, husbands decided how much the woman could spend. Although when women did earn an income, (albeit a low income), they handed their wage packets over to their husbands and their husbands decided how women's earnings were to be spent.

> Even though I work for the money, because it's for the family then I don't mind if my husband is the one who says what to spend it on...it has to be spent properly because we haven't got much of it and so he can look after it (26).

There is an 'internal economy' of households and that economy is based upon the domestic financial organisation that takes place within households. The 'internal economy' of households varies by gender, status and 'race'. Earning an income gives some women in higher income households the access and right to discuss issues of finance, where money comes from, how it is spent and who spends it. The greater a woman's control of income, the greater her bargaining power over the distribution of that income. Also the greater her leverage in other household economic and domestic decisions. An increase in educational levels and employment rates enables women to provide sizeable shares of family income. For some women, (those in lower income households), the mere fact of women earning an independent income does not necessarily indicate a revolutionary change in authority relations between husbands and wives. Furthermore, some women who were machinists worked part-time as they were able to combine child care with paid work. This supports findings by Morris (1984) and Vogler and Pahl (1993) who have shown part-time work does little to increase women's power within the home and it is only full-time work which gives women power both financially and broadly within the relationship. However, some South Asian women worked full-time in lower income households, yet this did not give them power within the home. Furthermore, many of these women did not know how much their husbands earned. This also confirms findings from previous research (Cragg and Dawson 1984, Gray 1979, Marsh 1979).

Where funds were obtained to purchase a washing machine

Access to large amounts of money indicates if women have savings themselves and are able to use these savings as they please. Or, do they have to ask their husband/partner for large amounts of money? How much access do women have to large amounts of money such as that required to purchase a washing machine? Where would they obtain funds to purchase a washing machine from? Would it be their decision or the decision of their husband/partner?

Table 7.3
Where funds were obtained to purchase a washing machine

Where obtained funds	n	%
Self/own earnings	2	3
Husband	27	45
With husband/partner	26	44
No partner (N/A)	5	8
Total (N)	60	100

Most respondents said they would ask their husbands to purchase a washing machine for them (45 per cent).

I would talk to my husband about it, and if he thought we needed it, then he would get it for me, but I would have to ask him to buy it for me, I don't have that much money and he's the one who has all the money anyway...so he would buy it (9).

I would ask my husband to buy it for me, where would I get that sort of money from? He's the one who decides the big things to buy, because he knows what we should be spending the money on and he decides where large sums of money go...and so he would probably buy it for me if I wanted it (26).

Other respondents said they would purchase a washing machine together with their partner (44 per cent).

> We would both discuss it together and then go out and buy it...it would be a joint decision and we would pay for it halfway...that's the way we do things, we believe in doing things together, as a partnership (37).

> I would talk to my partner about it and it would be a joint decision we make together...and we would pay for it together and that would be fair, half each...but if I didn't have the money then he would pay for it and I would pay him back from my share...so the washing machine would be both of ours and not just his (20).

Previous researchers (Edwards 1981, Pahl 1989) have made a distinction between 'control', 'management' and 'budgeting' of household income. The 'control' of money is concerned with decisions about how income is allocated. The 'management' of money refers to how control decisions are put into practise. The 'budgeting' of money refers to spending within different spheres of expenditure. My research also found a distinction between the 'control' and 'management' of money. However, the *'distribution'* of income was also found to be a significant part of financial organisation. This was related to earning and spending. Women in higher income households distributed their own income, yet women in lower income households who handed their wage packets over to their husbands, also handed over the distribution of that income. Previous research (Morris 1984, 1990) has made a distinction between 'household' and 'domestic' income. 'Household' income refers to the total amount of money received by different members of the households from different sources. 'Domestic' income refers to the total income available for spending on the household as a collectivity. My research also found a distinction between 'household' and 'domestic' income, but such a distinction was only found in higher income households where women had higher levels of education and were in high positions in the labour market. For women in lower income households, their earnings were placed into a *'family'* income where husbands decided how money was spent.

Decision to spend money earned by female

Who decides to spend the money women earn indicates the extent to which women have control over their own earnings or whether earnings are controlled by their husband/partner. Who decides to spend the money earned by the female? Does she decide herself or does her husband/partner decide for her?

Table 7.4
Decision to spend money earned by female

Who decides	n	%
Self	18	30
Self & husband/partner	22	37
Husband/partner	14	23
Mother-in-law	1	2
No partner (N/A)	5	8
Total (N)	60	100

Most respondents said they decided together with their husband/partner what to spend their earnings on (37 per cent).

> We both decide what to spend the money on...we put the money together and we share everything and it's what we feel works right for us and we can share everything down the middle...it makes us feel as though we have an equal relationship (34).

> I think it's better if we both sit down and discuss the money, because it means we're both taking a part in what is going on and we both care about it, so it's like a partnership really (59).

However, some respondents said they themselves decided what to spend their earnings on (30 per cent).

> If I am the one who is able to decide what to spend my money on, then I am showing my partner I don't want him to control me and what I do...if he did, then I would have less control than him and would probably have to do what he said...and I don't want that to happen...and so I make sure he always knows that and doesn't get a chance to try and say what I should spend my money on (14).

> I do and that's simple because I earned it and I worked hard for it and so it should be me who decides what to spend it on...I think it's wrong when men tell women what they can spend money on...and when she's earned the money herself (32).

Other respondents said it was their husband/partner who decided what to spend their earnings on (23 per cent).

> ...my husband decides what to spend the money on, he takes care of all that business in the home...he looks after it all and he decides what it's spent on and what is being saved...I'm glad he takes care of it, I wouldn't know what to do with it...he makes sure we have enough money and he makes sure the bills get paid (29).

> ...because I work for the family business, I don't mind what happens to the money, because it all goes back into the family and it's all for us and the children...and so the money I make, my husband is the one who decides what to do with it, sometimes he may use it to pay a big bill or something, but most of the time I don't see it and he looks after it (25).

The system of domestic financial management is a reflection of power within a relationship. In the 'traditional' family, many women said they spent money on the family and children (a 'maternal altruism'), whereby the needs of the family and children are always treated as being paramount, coming before those of the wife and mother. Women do not use their wages exclusively for personal consumption. This confirms findings from previous research (Edwards 1981, Graham 1985, Gray 1979, Pahl 1989, Wilson 1987). Whereas in the 'co-habiting' family, spending money was discussed by both partners. This has also been found in previous research (Pahl 1989, Wilson 1987). Although many women in the sample did work, for some of them, (those in lower income households), work did not increase their sense of self-worth. The mere fact that they held jobs did not have fundamental effects upon relations between husbands/partners and wives. For example, women who were machinists handed their wage packets over to their husbands and husbands decided how it was spent. These findings indicate that there are significant differences in the organisation of domestic finance in South Asian and white households.

Whether wife/partner knows her husband/partner's earnings

Knowledge of each other's earnings indicates the extent to which each partner wants to disclose the amount of money they earn and the degree to which they want their partner to share in this and have some control over it. Did respondents know how much their husband/partner earned?

Table 7.5
Whether wife/partner knows her husband/partner's earnings

Know earnings	n	%
Yes		
Discuss finance	41	69
No		
Will worry	5	8
Male controls finance	9	15
No partner (N/A)	5	8
Total (N)	60	100

The majority of respondents (69 per cent) said they knew how much their husband/partner earned.

We both tell each other what we earn, we believe in having an equal relationship and that means telling each other these things...it doesn't bother me at all, I think it bothers him more than it bothers me...he gets afraid I might be earning more than him one day (40).

Yes I know how much he earns, although sometimes he's reluctant to tell me, but I always know...I always look at his payslip and so I know exactly how much he earns...and I think I have a right to know, why shouldn't I know? He knows how much I earn and so I should know how much he earns, we should both follow the same rules and not just do what he says...he wants to know what I earn, then he should expect to tell me what he earns (16).

Other respondents (23 per cent) said they did not know how much their husband/partner earned. A number of reasons were given for this. Some respondents (15 per cent) said their husband/partner controlled the finances in the home.

I think looking after the money is the man's job...and it should be...I don't get involved and so he doesn't tell me how much he earns...I don't think he needs to, what do I want to know for anyway? It's his job and I let him get on with it, he's the one who says what we can spend money on and that doesn't bother me at all...it's the way I like it (27).

I don't think he wants to tell me, because then it wouldn't be his job if he involved me would it? He wants to take control of it and he does...it makes him know he is the head of the family and he has an important job to do, handling money is an important job...and it makes him feel good. I don't think I would like to do it, it would make me think about money too much and how much we *haven't got* (respondent's emphasis) (48).

Other respondents (8 per cent) said their husband/partners did not tell them how much they earned, as they did not want their wives/partners to worry.

I don't know what he earns and I don't want to know...he knows what I'm like, because if he told me, then I would start to worry and wonder about how much money we have and what we are doing with it...I don't want him to tell me, it's better the way it is, he looks after it and I don't have to worry about it then (41).

Earning an income makes a significant difference to knowledge of earnings and how money is spent. In 'co-habiting' households, individuals are able to spend more money on consumer items. Financial status can be revealed indirectly by standard of lifestyle. Sometimes, in cases where wives did not know how much their husbands earned, (in 'traditional' households), money remained a taboo issue for many couples because when people talk about money, they are really talking about authority relations inside households and how these authority relations are controlled and *by whom*. Authority relations reflect how much men and women earn and the form of budgeting symbolises how power is distributed in the family. Men have traditionally derived their authority from status and resources acquired *outside* the family and have transformed their status and these resources into authority relations *inside* the family. What happens to women's income and how they view it, is important. Autonomy is gained by the expenditure of individual income and the structure of the accounting system questions the traditional authority of men to make financial decisions and allows women to assert the same authority over discretionary income that men have had in the past.

The significance of religion, education and employment

The religious background of respondents did not influence the amount of control women had over domestic finance and whether they had access to money. Different types of financial systems in South Asian households were related to women's level of education and their position in the labour market. Women in lower income households were more likely to be in 'traditional' families. These households adopted the whole wage system, but it was the *man* and not the woman who was most likely to control domestic finance. This is contrary to previous research (Edwards 1981, Graham 1985, Gray 1979, Land 1979, Pahl 1989, Wilson 1987) which indicates that it is *women* who are more likely to be in control of domestic finance in the whole wage system. Women in lower income households who employed the whole wage system had lower levels of education and were in low positions in the labour market, (see Appendix 3 for chi square tables on education and employment).

Women in 'co-habiting' families were in higher income households. These women had high levels of education and were in high positions in the labour market. They were more likely to employ the independent management system of domestic financial organisation. This confirms findings from previous research (Edwards 1981, Hertz 1986) which indicates that the independent management system is found among couples where both partners are in employment and where both earn relatively high incomes. However some women in 'co-habiting' families also had a joint management system. Those who had a joint management system were more likely to have a joint bank account. This has also been found in previous research (Hunt 1980, Pahl 1989). The allowance system was more likely to be found in 'traditional' families where women were non-employed housewives. Women were given a housekeeping allowance and had to ask their husbands for personal spending money. This has also been found in previous research where wives are given a fixed sum of money for housekeeping expenses and where the husband is the sole earner (Edwards 1981, Gray 1979, Pahl 1989).

The different financial systems were associated with level of education and position in the labour market as well as family type. This was also related to level of income. Those who had higher levels of income were more likely to have high levels of education and be in high positions in the labour market. This confirms findings from previous research (Pahl 1989, Vogler and Pahl 1993) which indicates that household allocative systems are clearly related to both spouses' employment status. In my research women in 'co-habiting' families were more likely to be in high positions in the labour market, as were their partners. Furthermore, previous research (Laurie and Rose 1994, Vogler and Pahl 1993) has shown that pooling systems are predominant where both partners are from the service class, that is among professionals and managers. This was also found in my research. Women who were in professional or semi-professional occupations were more likely to use the pooling systems and their partners were more likely to be from similar occupational backgrounds as them.

Previous research (Vogler and Pahl 1993) has shown that household allocative systems are related to husbands' but not wives' educational qualifications. Highly qualified husbands (with 'A' levels) are more likely to use the joint pool, whereas those with no qualifications or 'O' levels are more likely to use the female whole wage system. However, my research found that financial systems were related to *both partners'* educational qualifications. Both partners were more likely to have similar levels of education. Women with high levels of education were more likely to use the joint pool, but women with lower levels of education were more likely to use the whole wage system. In contrast to previous research (Vogler and Pahl 1993), the more egalitarian system of financial organisation was more likely to be found in households where *women and men* were highly educated. Couples who pooled their money were more likely to be co-habiting. This confirms findings from previous research (Vogler and Pahl 1993) which indicates that couples who pool their money were less traditional than those who used other allocative systems.

Conclusion

The different types of financial systems employed in South Asian households were related to level of education, position in the labour market as well as family type. Women in lower income households who worked were more likely to be in 'traditional' families, have a lower level of education and be in low positions in the labour market. These households employed a whole wage system, where men were more likely to control domestic finance. The allowance system however, was more likely to be found in 'traditional' families where women were non-employed housewives and given a housekeeping allowance and had to ask their husbands for personal spending money. Married women's earnings in 'traditional' families are seen as a supplementary income, rather than as a necessity. Women's role within the home limits the freedom they have outside of it and helps to sustain their social and economic dependency upon their husbands. Wives remain financially dependent upon their husbands even when they themselves are employed and they lack the economic freedom that his work gives him. Women in 'co-habiting' families were more likely to employ an independent or joint management system where finances were shared between both partners. Here, there is no privileged position of power. This is a model based upon equal access and joint responsibility which depends on a high level of trust and agreement about priorities for spending. However, it cannot be assumed that a high level of income for one partner necessarily benefits the living standards of the other.

Where men were the primary earners ('traditional' families), they paid the bills and women were less likely to be involved in the distribution of income. Where both partners earned an income ('co-habiting' families), these couples were most notable for the presence of a surplus income over and above that of basic needs. Here there was a strong belief in an equal and shared partnership. For 'traditional' women, finance is controlled by the male, he decides how money is spent. These women experience private patriarchy inside the household through the organisation of domestic finance. For some 'independent' women where finances are handled jointly, these women are more likely to be employed. They experience a more public form of patriarchy outside the household. The present research indicates that there are significant differences between white and South Asian households in domestic financial organisation. In lower income South Asian households men were more likely to control domestic finance, women handed over their wage packets to their husbands and husbands decided how women's earnings were spent. Furthermore, the type of financial system employed in South Asian households is related to *both partner's* educational qualifications. The organisation of domestic finance reflects the different

128

authority and power relations which translate into male power and female disadvantage. Women's participation in the labour market has not necessarily given them more power within the home to control how money is spent and by whom. The incomes women bring to households may not necessarily be a reflection of their allocation of power within households. For some women it may appear to be, but ultimately it is men who control and women who contribute to that control.

8 Education, employment and marital status

This chapter will examine Labour Force Survey (LFS) statistics on economic activity, highest educational qualification, marital status and ethnicity. The chapter will investigate whether my East London sample was representative of the national data and examine any correlations between my findings and LFS data. It will also look at comparisons within South Asian groups and between other ethnic groups (Afro-Caribbean and white), to investigate whether marriage has a differential impact for different ethnic groups and if there been any changes over time (1984-1994) in paid employment and education for women.

Labour Force Survey data

The relevant LFS data was sorted by gender (women), ethnic group (all ethnic groups), age (all ages and 25-30), education (highest qualification), employment (economic activity) and marital status (single, married, cohabiting and divorced). The LFS data was taken for 11 years (1984-1994). When examining correlations between marital status, economic activity, education and ethnicity it was taken for three years (1984, 1990 and 1994).

The LFS is a quarterly sample survey of around 60,000 households and people living in NHS accommodation (ie nurses). The questionnaire covers a wide range of demographic and employment-related information. Questions about economic activity (paid work, job search), are asked of all people aged 16 or over, and relate to a specific reference period (normally a period of one week or four weeks, depending upon the topic), immediately prior to interview. If any household member is unavailable for interview, information for that person is provided by a related adult member of the same household. Students living away from home in halls of residence are also included.

Each quarter's LFS sample of 60,000 households is made up of five 'waves' each of approximately 12,000 households. Each wave is interviewed in 5 successive quarters; in any one quarter one wave will be receiving their first interview, one wave their second and so on, with one wave receiving their fifth and final interview. Thus there is an 80 per cent overlap in the samples for successive quarters. The survey results are 'grossed up' to give the correct population total for Great Britain and reflect the distributions by sex, age and region shown by the population figures. Estimates relating to 10,000 people or fewer (after grossing up) are not shown, since they are based upon small samples and are therefore unlikely to be reliable. This is in line with current practice for all LFS based analyses (Sly 1994, 1995).

Ethnic origin

People interviewed in the quarterly LFS are asked to classify their own ethnic origin and that of others in their household by answering the question; 'To which of these groups do you consider.......belongs?'; White, Black-Caribbean, Black-African, Black-Other, Black-Mixed, Indian, Pakistani, Bangladeshi, Chinese and Other. However, LFS estimates relating to ethnic origin (or country of origin and nationality), are subject to high sampling errors as the populations in question are relatively small in number and tend to be highly clustered, both within particular geographical areas and within households. This limits the detail in which results can be presented.

Economic activity and classification

People in employment in the survey are regarded as those aged 16 and over who did some paid work in the reference week (whether as an employee or self-employed), those who had a job that they were temporarily away from (on holiday for example), those on government employment or training programmes and unpaid family workers.

Unemployed people in the survey are regarded as those aged 16 and over without a paid job, who said they were available to start work in the next two weeks and who either had looked for work at some time during the four weeks prior to the interview, or were waiting to start a job they had already obtained.

The 'economically active' population or labour force, comprises people in employment together with unemployed people. The 'economically inactive' population comprises people who are neither in employment nor unemployed. This group includes all people aged under 16, together with those who were looking after a home or retired, and also discouraged workers who were not seeking work, because they believe there were no jobs available.

Highest qualification

Educational qualifications in the LFS are asked of all people aged over 16. Individuals are asked to state their highest qualification, which ranges from higher degree to

GCSE down to no qualifications, as well as other qualifications such as nursing certificates, YTS and BTEC.

A comparison - findings from the East London study

Religion

In the East London study of 60 women, religion influenced whether South Asian women had an arranged marriage and were given a dowry. Moslem women were more likely to have had an arranged marriage and given a dowry (43 per cent), followed by Sikh (30 per cent) and Hindu women (27 per cent). However, religion did not influence women's attitudes to arranged marriages or dowries.

Education

Level of education influenced whether South Asian women had an arranged marriage and were given a dowry. Highly educated women were in high positions in the labour market, did not have an arranged marriage and were not given a dowry. Women with lower levels of education were in low positions in the labour market, had an arranged marriage and were given a dowry.

Employment

Position in the labour market is related to level of education and influenced South Asian women's position within households. Women in high positions in the labour market were highly educated. Women in low positions in the labour market had lower levels of education.

In order to make a comparison with LFS data and the East London study, it is necessary to map my own categories onto those used in the LFS. Since Hindu and Sikh women in my sample were Indian, and Moslem women were Pakistani or Bangladeshi, these categories can be mapped onto those used by the LFS (Indian=Hindu/Sikh, Pakistani/Bangladeshi=Moslem). However, as this is not an exact mapping, there may be possible discrepancies between the two data sets.

Labour Force Survey data

Economic activity

This section will compare data for the 25-30 age cohort in 1993, (this was the age range of respondents in the East London study, and they were interviewed in 1993), with data for all women. It is important to make a comparison between the 25-30 age cohort and all women, as data from this age cohort will produce a different picture from data for all women. The rapidity of social change for the 25-30 age cohort, may be greater than for all women, hence it is important to examine both groups.

The LFS suggests that the East London study of 60 women is representative of the national data and indicates that Pakistani/Bangladeshi (Moslem) women have the lowest proportion of women who are in employment compared to all other ethnic groups. Whereas Indian (Hindu and Sikh) women, have a very high number of women who are in employment, this is shown for all women and women aged 25-30.

Table 8.1
Economic activity and ethnicity, 1993 (all women)

Economic activity (All Women) 1993	Ethnic group (per cent)			
	All	White	Afro-Caribbean	Indian	Pakistani/ Bangladeshi
Economically active	53	53	62	56	24
In employment	49	50	49	50	17
ILO[1] Unemployed	4	4	13	6	7
Inactive	47	47	38	44	76

Source: LFS 1993

Table 8.2
Economic activity and ethnicity, 1993 (women aged 25-30)

Economic activity (Women aged 25 -30) 1993	Ethnic group (per cent)				
	All	White	Afro-Caribbean	Indian	Pakistani/ Bangladeshi
Economically active	72	73	65	70	29
In employment	66	67	50	60	22
ILO unemployed	6	6	15	10	7
Inactive	28	27	35	30	71

Source: LFS 1993

As shown in table 8.2, 60 per cent of Indian women in the 25-30 age cohort were in employment which is slightly lower than the numbers of white women. Pakistani/Bangladeshi women have the lowest number of women in employment. The LFS data indicates that women aged 25-30 were more likely to be working than all women. The LFS data suggests that the East London study is representative of the national data. Hindu and Sikh women (Indian) were more likely to be employed than Pakistani/Bangladeshi (Moslem) women.

Highest qualification

This section will examine data for the 25-30 age cohort for highest educational qualification and ethnic origin (1993) and compare data for all women.

Table 8.3
Highest qualification and ethnicity, 1993 (women aged 25-30)

Highest qualification[2] (Women aged 25 - 30) 1993	Ethnic group (per cent)				
	All	White	Afro-Caribbean	Indian	Pakistani/Bangladeshi
First degree	9	9	8	14	4
'A' Levels	7	7	7	8	6
'O' Levels	26	27	17	13	10
CSE below grade 1	9	10	8	6	2
No qualifications	17	16	20	27	50

Source: LFS 1993

The LFS data demonstrates that Indian (Hindu and Sikh) women were more likely to have degrees than white and other women in 1993. Pakistani/Bangladeshi (Moslem) women were less likely to have degrees than any other ethnic group.

Table 8.4
Highest qualification and ethnicity, 1993 (all women)

Highest qualification (All Women) 1993	Ethnic group (per cent)				
	All	White	Afro-Caribbean	Indian	Pakistani/Bangladeshi
First degree	3	3	4	5	1
'A' Levels	4	4	4	4	2
'O' Levels	12	12	10	9	5
CSE below grade 1	3	3	3	2	2
No qualifications	19	18	19	26	32

Source: LFS 1993

When comparing the numbers for all women, the LFS data indicates that the East London study is representative of the national data. Indian (Hindu and Sikh) women were more likely to have degrees than Pakistani/Bangladeshi (Moslem) women. Pakistani/Bangladeshi (Moslem) women were more likely to have no qualifications than other women. There are significant differences between ethnic groups in terms of educational qualifications. Indian (Hindu and Sikh) women were more educated than white women, followed by Afro-Caribbean women. Pakistani/Bangladeshi (Moslem) women were the least educated. Education has a similar impact for women of all ethnic groups, enabling them to enter employment, however women from different ethnic groups have differential access to education.

Highest qualification, marital status and ethnicity

The following tables provide figures from 1984, 1990 and 1994[3] for highest qualification (degrees), marital status and ethnicity, for all women and for women aged 25-30.

Table 8.5
Highest qualification (degrees), marital status and ethnicity (all women)

Ethnic group	Degrees				
Year	Marital status (per cent)				
	All	Single	Cohabiting	Married	Divorced
All women					
1984	3	4	3	-	3
1990	4	3	5	9	4
1994	4	3	3	9	3
White women					
1984	3	4	3	-	3
1990	4	3	4	9	4
1994	4	3	4	9	3
Indian women					
1984	5	3	6	-	13
1990	7	2	11	-	14
1994	4	4	4	19	6
Pakistani/Bangladeshi women					
1984	3	-	4	-	-
1990	2	1	4	-	-
1994	2	2	2	-	-
Afro-Caribbean women					
1984	-	-	-	-	-
1990	5	2	8	7	7
1994	3	2	5	9	4

Source: LFS 1984, 1990 and 1994

Table 8.6
Highest qualification (degrees), marital status and ethnicity
(women aged 25-30)

| Ethnic group | Degrees | | | | |

Year	Marital status (per cent)				
	All	Single	Cohabiting	Married	Divorced
All women					
1984	7	14	6	-	2
1990	8	16	6	11	1
1994	10	15	8	13	1
White women					
1984	7	15	6	-	2
1990	8	16	6	11	1
1994	10	14	8	13	1
Indian women					
1984	12	7	13	-	-
1990	10	44	6	-	-
1994	21	43	11	32	41
Pakistani/Bangladeshi women					
1984	2	-	2	-	-
1990	1	-	1	-	-
1994	5	29	2	-	-
Afro-Caribbean women					
1984	1	2	-	-	-
1990	4	6	-	-	-
1994	8	9	5	9	-

Source: LFS 1984, 1990 and 1994

Tables 8.5 and 8.6 demonstrate the relationship between education, ethnicity and the impact of marital status upon women's lives. The tables indicate that there are differences between ethnic groups and within the South Asian category. Marital status has a disproportionate impact for Pakistani/Bangladeshi and Indian groups than white and Afro-Caribbean groups. This suggests that the East London study is representative of the national data where Hindu and Sikh (Indian) cohabiting women were more likely to have degrees than Moslem (Pakistani/Bangladeshi) women. Moslem (Pakistani/Bangladeshi) women were more likely to have had an arranged marriage than Hindu or Sikh (Indian) women.

The significance of religion and marital status

In the East London study, religion influenced whether women had an arranged marriage and were given a dowry. Moslem women were more likely to have had an arranged marriage (43 per cent), followed by Sikh (30 per cent) and Hindu (27 per cent) women. What is the relationship between marital status, ethnicity, economic activity and education?

Economic activity, marital status and ethnicity

The following tables provide figures from 1984, 1990 and 1994 for economic activity, marital status and ethnicity, for all women and women aged 25-30. Abbreviations used are; Cohab = cohabiting and Divor = divorced.

Table 8.7
Economic activity, marital status and ethnicity (all women)

Ethnic group	In employment					ILO/OECD unemployed				
	Marital status (per cent)					Marital status (per cent)				
Year	All	Single	Married	Co-hab	Divor	All	Single	Married	Co-hab	Divor
All women										
1984	35	24	47	-	44	4	4	4	-	9
1990	40	27	54	77	53	3	2	3	6	6
1994	39	24	55	71	50	3	3	3	6	7
White women										
1984	35	25	47	-	49	4	4	4	-	9
1990	41	28	54	77	53	3	2	3	6	6
1994	40	25	54	71	51	3	3	3	6	6
Indian women										
1984	30	12	47	-	34	7	4	9	-	37
1990	35	13	54	79	33	5	3	6	21	11
1994	35	18	51	82	46	5	2	6	18	35
Pakistani/Bangladeshi women										
1984	9	2	18	-	59	7	7	6	-	-
1990	11	6	17	-	33	4	2	6	-	-
1994	11	7	16	36	25	4	3	4	31	26
Afro-Caribbean women										
1984	43	28	64	-	60	8	7	9	-	16
1990	46	36	70	57	54	6	6	5	9	5
1994	36	25	57	70	42	8	8	7	4	15

Source: LFS 1984, 1990 and 1994

Table 8.8
Economic activity, marital status and ethnicity (women aged 25-30)

Ethnic group	In employment					ILO/OECD unemployed				
	Marital status (per cent)					Marital status (per cent)				
Year	All	Single	Married	Co-hab	Divor	All	Single	Married	Co-hab	Divor
All women										
1984	53	77	48	-	47	8	8	8	-	11
1990	65	76	61	80	47	6	6	6	6	8
1994	65	68	64	76	41	6	8	5	5	10
White women										
1984	54	79	49	-	47	8	8	8	-	11
1990	66	77	62	81	47	6	5	6	5	8
1994	67	69	67	76	42	6	7	5	5	9
Indian women										
1984	47	77	44	-	66	11	14	11	-	34
1990	64	93	60	100	100	8	7	7	-	-
1994	65	88	55	100	49	7	3	7	-	25
Pakistani/Bangladeshi women										
1984	13	-	13	-	-	5	-	5	-	-
1990	22	-	22	-	51	6	-	7	-	-
1994	25	72	19	-	21	4	19	1	-	20
Afro-Caribbean women										
1984	52	52	51	-	63	14	13	13	-	37
1990	66	65	80	37	41	10	13	-	25	-
1994	56	58	53	66	27	12	17	10	-	-

Source: LFS 1984, 1990 and 1994

As shown in table 8.7, single women from all ethnic groups, (with the exception of Afro-Caribbean), had significantly higher numbers of women who were in employment compared to married women, which is similar to those cohabiting. Single women, (from all ethnic groups), and cohabiting women, (from all ethnic groups, with the exception of Afro-Caribbean in 1990), were more likely to be in employment than married women. This suggests that the East London study is representative of the national data, where single and cohabiting women were more likely to be in employment than married women. Marital status has a disproportionate impact upon economic activity for different ethnic groups. When we control for age (table 8.8), the findings suggest that marital status has more impact upon Indian and Pakistani/Bangladeshi women than for Afro-Caribbean and white women. There are differences between ethnic groups and there are also differences within the South Asian category.

Changes over time

The following sections will examine data from the LFS for 11 years (1984-1994) on economic activity, education and marital status, to investigate whether changes for different ethnic groups are occurring at different rates. As the 25-30 age cohort in East London indicates that rapid social change is taking place amongst this age group, does data from the LFS also demonstrate this?

Economic activity

The following tables provide figures for all women from 1984-1994 and women aged 25-30 for economic activity and ethnic origin.

Table 8.9
Economic activity and ethnicity (all women)

Year	Ethnic origin (per cent)				
	All	White	Afro-Caribbean	Indian	Pakistani/Bangladeshi
1984	35	35	43	30	6
1985	36	36	40	28	5
1986	36	36	40	31	7
1987	37	37	45	30	8
1988	38	39	48	34	9
1989	40	40	49	37	10
1990	40	41	46	35	11
1991	40	40	49	34	11
1992	49	49	54	52[4]	16
1993	49	50	49	50	17
1994	49	50	51	49	20

Source: LFS 1984-1994[5]

142

Table 8.10
Economic activity and ethnicity (women aged 25-30)

Year	All	White	Afro-Caribbean	Indian	Pakistani/Bangladeshi
			Ethnic origin (per cent)		
1984	53	54	52	47	11
1985	54	54	56	47	10
1986	54	55	52	50	13
1987	56	57	63	41	10
1988	59	59	66	58	12
1989	63	64	72	67	10
1990	65	66	66	64	22
1991	64	65	68	56	16
1992	64	66	59	61	15
1993	66	67	50	60	22
1994	66	67	57	66	25

Source: LFS 1984-1994

As shown in table 8.9, there has been an increase in economic activity for women from all ethnic groups in the last 11 years. The numbers of white and Indian women who are economically active are similar, for Afro-Caribbean women the numbers are higher. For Pakistani/Bangladeshi women, the numbers remain low, but there has been a dramatic increase. The numbers of Pakistani/Bangladeshi women who are economically active remain less than half of those from all other ethnic groups. However for the 25-30 age cohort (table 8.10), the increase is more apparent. There are different rates of change for different ethnic groups, the greatest being for Pakistani/Bangladeshi women.

Highest qualification

The following tables provide figures from 1984-1994 for highest qualification and ethnic origin for all women and for women aged 25-30.

Table 8.11
Highest qualification (degrees) and ethnicity (all women)

Year	Ethnic origin (per cent)				
	All	White	Afro-Caribbean	Indian	Pakistani/Bangladeshi
1984	3	2	3	5	2
1985	3	3	3	4	2
1986	3	3	3	4	1
1987	3	3	4	5	2
1988	3	3	4	5	2
1989	3	3	4	5	2
1990	4	4	5	7	2
1991	4	4	6	6	3
1992	3	3	3	4	2
1993	3	3	4	5	1
1994	4	4	3	4	2

Source: LFS 1984-1994

Table 8.12
Highest qualification (degrees) and ethnicity (women aged 25-30)

Year	Ethnic origin (per cent)				
	All	White	Afro-Caribbean	Indian	Pakistani/Bangladeshi
1984	9	9	3	13	2
1985	10	10	1	11	8
1986	9	9	4	7	3
1987	9	9	3	6	5
1988	8	9	3	8	3
1989	9	9	2	15	1
1990	9	10	5	13	3
1991	9	9	6	16	7
1992	9	9	9	15	3
1993	9	9	8	14	4
1994	10	10	8	21	5

Source: LFS 1984-1994

As shown in table 8.11, the numbers of white women obtaining degrees has slightly increased. For Afro-Caribbean and Indian women the numbers have fluctuated. For the 25-30 age cohort (table 8.12), the numbers of Afro-Caribbean, Indian and Pakistani/Bangladeshi women have fluctuated, but have shown an increase. In comparison to other ethnic groups, the numbers of Indian women obtaining degrees is relatively high. They are more likely to obtain a degree than any other ethnic group. Although, the numbers of Pakistani/Bangladeshi women are comparatively low, overall there has been an increase. This suggests that the East London study is representative of the national data where Hindu and Sikh (Indian) women were more likely to have degrees than Moslem (Pakistani/Bangladeshi) women.

Conclusion

The LFS indicates the East London study is representative of the national data and has enabled me to make a comparison, examining the effect of social change and whether there are differences between ethnic groups. Marital status has a differential impact upon economic activity and education for different ethnic groups. When controlling for age (25-30), marital status has more impact upon Indian and Pakistani/Bangladeshi groups, than it does for Afro-Caribbean and white groups. There are differences *between* ethnic groups and there are also differences *within* the South Asian category. The data has also indicated the extent of rapid social change for women from the 25-30 age cohort.

Education and employment influence women's marital status. Women are less likely to marry if they are highly educated and employed. Marital status has a significant impact upon women's lives. However, marital status has a differential impact for different ethnic groups. High numbers of white and Indian (Hindu and Sikh) women who are not married, (single/cohabiting/divorced), are more likely to be employed and educated than Pakistani/Bangladeshi (Moslem) women who are married. Indian women (Hindu and Sikh), if they are highly educated, are less likely to marry than Pakistani/Bangladeshi (Moslem) women. This is demonstrated in the LFS data and in the East London study, where Moslem women were more likely to have had an arranged marriage than Hindu or Sikh women, and all single women from all three groups (Hindu, Sikh, Moslem), were highly educated and in high positions in the labour market.

In the last 11 years, there has been a significant change in economic activity for South Asian women. The numbers of Indian (Hindu and Sikh) women in employment has shown a gradual increase and is comparable to white women. There has been a rapid increase for Pakistani/Bangladeshi (Moslem) women, however these numbers remain low. South Asian women are more likely to be employed, although there are differences within the South Asian category. The numbers of Indian women in employment are similar to those of white and Afro-Caribbean women, yet the numbers for Pakistani/Bangladeshi women are less than half that of women from other ethnic groups. This indicates that the 25-30 age cohort are an important group, since they demonstrate the extent of rapid social change.

There are more Indian women who have degrees than women in other ethnic groups. However, there are differences for the South Asian category. The numbers for Pakistani/Bangladeshi have increased, but remain low. For the 25-30 age cohort, the numbers have fluctuated for all ethnic groups, but shown an overall increase. Indian women are still the highest group obtaining degrees in the 25-30 age cohort. This data also indicates that the 25-30 age cohort are the most important group in which rapid social change is taking place.

Religion has a significant impact upon whether women get highly educated and enter employment. The LFS data indicates that Pakistani/Bangladeshi (Moslem) women have the lowest levels of education and the lowest rates of employment compared to all other ethnic groups. This suggests that the East London study is representative of the national data, where Moslem women had lower levels of education compared to Hindu and Sikh women and were less likely to be employed.

The LFS indicates that the East London study is representative of the national data. Marital status has a differential impact upon economic activity and education for different ethnic groups. When controlling for age (25-30), marital status has more impact upon Indian and Pakistani/Bangladeshi groups than it does for Afro-Caribbean and white groups. There are differences within the ethnic groups and there are also differences within the South Asian category. The data also indicates the extent of rapid social change which is taking place for the 25-30 age cohort of South Asian women. These women are rejecting arranged marriages and instead are cohabiting with their partners. They are leaving private patriarchy at the expense of entering public patriarchy.

Notes

1   This figure is laid down by the International Labour Organisation (ILO), and is also used by the OECD (Organisation for Economic Co-operation and Development), and includes those aged 16 and over without a paid job, who said they were available to start work in the next two weeks.

2   These educational qualifications were used for analysis (first degree, 'A' levels, 'O' levels, CSE below grade 1 and no qualifications), as these were the qualifications that respondents reported in the East London study. Hence it was possible to make a direct comparison between the two data sets.

3   The three years 1984, 1990 and 1994 were taken for analysis. 1990 was taken as a mid-point and 1994 were the most recent statistics available at the time of writing.

4   There has been a dramatic increase for Indian women who are
        economically active from 1991 to 1992. This may be due to the changing
        of LFS data collection. Between 1984 and 1991, the survey was carried out
        annually, with results published relating to the March to May quarter.
        From 1992, the LFS questionnaire changed and has been carried out every
        quarter with a sample size of 60,000 households. There are methodological
        and quarterly differences between the annual and quarterly series which
        may affect comparability. Quarterly estimates for the population of Indian
        origin have been more variable than other ethnic groups, probably as a
        result of sampling variability. This change should not be taken as
        indicative of a trend. Furthermore, there has also been a change in the
        question on ethnic definition since 1991 (Sly 1994,1995).

5   There is a discrepancy between the figures in this table and those in table
        8.7. The figures in table 8.7 separate those who are employed and
        unemployed, whereas the figures in this table are for those who are
        economically active.

9 Conclusions

The research suggests that amongst South Asian women in British society there are two forms of patriarchy (private and public). Patriarchy can be defined as a form of social organisation in which men hold power and are able to control and dominate women through the social systems of organisation. These may be internal to the household (arranged marriages, dowries, domestic labour and domestic finance), or external to the household (the labour market). The pattern of gender relations for South Asian women indicates that ethnicity has an impact upon the different forms of patriarchy experienced by South Asian women. Moslem women experience an intense form of private patriarchy, followed by Sikh and Hindu women. Other 'independent' women experience a public form of patriarchy. There are significant changes occurring for the younger women in the sample, indicating a move from private to public patriarchy.

Private patriarchy is based upon the household as the main site of women's oppression, this takes place through arranged marriages, the giving of dowries, the distribution of domestic labour and domestic financial organisation. This form of patriarchy was experienced by 'traditional' women. 'Traditional' women had an arranged marriage and were given a dowry, they performed the majority of domestic labour tasks and had little or no control over domestic finance. They had low levels of education (those who had 'O' levels or no qualifications), and were in low positions in the labour market.

Public patriarchy is based upon the labour market (employment) as the main site of women's oppression. The household is no longer the main site of these women's oppression, but still exists as a patriarchal structure. This form of patriarchy was experienced by 'independent' women. 'Independent' women were highly educated (those who had a BA or MA) and in high positions in the labour market (professional, semi-professional). They had not had an arranged marriage and were not given a dowry, they shared domestic labour tasks and jointly controlled domestic finance.

Education and employment influenced the forms of patriarchy experienced by South Asian women. Education is linked to employment. Highly educated women were in high positions in the labour market. If women had lower levels of education, they were in low positions in the labour market.

Influences on forms of patriarchy experienced by South Asian women

Religion

Religion influenced whether South Asian women had an arranged marriage and were given a dowry. Moslem women were more likely to have an arranged marriage, followed by Sikh and Hindu women. Moslem women experienced an intense form of private patriarchy, followed by Sikh and Hindu women. Religion did not influence attitudes on arranged marriages, but it did influence practices.

Education

Level of education influenced the position of South Asian women within households and the forms of patriarchy they experienced. Once women become educated, this has a significant impact upon their lives. Education influenced whether women were 'traditional' or 'independent' and whether they had an arranged marriage.

Employment

Women's position in the labour market influenced their position within households. The link between education and employment is important. Education affects women's employment levels. The relationship between education and employment is reflected in the degree to which South Asian women are 'independent' and the extent to which they will have an arranged marriage. Education influenced forms of patriarchy experienced by women, which in turn influenced how women were defined.

Structures of patriarchy

The household

The household is the main site in which private patriarchy exists. It includes the family which is a central part of society's power structure where women are disadvantaged. The household includes;

Domestic labour Men benefit from women performing domestic labour for them, their resistance to change and their refusal to participate is a demonstration of their power over women. Domestic labour is a female activity. Men do not perform domestic labour to a significant extent. Level of education influenced respondents' views on domestic labour. Highly educated respondents (those who had a BA or

MA), emphasised a sharing of roles and said their partners participated in domestic labour. Respondents with lower levels of education (those who had 'O' levels or no qualifications), performed the majority of domestic labour tasks. Women's position in the labour market influenced their views on domestic labour. Respondents in high positions in the labour market (semi-professional, non-manual, students), were more likely to share domestic labour tasks and indicated similar responses to those who were highly educated. Respondents in low positions in the labour market, (housewives, skilled manual, semi-skilled), carried out the majority of domestic labour tasks and indicated similar responses to those with low levels of education, (those who had 'O' levels or no qualifications).

Arranged marriages Marriage is an area where 'traditional' South Asian women are disadvantaged. 'Traditional' women felt arranged marriages were part of their cultural identity and wanted their own children to have arranged marriages. However, 'independent' women felt arranged marriages degraded and humiliated women and wanted to reject the tradition of arranged marriages. Level of education influenced respondents' views on arranged marriages. Highly educated women (those with a BA or MA), regarded arranged marriages as being negative for women. They did not have, or intend to have an arranged marriage. Women with lower levels of education, (those with 'O' levels or no qualifications), regarded arranged marriages as being positive for women and had an arranged marriage. Women's position in the labour market influenced their views on arranged marriages. Respondents in low positions in the labour market (skilled manual), indicated similar responses to those with low levels of education. Respondents in high positions in the labour market (semi-professional, professional), indicated similar responses to those who were highly educated. Religion did not influence respondents' views on arranged marriages, but did affect whether South Asian women would have an arranged marriage.

Dowries Arranged marriages include a financial contract (dowry) in which money and/or material possessions are exchanged. Dowries are related to arranged marriages and are used to sell women as property for men's advantage. 'Traditional' women felt dowries were part of their South Asian identity and would give their own daughters a dowry and expected to receive one for their sons. However, 'independent' women said dowries were used to sell women as property for marriage and did not want to continue the tradition of giving or receiving dowries. Level of education influenced respondents' views on dowries. Highly educated women (those who had a BA or MA), said dowries degraded and humiliated women. These women had not had an arranged marriage and were not given a dowry. Respondents with lower levels of education (those who had 'O' levels or no qualifications), said dowries were part of the tradition, custom and identity of South Asian people. These women had an arranged marriage and were given a dowry. Women's position in the labour market influenced their views on dowries. Respondents in low positions in the labour market (skilled manual), indicated similar responses to those with low levels of education.

150

Respondents in high positions in the labour market (semi-professional, professional), indicated similar responses to those who were highly educated. Religion did not influence respondents' views on dowries. However, religion did affect whether South Asian women were given a dowry.

Domestic finance The distribution of domestic finance indicates who has power over whom and who controls whom. Highly educated respondents, (those who had a BA or MA), had their own bank accounts and both partners knew each other's earnings. Respondents with lower levels of education, (those who had 'O' levels or no qualifications), did not have their own bank accounts and did not know how much their husbands earned. Women's position in the labour market influenced their views on domestic finance. Respondents in high positions in the labour market, (non-manual, semi-professional, students), had greater control over domestic finance and indicated similar responses to those who were highly educated. Respondents in low positions in the labour market (skilled manual), had little or no control over domestic finance and indicated similar responses to those with low levels of education. Religion did not influence respondents' views on domestic finance.

The state

The state is an instrument of patriarchal domination, it is sexist, racist and capitalist. It is part of an unequal society and is important in the transformation of private to public patriarchy. It provides 'independent' South Asian women with access to education which enables them to enter the labour market.

The labour market

Women's position in the labour market, their lower pay and marginalisation leads to their dependence upon men, pushing women to serve men's domestic and economic needs. However, the labour market enables 'independent' women to leave households (private patriarchy), but at the expense of entering public patriarchy.

Culture

The dominant norms and values of South Asian culture disadvantage South Asian women. Women are expected to be homemakers, participate in an arranged marriage and engage in dowry practice.

South Asian women and patriarchy

In comparison to Walby (1990), firstly, I would argue there are four main structures of patriarchy (household, state, labour market and culture), instead of Walby's six (household, state, employment, culture, sexuality and violence). Violence and sexuality are important to women's position within households, but they can be included in the household rather than being separate structures. Violence and sexuality are directly linked to arranged marriages. As 'traditional' South Asian women have arranged marriages and are given dowries, this indicates the situation is different for South Asian and white women. The household is an important structure for South Asian women and their position within it affects what they will do with their lives, (whether they become educated, employed or have an arranged marriage). Secondly, the forms of patriarchy experienced by South Asian women are extreme forms of public and private patriarchy. Finally my theory of patriarchy applies specifically to one ethnic group (South Asian women).

In the present research, patriarchy was either private or public and women were either 'traditional' or 'independent'. The form of patriarchy is directly mapped onto the type of woman, because different women experience different forms of patriarchy. The type of woman and the form of patriarchy they experience is dependent upon their level of education and in turn, their position in the labour market. Patriarchy exists along a continuum and is not necessarily based upon a rigid dichotomy. The form of patriarchy women experience depends upon which is the dominant structure in their lives at one particular time. It could be the household (private patriarchy) or the state (public patriarchy). Women are included within the public sphere, but at the same time, are disadvantaged within it. The household is related to the state, as it is in the household where South Asian women decide if they become educated, whether they have an arranged marriage and if they become employed. Their educational level in turn affects their position within households. In the household South Asian women learn the cultural standards of acceptable behaviour. In public spheres, these ideas of culture are reinforced through religion, education and the media. The household is related to other structures of patriarchy and affects whether South Asian women will participate in paid employment and/or have an arranged marriage. There are different patterns of patriarchy for the different South Asian groups. Moslem women experience extreme forms of private patriarchy, followed by Sikh and Hindu. Other 'independent' women experience public patriarchy. A change is beginning to take place, with South Asian women moving out of the private sphere into the public arena. In private patriarchy, the expropriation of women's labour takes place primarily by individual patriarchs within the household. Whilst in public patriarchy it is collective. In private patriarchy, the principle strategy is exclusionary and in public it is segregationist. In private patriarchy, household production is the dominant structure, in the public form it is replaced by the state and the labour market (Walby 1990).

The significance of the state is different for South Asian women and men than for white women and men. White men have access to the state in which they are able to control white women. South Asian men do not have access to the state to control South Asian women. Racism and minority status mean South Asian men do not benefit from patriarchal social structures in the same way as white men do. South Asian women have been dominated patriarchally in different ways by men of different colours. The state is both patriarchal and racist. The state divides and separates different ethnic groups (South Asian and white). Despite the fact that the state supports systems of domination, nevertheless by its function of developing education, it has provided an avenue for women's emancipation.

Culture is another structure of patriarchy which includes the different norms and values of expected behaviour for South Asian women, such as participating in the practices of arranged marriages and dowries. 'Independent' women who become educated are not having arranged marriages. Even though some women are moving away from a private form of patriarchy, they are included in the public world but are subordinated within it (social closure, segregation). The reason for change is 'independent' South Asian women's access to education. Level of education affects women's access to employment and influences their position in the labour market. The link between education and employment is important, as education is the primary determinant of women's position in the labour market. The change from private to a more public form of patriarchy is evident. 'Traditional' South Asian women want to retain the custom of arranged marriages and the partaking of dowries, they want to hold on to these traditions as part of their South Asian identity. 'Independent' South Asian women become highly educated and enter the labour market, they no longer want to have arranged marriages, instead they want to co-habit with their partners. Education is an avenue which enables 'independent' women to enter the labour market in which they are now experiencing a more public form of patriarchy.

Appendix 1

Background information of subjects

Table A1.1

Hindu women

Definition of subject	Age	Occupation	Marital status	Highest qualification
1	26	Skilled manual	Married	BTEC
2	26	Skilled manual	Married	BTEC
3	26	Skilled manual	Married	'O' levels
4	29	Semi-skilled	Married	'O' levels
5	27	Semi-skilled	Married	'A' levels
6	25	Semi-skilled	Married	'O' levels
7	25	Non-manual	Married	'O' levels
8	28	Skilled manual	Married	'O' levels
9	25	Non-manual	Single	BA
10	26	Non-manual	Single	'O' levels
11	26	Student	Single	MA
12	27	Semi-professional	Single	BA
13	27	Semi-professional	Single	BA
14	27	Semi-professional	Single	MA
15	28	Student	Single	MA
16	27	Professional	Single	MA
17	26	Semi-professional	Single	MA
18	27	Semi-professional	Single	MA
19	25	Student	Single	BA
20	25	Student	Single	MA

Table A1.2
Sikh women

Definition of subject	Age	Occupation	Marital status	Highest qualification
21	25	Skilled manual	Married	'O' levels
22	25	Skilled manual	Married	'O' levels
23	26	Skilled manual	Married	'O' levels
24	27	Semi-skilled	Married	BTEC
25	28	Self-employed	Married	'O' levels
26	26	Semi-skilled	Married	'O' levels
27	30	Semi-skilled	Married	'O' levels
28	30	Skilled manual	Married	'O' levels
29	29	Semi-skilled	Married	'O' levels
30	25	Semi-skilled	Single	'O' levels
31	26	Semi-skilled	Single	BTEC
32	26	Student	Single	BA
33	25	Student	Single	BA
34	28	Non-manual	Single	BA
35	26	Non-manual	Single	BA
36	25	Non-manual	Single	BA
37	30	Semi-professional	Single	MA
38	26	Non-manual	Single	BA
39	30	Semi-professional	Single	MA
40	26	Non-manual	Single	BA

Table A1.3
Moslem women

Definition of subject	Age	Occupation	Marital status	Highest qualification
41	29	Skilled manual	Married	CSE's
42	30	Housewife	Married	None
43	27	Skilled manual	Married	None
44	29	Housewife	Married	None
45	28	Skilled manual	Married	None
46	26	Skilled manual	Married	CSE's
47	30	Housewife	Married	None
48	30	Housewife	Married	None
49	27	Skilled manual	Married	None
50	26	Skilled manual	Married	'O' levels
51	26	Non-manual	Married	BTEC
52	27	Non-manual	Married	'A' levels
53	26	Non-manual	Married	BTEC
54	26	Student	Single	BA
55	25	Student	Single	'A' levels
56	25	Student	Single	'A' levels
57	28	Student	Single	BA
58	28	Semi-professional	Single	BA
59	27	Non-manual	Single	BA
60	26	Student	Single	BA

Appendix 2

The interview schedule

1. General background

a. What is your name?
b. How old are you?
c. Who are the people that live in your household?
c.i. Ages and sexes of children?
d. Are you married?
e. If not, are you single/divorced/separated/widowed/living with your partner?

2. Employment

a. Do you have a job?
b. What is your occupation?
        If work;
c. How many hours a week do you work?
c.i. Do you enjoy your work? Explain.
c.ii. What are your reasons for working? Explain.
        If married or living with partner;
d. What is your husband's/partner's occupation?
d.i. Does your husband/partner think it's a good idea for you to work? Explain.
d.ii. Would your husband/partner mind if you changed your job? Explain.
d.iii. Have you ever done any work at home that you were paid for (homeworking)? Explain.
e. Does your work affect your family life (housework/looking after the children, you husband/partner)? Explain.
f. Do you think it's a good idea for South Asian women to go out to work? Why? Explain.

3. Education

a. What are your academic qualifications (number of and grades).

> CSE
> GCSE/'O' Levels
> **'A' Levels**
> **'S' Levels**
> HND/Diploma
> Access Course
> Bachelors Degree
> Masters Degree
> MPHIL
> PhD
> Other.

b. Is this the standard of education you wanted to achieve? Why? Explain.

c. Does a woman's standard of education affect her position regarding marriage in South Asian society (who she marries, when she marries)? How? Explain.

d. How are highly educated women (Bachelors and Masters level and beyond) regarded by men and women in South Asian society? Explain.

e. Is education for men and women viewed differently in South Asian society? Explain.

f. Who/What decides how far women are educated in South Asian society? Explain.

g. Do you think it is important for South Asian women to be educated up to and beyond degree level? Why? Explain.

4. The division of labour

a. Who does the following tasks?

i. If married or living with partner (husband or partner/wife/both same/husband or partner more/wife more/neither)?

ii. If not married who does it?

iii. How often (once a day/once a week/twice a week/once a month/other/neither)?

iv. Who performed the activity on the last occasion?

> Shopping (food/groceries)
> Cooking (breakfast/lunch/dinner)
> Cleaning table/setting table
> Washing dishes/drying dishes
> Cleaning (vacuuming/dusting)
> (oven/fridge)
> (bathroom/toilet)
> Washing (changing sheets/folding/ironing)

Childcare if under 5 (bathes/changes nappies/feeds)
Childcare all ages (bathes/takes to school/plays with)
Homecare (plugs/gardening/taking out rubbish).

b. Approximately how many hours a day do you spend on housework?
c. How many hours a day does your husband/partner spend on housework?
d. Who do you think should do the housework? Why? Explain.
e. Why do you think it's mostly women in South Asian society who do the housework? Explain.
f. Do you think a woman's place is in the home? Why? Explain.
g. Does your culture influence whether women should stay at home and be housewives? How and why? Explain.

5. Financial organisation

If work;
a. Who decides what the money you earn is spent on?
a.i. Are you able to spend the money you earn on whatever you want?
a.ii. What do you spend the money on?
If work and married;
b. What does your husband spend his money on?
b.i. Do you tell your husband/partner what you spend your money on?
b.ii. Does your husband/partner know how much you earn?
b.iii. Do you know how much your husband/partner earns?
b.iv. Do you have a bank account?
If yes; If no, go to d.
c. Is it your own or is it a joint account?
c.i. Can you access money any time you want from the account?
d. Where do you get the money from if you want to buy something for yourself (clothes/shoes/make-up)?
e. If you wanted to buy a washing machine, would you ask your husband/partner to buy it, or would you save up for it yourself? Why?

Unstructured interview questions

6. Marriage

Description of marriage; when, type, contact with husband?
Definition and views of arranged marriages; importance, common, who decides?
Parental/cultural influence of arranged marriages?
Views/cultural views on position of single women; free choice of partner?

7. Dowries

Definition/views of dowries; importance, common, why given?
Parental/cultural view of giving dowries; how decide?
Relationship of position of women and dowry?
Given dowry; description, monetary value?
Own children and dowry; sons (expect to receive), daughters (except to give), why?

8. Religion

How religious; temples, pray, read?
Influence of religion on life; how, why?
Views on religion; importance, why?
Culture/religion; relationship, expectations of, why?
Family/religion; relationship, expectations of, why?

9. Views on traditional/independent women

Feelings regarding independent women/cultural view?
Feelings regarding traditional women/cultural view?
What is the difference; why?
Best position for South Asian women; why?

Appendix 3

Chi square tables

The following tables provide tables for chi square values for education and employment. Chi square tests of significance were used to test for associations. If the chi square value was less than .05 the correlation was shown to be highly significant. The figures in each row add up to 100%. The figures in each column indicate the total number of respondents who had no qualifications, CSE's etc for education. For employment the figures indicate the numbers of respondents who were from self-employed, skilled manual occupations etc. See keys for explanation.

Table A3.1
The relationship between education and women's responses on the importance of an arranged marriage

Education (per cent)

Important	1	2	3	4	5	6	7	Row Total
Culture	20	7	27	13	7	20	6	25
Respect	10	-	60	10	20	-	-	17
Work	25	-	25	25	25	-	-	6
Family bond	67	-	33	-	-	-	-	5
Religion	-	-	100	-	-	-	-	2
Not important								
Pressure	-	5	11	-	5	53	26	32
No choice	-	-	-	-	-	33	67	5
Unhappiness	-	-	33	-	33	33	-	5
Degrade women	-	-	-	-	-	50	50	3
Column total	11	3	27	7	10	27	15	100

Education, Chi square value (48 degrees of freedom) = 0.01224

1 = None
2 = CSE's
3 = 'O' levels
4 = 'A' levels
5 = BEC/HND
6 = BA/BSc
7 = MA/MSc

Table A3.2
The relationship between education and whether respondents wanted their own children to have an arranged marriage

Education (per cent)

Arranged marriage	1	2	3	4	5	6	7	Row Total
Continue traditions	15	7	62	16	-	-	-	40
Demonstrate love	65	-	25	-	10	-	-	5
Obedience	45	30	-	-	25	-	-	5
Non-arranged marriage								
Choice	-	-	-	-	-	50	50	17
Degrading	-	-	-	-	33	33	33	23
Disagree	-	-	-	-	-	50	50	7
Don't know	-	-	-	-	100	-	-	3
Column total	11	3	27	7	10	27	15	100

Education, Chi square value (36 degrees of freedom) = 0.00004

1 = None
2 = CSE's
3 = 'O' levels
4 = 'A' levels
5 = BEC/HND
6 = BA/BSc
7 = MA/MSc

Table A3.3
The relationship between education and respondents' views on women and the giving of dowries

Education (per cent)

Relationship	1	2	3	4	5	6	7	Row Total
Burden/disrespect	-	-	-	3	8	21	68	22
Sold to men	-	-	-	10	24	56	10	42
Have to be looked after	10	70	20	-	-	-	-	17
Cultural/historical	26	-	74	-	-	-	-	8
Parents demonstrate love/duty	33	-	67	-	-	-	-	12
Column total	11	3	27	7	10	27	15	100

Chi square value (24 degrees of freedom) = 0.00000

1 = None
2 = CSE's
3 = 'O' levels
4 = 'A' levels
5 = BEC/HND
6 = BA/BSc
7 = MA/MSc

Table A3.4
The relationship between education and respondents' views on whether they would give their own children dowries

Own children	Education (per cent)							Row Total
	1	2	3	4	5	6	7	
Would give								
Continue traditions	21	11	35	23	10	-	-	40
Demonstrate love	60	-	40	-	-	-	-	5
Want daughters to be obedient	60	-	40	-	-	-	-	5
Would not give								
Own choice	-	-	-	-	13	87	-	17
Inferior to men	-	-	-	-	-	53	47	23
Disagree	-	-	-	-	35	-	65	7
Don't know								
Unsure	-	-	-	-	100	-	-	3
Column total	11	3	27	7	10	27	15	100

Chi square value (36 degrees of freedom) = 0.00004

1 = None
2 = CSE's
3 = 'O' levels
4 = 'A' levels
5 = BEC/HND
6 = BA/BSc
7 = MA/MSc

Table A3.5
The relationship between education and who respondents felt should do the housework

	Education (per cent)							
Women	1	2	3	4	5	6	7	Row Total
Female role	33	-	67	-	-	-	-	15
Female more capable	33	17	17	33	-	-	-	10
If female at home	25	-	50	25	-	-	-	7
Both								
Equal sharing	2	2	10	18	10	36	22	68
Column total	11	3	27	7	10	27	15	100

Chi square value (18 degrees of freedom) = 0.00033

1 = None
2 = CSE's
3 = 'O' levels
4 = 'A' levels
5 = BEC/HND
6 = BA/BSc
7 = MA/MSc

Table A3.6

The relationship between education and whether respondents felt a woman's place was in the home

	Education (per cent)							
	1	2	3	4	5	6	7	Row Total
In the home								
Yes								
To look after home/children	37	5	42	16	-	-	-	32
Cultural expectation	-	-	50	-	-	50	-	7
No								
Choice/independence	-	4	14	-	24	29	29	35
Traps/imprisons women	-	-	-	-	20	40	40	8
Career/job satisfaction	-	-	27	9	-	55	9	18
Column total	11	3	27	7	10	27	15	100

Chi square value (24 degrees of freedom) = 0.00095

1 = None
2 = CSE's
3 = 'O' levels
4 = 'A' levels
5 = BEC/HND
6 = BA/BSc
7 = MA/MSc

Table A3.7
The relationship between education and type of account

Account	1	2	3	4	5	6	7	Row Total
Own	-	-	14	6	11	44	25	60
Joint	-	-	33	67	-	-	-	5
None	33	10	48	-	10	-	-	35
Column total	11	3	27	7	10	27	15	100

Education (per cent)

Chi square value (12 degrees of freedom) = 0.00000

1 = None
2 = CSE's
3 = 'O' levels
4 = 'A' levels
5 = BEC/HND
6 = BA/BSc
7 = MA/MSc

The relationship between education and where respondents obtain money for personal items

Where from	Education (per cent)							Row Total
	1	2	3	4	5	6	7	
Self/own earnings	-	5	13	8	10	41	23	65
Husband	35	-	55	5	5	-	-	33
Mother-in-law	-	-	-	-	100	-	-	2
Column total	11	3	27	7	10	27	15	100

Chi square value (12 degrees of freedom) =0.00001

1 = None
2 = CSE's
3 = 'O' levels
4 = 'A' levels
5 = BEC/HND
6 = BA/BSc
7 = MA/MSc

The relationship between occupation and respondents' views on single, independent women

	Occupation (per cent)								
Single women	1	2	3	4	5	6	7	8	Row Total
Strong/independent	-	-	-	-	-	45	25	30	27
Risk losing family	-	-	-	-	80	-	-	20	20
Sexually promiscuous	20	20	30	30	-	-	-	-	25
Ruin family name	6	-	60	10	24	-	-	-	28
Column total	7	2	23	15	20	13	2	18	100

Chi square value (14 degrees of freedom) = 0.02421

1 = Unemployed housewife
2 = Self-employed
3 = Skilled manual
4 = Semi-skilled
5 = Non-manual
6 = Semi-professional
7 = Professional
8 = Student

Table A3.10

The relationship between occupation and respondents' opinions on the cultural view of single, independent women

Single women cultural view	Occupation (per cent)								Row Total
	1	2	3	4	5	6	7	8	
Broken rules	10	-	7	-	10	-	20	53	25
Ruined 'izzat'	12	12	43	14	19	-	-	-	43
Should be punished	25	-	61	7	7	-	-	-	16
Sexually loose	-	-	-	-	-	80	10	10	16
Column total	7	2	23	15	20	13	2	18	100

Chi square value (14 degrees of freedom) = 0.03272

1 = Unemployed housewife
2 = Self-employed
3 = Skilled manual
4 = Semi-skilled
5 = Non-manual
6 = Semi-professional
7 = Professional
8 = Student

Table A3.11
The relationship between occupation and respondents' views on the relationship of women and the giving of dowries

Relationship	Occupation (per cent)								Row Total
	1	2	3	4	5	6	7	8	
Burden/disrespected	-	-	-	-	12	25	30	33	22
Sold to men	-	-	-	-	35	20	30	15	42
Have to be looked after	9	76	15	-	-	-	-	-	17
Cultural/historical	-	64	14	14	8	-	-	-	8
Parents demonstrate love/duty	10	30	12	12	36	-	-	-	12
Column total	7	2	23	15	20	13	2	18	100

Chi square value (28 degrees of freedom) = 0.03977

1 = Unemployed housewife
2 = Self-employed
3 = Skilled manual
4 = Semi-skilled
5 = Non-manual
6 = Semi-professional
7 = Professional
8 = Student

Table A3.12
The relationship between occupation and whether respondents would give their own children dowries

Own children	Occupation (per cent)								Row Total
	1	2	3	4	5	6	7	8	
Would give									
Continue traditions	4	54	12	4	26	-	-	-	40
Demonstrate love	-	-	-	-	100	-	-	-	5
Want daughters to be obedient	-	-	-	-	100	-	-	-	5
Would not give									
Own choice	-	-	-	-	-	40	60	-	17
Inferior to men	-	-	-	-	-	20	60	20	7
Disagree	-	-	-	-	30	-	50	20	7
Don't know									
Unsure	-	-	-	-	-	-	-	100	3
Column total	7	2	23	15	20	13	2	18	100

Chi square value (42 degrees of freedom) = 0.02326

1 = Unemployed housewife
2 = Self-employed
3 = Skilled manual
4 = Semi-skilled
5 = Non-manual
6 = Semi-professional
7 = Professional
8 = Student

The relationship between occupation and who respondents felt should do the housework

	Occupation (per cent)								
	1	2	3	4	5	6	7	8	Row
Women									Total
Female role	-	-	56	33	11	-	-	-	15
Female more capable	-	17	49	17	17	-	-	-	10
If female at home	50	25	-	25	-	-	-	-	7
Both									
Equal sharing	5	-	12	12	22	20	2	27	68
Column total	7	2	23	15	20	13	2	18	100

Chi square value (21 degrees of freedom) = 0.00408

1 = Unemployed housewife
2 = Self-employed
3 = Skilled manual
4 = Semi-skilled
5 = Non-manual
6 = Semi-professional
7 = Professional
8 = Student

Table A3.14
The relationship between occupation and whether respondents felt a woman's place was in the home

In the home	Occupation (per cent)								Row Total
	1	2	3	4	5	6	7	8	
Yes									
To look after home/children	11	5	47	21	16	-	-	-	32
Cultural expectation	-	-	-	25	50	-	-	25	7
No									
Choice/independence	5	-	14	10	14	24	-	33	35
Traps/prisons women	-	-	20	-	20	20	-	40	8
Job satisfaction	9	-	9	18	27	18	10	9	18
Column total	7	2	23	15	20	13	2	18	100

Chi square value (28 degrees of freedom) = 0.02398

1 = Unemployed housewife
2 = Self-employed
3 = Skilled manual
4 = Semi-skilled
5 = Non-manual
6 = Semi-professional
7 = Professional
8 = Student

Table A3.15
The relationship between occupation and where respondents obtain funds to purchase a washing machine

Where from	Occupation (per cent)								Row Total
	1	2	3	4	5	6	7	8	
Self/own earnings	-	-	-	-	100	-	-	-	3
Husband	14	4	44	19	19	-	-	-	45
Together with husband/partner	-	-	8	12	23	31	4	23	44
No partner (n/a)	-	-	-	100	-	-	-	-	8
Column total	7	2	23	15	20	13	2	18	100

Chi square value (21 degrees of freedom) = 0.00020

1 = Unemployed housewife
2 = Self-employed
3 = Skilled manual
4 = Semi-skilled
5 = Non-manual
6 = Semi-professional
7 = Professional
8 = Student

Table A3.16
The relationship between occupation and who decides to spend money earned by female

Who decides	Occupation (per cent)								Row Total
	1	2	3	4	5	6	7	8	
Self	-	-	6	17	6	17	-	56	30
Self and husband/ partner	-	-	18	9	41	23	5	5	37
Husband/partner	-	7	50	29	14	-	-	-	23
Mother-in-law	-	-	100	-	-	-	-	-	2
No partner	80	-	20	-	-	-	-	-	8
Column total	7	2	23	15	20	13	2	18	100

Chi square value (28 degrees of freedom) = 0.00000

1 = Unemployed housewife
2 = Self-employed
3 = Skilled manual
4 = Semi-skilled
5 = Non-manual
6 = Semi-professional
7 = Professional
8 = Student

Bibliography

Abel, E. and Newson, M. (eds.) (1990), *Circles of Care: work and identity in women's lives,* New York State University Press: New York.

Abramson, H. (1979), 'Migrants and Cultural Diversity: on ethnicity and religions in society', *Social Compass,* Vol. 26, No.1, pp.5-29.

Acker, J. (1983), 'Objectivity and truth: problems in doing feminist research', *Women's Studies International Forum,* Vol. 6, pp.423-435.

Acker, J. (1992), 'The Future of Women and Work: ending the twentieth century', *Sociological Perspectives,* Vol. 35, No. 1, pp.53-68.

Adamson, O. et al (1976), 'Women's Oppression Under Capitalism', *Revolutionary Communist,* No. 5.

Afshar, H. (1989), 'Gender Roles and the Moral Economy of Kin among Pakistani Women in Yorkshire', *New Community,* Vol. 15, No. 2.

Agarwal, B. (1988), 'Neither Sustenance nor Sustainability: agricultural strategies, ecological degradation and Indian women in poverty', in Agarwal, B. (ed.), *Structures of Patriarchy: state, community and household in modernising Asia,* Indrapratstha Press: New Delhi.

Alcoff, L. (1988), 'Cultural Feminism Versus Poststructuralism: the identity crisis in feminist theory', *Signs,* Vol. 13, pp.405-436.

Alexander, S. (1976), 'Women's Work in Nineteenth Century England: a study of the years 1820-1850', in Oakley, A. and Mitchell, J. (eds.), *The Rights and Wrongs of Women,* Penguin: Harmondsworth.

Ali, Y. (1992), 'Muslim Women and the Politics of Ethnicity and Culture', in Sahgal, G. and Yuval-Davis, N. (eds.), *Refusing Holy Orders: women and fundamentalism in Britain*, Virago: London.

Allan, G. (1985), *Family Life: domestic roles and social obligation,* Basil Blackwell: Oxford.

Allan, G. and Crow, G. (eds.) (1989), *Home and Family: creating the domestic sphere,* Macmillan: London.

Amos, V. and Parmar, P. (1981), 'Resistance and Responses: the experiences of black girls in Britain', in McRobbie, A. and McCabe, T. (eds.), *Feminism for Girls: an adventure story,* Routledge Kegan Paul: London.

Amos, V. and Parmar, P. (1984), 'Challenging Imperial Feminism', *Feminist Review,* Vol. 17, pp.3-20.

Anthias, F. and Yuval-Davis, N. (1989), 'Introduction', in Anthias, F. and Yuval-Davis, N. (eds.), *Woman-Nation-State,* Macmillan: London.

Anthias, F. and Yuval-Davis, N. (1992), *Racialised Boundaries: race, nation, gender, colour and class and the anti-racist struggle,* Routledge: London.

Anwar, M. (1979), *The Myth of Return,* Heinemann: London.

Anwar, M. (1981), *Between Two Cultures,* Commission For Racial Equality: London.

Anwar, M. (1985), *Pakistanis in Britain: a sociological study,* New Century Publishers: London.

Bacchi, C. (1990), *Same Difference: feminism and sexual difference,* Allen and Unwin: London.

Ball, S. (1981), *Beachside Comprehensive: a case study of a secondary school,* Cambridge University Press: Cambridge.

Ballard, C. (1978), 'Arranged Marriages in the Social Context', *New Community,* Vol. 6, No. 3, pp.181-195.

Ballard, R. (1990), 'Migration and Kinship', in Clarke, C. (ed.), *South Asians Overseas,* Cambridge University Press: Cambridge.

Ballard, R. (1992), 'New Clothes for the Emperor: the conceptual nakedness of the race relations industry in Britain', *New Community,* Vol. 8, No. 3, pp.481-491.

Ballard, R. (1994a), 'Introduction: The emergence of Des Pardesh', in Ballard, R. (ed.), *Des Pardesh: the South Asian presence in Britain,* Hurst and Company: London.

Ballard, R. (1994b), 'Difference and Disjunction among the Sikhs', in Ballard, R. (ed.), *Des Pardesh: the South Asian presence in Britain,* Hurst and Company: London.

Ballard, R. and Ballard, C. (1977), 'The Development of South Asian Settlements in Britain', in Watson, J. (ed.), *Between Two Cultures,* Basil Blackwell: Oxford.

Ballard, R. and Vellins, S. (1985), 'South Asian Entrants to British Universities: a comparative note', *New Community,* Vol. 12, No. 2, pp.260-265.

Banton, M. (1983a), *Racial and Ethnic Competition,* Cambridge University Press: Cambridge.

Banton, M. (1983b), 'The influence of Colonial status upon Black-White Relations in England', *Sociology,* Vol. 17, No. 4, pp.547-559.

Bardhan, K. (1980), 'Women's Work in Relation to Family Strategies in South and South East Asia', *Samya Shakti,* Vol. 4, No. 5, pp.83-120.

Barot, R. (1987), 'Caste and Sect in the Swaminarayan Movement', in Burghart, R. (ed.), *Hinduism in Great Britain,* Tavistock: London.

Barrett, M. (1980), *Women's Oppression Today: problems in Marxist Feminist analysis,* Verso: London.

Barrett, M. and Mackintosh, M. (1985), 'Ethnocentrism and Socialist Feminist Theory', *Feminist Review,* Vol. 20, pp.23-48.

Barton, S. (1986), *The Bengali Muslims of Bradford,* University of Leeds: Department of Theology and Religious Studies.

Becker, H. (1963), *Outsiders: studies in the sociology of deviance,* Free Press: New York.

Beechey, V. (1977), 'Some Notes on Female Wage Labour in Capitalist Production', *Capital and Class,* Vol. 3, pp.45-66.

Beechey, V. (1978), 'Women and Production: a critical analysis of some sociological theories of women's work', in Kuhn, A. and Wolpe, A. (eds.), *Feminism and Materialism: women and modes of production,* Routledge Kegan Paul: London.

Beechey, V. (1986), 'Women's Employment in Contemporary Britain', in Beechey, V. and Whitelegg, E. (eds.), *Women in Britain today,* Open University Press: Milton Keynes.

Bender, D. (1967), 'A Refinement of the Concept of the Household: family, co-residence and domestic functions', *American Anthropologist,* Vol. 70, pp.309-320.

Bennett, L. (1983), *Dangerous Wives and Scared Sisters: social and symbolic role of high class women in Nepal,* Colombia University Press: New York.

Bergmann, B. (1980a), 'Occupational Segregation, Wages and Profits when Employers Discriminate by Race or Sex', in Amsden, A. (ed.), *The Economics of Women and Work,* Penguin: Harmondsworth.

Bergmann, B. (1980b), 'Curing High Unemployment Rates among Blacks and Women', in Amsden, A. (ed.), *The Economics of Women and Work,* Penguin: Harmondsworth.

Berk, A. (1980), *Women and Household Labour,* Sage: Beverley Hills.

Berk, S. (1985), *The Gender Factory: the apportionment of work in American households,* Penguin: New York.

Berk, S. and Shih, S. (eds.) (1980), *Women and Household Labour,* Sage: Newbury Park.

Bernard, J. (1982), *The Future of Marriage,* Yale University Press: New Haven.

Bernardes, J. (1986), 'In Search of "The Family", analysis of the 1981 UK Census: a research note', *Sociological Review,* Vol. 34, No. 4, pp.828-836.

Bhachu, P. (1985), *Twice Migrants: East African Sikh settlers in Britain,* Tavistock: London.

Bhachu, P. (1988), 'Apni Marzi Kardhi, Home and Work: Sikh women in Britain', in Westwood, S. and Bhachu, P. (eds.), *Enterprising Women: ethnicity, economy and gender relations,* Routledge: London.

Bhachu, P. (1991), 'Culture, Ethnicity and Class Among Punjabi Sikh Women in the 1990's', *New Community,* Vol. 17, No. 3, pp.401-412.

Bharanti, A. (1972), *The Asians in East Africa: Jayhind and Uhuru,* Nelson Hall: Chicago.

Bhavnani, K. and Coulson, M. (1986), 'Transforming Socialist Feminism: the challenge of racism', *Feminist Review,* Vol. 23.

Bhavnani, R. (1994), *Black Women in the Labour Market,* Equal Opportunities Commission: Manchester.

Bidney, D. (1953), *Theoretical Anthropology*, Colombia University Press: New York.

Bigger, H. (1987), *Hindu Nature: the historical traditional of the British reality*, unpublished MA Thesis: University of Lancaster.

Blumberg, R. (ed.) (1991), *Gender, Family and Economy: the triple overlap*, Sage: Newbury Park.

Blumstein, R. and Schwartz, P. (1983), *American Couples*, Morrow: New York.

Bordewich, F. (1986), 'Dowry Murders', *Atlantic Magazine*, pp.21-27.

Bose, C. (1979), 'Technology and Changes in the Division of Labour in the American Home', *Women's Studies International Quarterly*, Vol. 2, pp.295-304.

Bott, E. (1975), *Family and Social Network*, Tavistock: London.

Brah, A. (1978), 'South Asian Teenagers in Southall: their perceptions of marriage, family and ethnic identity', *New Community*, Vol. 6, No. 3, pp.197-215.

Brah, A. (1992), 'Difference, diversity, differentiation', in Donald, J. and Rattansi, A. (eds.), *'Race', Culture and Difference*, Sage: London.

Brah, A. (1993), 'Race and Culture in the Gendering of Labour Markets: South Asian young Muslim women and the labour market', *New Community*, Vol. 19, No. 3, pp.441-458.

Brah, A. and Minhas, R. (1985), 'Structural Racism or Cultural Conflict: Asian girls in British schools', in Weiner, G. (ed.), *Just a Bunch of Girls*, Open University Press: Milton Keynes.

Brah, A. and Shaw, S. (1992), *Working Choices: South Asian young Muslim women and the labour market*, Department Of Employment Research Paper No. 91.

Braidotti, R. (1992), 'The exile, the nomad and the migrant: reflections on international feminism', *Women's Studies International Forum*, Vol. 15, No. 1, pp.7-10.

Brannen, J. (1988), 'The study of sensitive subjects', *Sociological Review*, Vol. 36, pp.552-563.

Brannen, J. and Wilson, G. (eds.) (1987), *Give and Take in Families: studies in resource distribution*, Allen and Unwin: London.

Braverman, H. (1974), *Labour and Monopoly Capital: the degradation of work in the twentieth century*, Monthly Review Press: New York.

Brennan, J. and McGeevor, P. (1990), *Ethnic Minorities and the Graduate Labour Market*, Commission For Racial Equality: London.

Brittan, E. (1976), 'Multicultural Education: teacher opinions on aspects of school life, Part 2', *Educational Research*, Vol. 18, No. 3, pp.182-194.

Brittan, A. and Maynard, M. (1984), *Sexism, Racism and Oppression*, Basil Blackwell: Oxford.

Brooks, D. and Singh, K. (1978), 'Ethnic Commitment Versus Structural Reality: South Asian immigrant women in Britain', *New Community*, Vol. 7, No. 1, pp.19-29.

Brown, C. (1984), *Black and White Britain: the third PSI survey*, Heinemann: London.

Brown, L. and Selznick, P. (1955), *Sociology*, Harper and Row: New York.

Brown, P. et al (1981), 'A Daughter: a thing to be given away', in Chicago Women's Studies Group, *Women in Society: Interdisciplinary Essays*, Virago: London.

Brown, S. and Riddell, S. (eds.) (1992), *Class, Race and Gender In Schools: a new agenda for policy and practice in Scottish education*, Scottish Council For Research In Education: Glasgow.

Brownmiller, S. (1976), *Against Our Will: men, women and rape*, Penguin: Harmondsworth.

Bruegel, I. (1979), 'Women as a Reserve Army of Labour: a note on recent British experience', *Feminist Review*, Vol. 3, pp.12-23.

Bruegel, I. (1988), *Sex and Race in the Labour Market*, unpublished paper presented at the CSE Sex and Class Group.

Bruegel, I. (1994), 'Labour Market Prospects for Women from Ethnic Minority backgrounds', in Lindley, R. (ed.), *Labour Market Structures and Prospects for Women*, Institute For Employment Research, Equal Opportunities Commission.

Bryan, B. et al (1985), *The Heart of the Race: black women's lives in Britain*, Virago: London.

Bujra, J. (1978), 'Introduction: Female Sexuality and the Sexual Division of Labour', in Caplan, P. and Bujra, J. (eds.), *Women United: Women Divided*, Tavistock: London.

Bulbeck, C. (1988), *One World Women's Movement*, Pluto Press: London.

Burghart, R. (ed.) (1987), *Hinduism in Great Britain*, Tavistock: London.

Byford, D. and Mortimore, P. (1985), *School Examination Results in the ILEA 1984*, Rs 977/85, Inner London Education Authority: London.

Caldwell, J. et al (1984), 'The Determinants of Family Structure in Rural South India', *Journal of Marriage and the Family*, Vol. 46, pp.215-229.

Camaroff, J. (ed.) (1980), *The Meaning of Marriage Payments*, Academic Press: Chicago.

Cameron, A. and Kuhrt, A. (eds.) (1983), *Images of Women in Antiquity*, Croom Helm: London and Canberra.

Caplan, L. (1994), 'Bridegroom Price in North India: caste, class and dowry evil among Christians in Madras', in Uberoi, P. (ed.), *Family, Kinship and Marriage in India*, Oxford University Press: Delhi.

Caplan, P. (1985), *Gender and Class in India: women and their organisations in a south Indian city*, Tavistock: London.

Carby, H. (1982), 'White women listen! Black feminism and the boundaries of sisterhood', in Centre For Contemporary Cultural Studies, *The Empire Strikes Back*, Hutchinson: London.

Carmody, S. (1979), *Women and World Religions*, Abingdon: Nashville, Tennessee.

Carter, A. (1984), 'Household Histories', in Netting, R. et al (eds.), *Households: comparative and historical studies of the domestic group*, University of California Press: Beverley Hills, California.

Centre for Contemporary Cultural Studies (1982), *The Empire Strikes Back*, Hutchinson: London.

Chandan, A. (1986), *Indians in Britain,* Sterling Publishers: New Delhi.

Charles, N. and Kerr, M. (1988), *Women, Food and Families,* Manchester University Press: Manchester.

Chekki, D. (1968), 'Mate Selection, Age At Marriage and Propinquity Among The Lingayats of India', *Journal of Marriage and the Family,* Vol. 30, pp.707-711.

Chester, R. (1986), 'The Conventional Family is Alive and Living in Britain', in Weeks, J. (ed.), *Family Directory: information resources on the family,* British Library Information Guide 1.

Chhachhi, A. (1986), *Concepts in Feminist Theory - consensus and controversy,* paper presented at Inaugural Seminar: University of West Indies, St Augustine.

Chodorow, N. (1978), *The Reproduction of Mothering: psychoanalysis and the sociology of gender,* University of California Press: Berkeley, California.

Clifford, J. and Marcus, G. (eds.) (1986), *Writing Culture: the poetics and politics of ethnography,* University of California Press: Berkeley, California.

Clough, E. and Drew, D. (1985), *Futures in Black and White: two studies of the experiences of young people in Sheffield and Bradford,* Park Publishers: Sheffield.

Cockburn, C. (1983), *Brothers: male dominance and technological change,* Pluto Press: London.

Cockburn, C. (1985), *Machinery Of Dominance: women, men and technical know-how,* Pluto: London.

Cohen, L. and Manion, L. (1983), *Multiracial Classrooms,* Croom Helm: London.

Cole, J. (ed.) (1986), *All American Women: lives that divide, ties that bind,* Macmillan: New York.

Coleman, J. (1968), 'The Concept of Equal Opportunity', *Harvard Educational Review,* Vol. 38, No. 1, pp.7-22.

Collard, A. (1988), *Rape of the Wild: man's violence against animals and the earth,* Women's Press: London.

Collins, P. (1990), *Black Feminist Thought: knowledge, consciousness and the politics of empowerment,* Harper Collins: London.

Coltrane, S. (1989), 'Household labour and the routine production of gender', *Social Problems,* Vol. 36, pp.473-490.

Connolly, C. (1991), 'Washing our Linen: one year of women against fundamentalism', *Feminist Review,* Vol. 37, pp.68-77.

Cook, J. and Fonow, M. (1990), 'Knowledge and Women's Interests: issues of epistemology and methodology in feminist sociological research', in Nielsen, J. (ed.), *Feminist research Methods,* West View: Boulder.

Coon, C. (1954), *The Study of Man,* Alfred Knopf: New York.

Cotterill, P. (1992), 'Interviewing Women: issues of friendship, vulnerability and power', *Women's Studies International Forum,* Vol. 15, No. 5, pp.593-606.

Cowan, R. (1983), *More Work For Mother: the ironies of household technology, from the open hearth to the microwave,* Basic Books: New York.

Craft, M. and Craft, A. (1983), 'The Participation of Ethnic Minority Pupils In Further and Higher Education', *Educational Research,* Vol. 25, No. 1, pp.10-19.

Cragg, A. and Dawson, T. (1984), *Unemployed Women: a study of attitudes and experience,* Department of Employment Research Paper 47.

Currell, M. (1974), *Political Woman,* Croom Helm: London.

Dahlerup, D. (1987), 'Confusing Concepts - Confusing Reality: a theoretical discussion of the patriarchal state', in Sassoon, A. (ed.), *Women and the State: the shifting boundaries between private and public,* Hutchinson: London.

Dahya, B. (1972), 'Pakistanis in England', *New Community,* Vol. 2, pp.25-33.

Dahya, B. (1974), 'Pakistanis in Britain: transients or settlers?', *Race,* Vol. 14, No. 3, pp.241-278.

Daniels, A. (1987), 'Invisible work', *Social Problems,* Vol. 34, pp.403-415.

Das Gupta, M. (1987), 'Selective Discrimination against Female Children in Rural Punjab, India', *Population and Development Review,* Vol. 13, pp.77-100.

Davidoff, L. (1976), 'The Rationalisation of Housework', in Leonard Barker, D. and Allen, S. (eds.), *Dependence and Exploitation in Marriage,* Hutchinson: London.

Davidoff, L. and Hall, C. (1987), *Family Fortunes: men and women of the English middle class 1780-1850,* Hutchinson: London.

Davidson, C. (1982), *A Woman's Work is Never Done: a history of housework in the British Isles 1650-1950,* Chatto and Windus: London.

Davie, G. (1990), 'An Ordinary God: the paradox of religion in contemporary Britain', *British Journal of Sociology,* Vol. 41, pp.395-421.

Davis, A. (1981), *Women, Race and Class,* Women's Press: London.

Davis, A. (1990), *Women, Culture and Politics,* Women's Press: London.

Dawson, A. (1988), 'Inner City Schools: unequal opportunity?' in Verma, G. and Pumfrey, P. (eds.), *Educational Attainments: issues and outcomes in multicultural education,* Falmer Press: London.

Deem, R. (1978), *Women and Schooling,* Routledge Kegan Paul: London.

Delphy, C. (1980), 'A Materialist Feminism *is* Possible', *Feminist Review,* Vol. 4, pp.79-105.

Delphy, C. and Leonard, D. (1992), *Familiar Exploitation: a new analysis of marriage in contemporary western societies,* Polity Press: Cambridge.

Dennis, N. et al (1956), *Coal Is Or Life: an analysis of Yorkshire mining,* Tavistock: London.

Devault, M. (1990), 'Talking and listening from a woman's standpoint: feminist strategies for interviewing and analysis', *Social Problems,* Vol. 37, No. 1, pp.96-116.

Devault, M. (1991), *Feeding the Family: the social organisation of caring as gendered work,* University of Chicago Press: Chicago.

Dex, S. (1983), 'The Second Generation: West Indian female school leavers', in Phizacklea, A. (ed.), *One Way Ticket: migration and female labour,* Routledge: London.

Dinnerstein, D. (1987), *The Rocking of the Cradle and the Ruling of the World,* Women's Press: London.

Donald, J. and Rattansi, A. (eds.) (1992), 'Introduction', in Donald, J. and Rattansi,

A. (eds.), *'Race', Culture and Difference,* Sage: London.

Drew, D. et al (1991), *Against The Odds: the education and labour market experiences of black young people,* TEED: Youth Cohort Series.

Drew, D. and Gray, J. (1989), *The Fifth Year Exam Achievements of Black People in England and Wales,* unpublished paper, Research Centre: University of Sheffield.

Driver, G. (1977), 'Cultural Competence, Social Power and School Achievement: West Indian secondary school pupils in the Midlands', *New Community,* Vol. 5, No. 4, pp.353-359.

Drury, B. (1991), 'Sikh Girls and the Maintenance of an Ethnic Culture', *New Community,* Vol. 17, No. 3, pp.387-399.

DuBois, B. (1983), 'Passionate Scholarship: notes on values, knowing and methods in feminist social science', in Bowles, G. and Klein, R. (eds.), *Theories of Women's Studies,* Routledge Kegan Paul: London.

Duncombe, J. and Marsden, D. (1993), 'Love and Intimacy: the gender division of emotion and emotion work', *Sociology,* Vol. 27, No. 2, pp.221-41.

Dworkin, A. (1981), *Pornography: men possessing women,* Women's Press: London.

Dwyer, J. (1988), *Formal Religious Nurture in Two Hindu Temples in Leicester,* unpublished PhD Thesis: University of Leicester.

Dyson, R. and Moore, M. (1983), 'Kinship Structure, Female Autonomy and Demographic Behaviour in India', *Population and Development Review,* Vol. 9, No. 1, pp.35-60.

Edgell, S. (1980), *Middle Class Couples: a study of domination and inequality in marriage,* Allen and Unwin: London.

Edwards, M. (1981), 'Financial Arrangements made by Husbands and Wives: findings of a survey', *Australia and New Zealand Journal of Sociology, 1981.*

Eichler, M. (1981), 'Power, Dependency, Love and the Sexual Division of Labour', *Women's Studies International Quarterly,* Vol. 4, No. 2, pp.201:219.

Eichler, M. (1988), *Non-sexist Research Methods,* Allen and Unwin: London.

Eisenstein, Z. (1981), *The Radical Future of Liberal Feminism,* Longmann: New York.

Elias, P. and Gregory, M. (1992), *The Changing Structure of Occupations and Earnings in Great Britain 1975-1990,* Institute for Employment Research: University of Warwick.

Essen, J. and Wedge, P. (1982), *Communities In Childhood Disadvantage,* Heinemann: London.

Evason, E. (1982), *Hidden Violence,* Farset Press: Belfast.

Feminist Review (1984), 'Many Voices, One Chant: Black Feminist Perspectives', *Feminist Review,* Vol. 17.

Fenton, S. and Sadiq, A. (1993), *The Sorrow in my Heart: sixteen Asian women speak about depression,* Commission For Racial Equality: Bristol.

Figuero, P. (1984), 'Race Relations and Cultural Differences: some ideas on a racial frame of reference', in Verma, G. and Bagley, C. (eds.), *Race Relations and Cultural Differences: educational and intercultural perspectives,* Croom Helm:

London.

Finch, J. (1983), *Married To The Job,* Allen and Unwin: London.

Finch, J. (1984), 'It's great to have someone to talk to: women interviewing women', in Bell, C. and Roberts, H. (eds.), *Social Researching: politics, problems, practice,* Routledge Kegan Paul: London.

Finch, J. (1989), *Family Obligations and Social Change,* Polity Press: Cambridge.

Finch, J. and Mason, J. (1993), *Negotiating Family Responsibilities,* Routledge: London.

Firestone, S. (1974), *The Dialectic of Sex: the case for feminist revolution,* Morrow: New York.

Flax, J. (1982), 'The Family in Contemporary Feminist Thought: a critical review', in Elshtain, J. (ed.), *The Family in Political Thought,* Harvester Press: Sussex.

Foster, E. (1992), 'Women and the Inverted Pyramids of the Black Churches in Britain', in Sahgal, G. and Yuval-Davis, N. (eds.), *Refusing Holy Orders: women and fundamentalism in Britain,* Virago: London.

Fox, G. (1975), 'Love Match and Arranged Marriage in a Modernising Nation', *Journal of Marriage and the Family,* Vol. 37, pp.180-193.

Frankenberg, R. (1993), *White Women Race Matters: the social construction of whiteness,* Routledge: New York.

Freed, S. and Freed, R. (1982), 'Changing Family Types in India', *Ethnology,* Vol. 21, pp.189-202.

Freed, S. and Freed, R. (1983), 'The Domestic Cycle in India', *American Etiologist,* Vol. 10, pp.312-327.

Freeman, C. (1982), 'The "Understanding" Employer', in West, J. (ed.), *Work, Women and the Labour Market,* Routledge Kegan Paul: London.

Frickle, T. (1987), *Himalayan Households: Tamang demography and domestic processes,* Ann Arbour: Michigan.

Fruzzetti, L. (1990), *The Gift of a Virgin: ritual and marriage in a Bengali society,* Oxford University Press: Delhi.

Fryer, P. (1984), *Staying Power: the history of black people in Britain,* Pluto Press: London.

Gardiner, J. (1976), 'Domestic Labour in Capitalist Society', in Leonard Barker, D. and Allen, S. (eds.), *Dependence and Exploitation in Marriage,* Hutchinson: London.

Gardner, K. and Shukur, A. (1994), 'I'm Bengali, I'm Asian and I'm Living Here: The changing identity of British Bengalis', in Ballard, R. (ed.), *Des Pardesh: The South Asian Presence in Britain,* Hurst: London.

Geerken, M. and Gove, W. (1983), *At Home and At Work: the family's allocation of labour,* Sage: Beverley Hills.

Geertz, C. (1973), *The Interpretation Of Culture,* Basic Books: New York.

Geertz, C. (1983), *Local Knowledge,* Basic Books: New York.

Gershuny, J. (1983), *Social Innovation and the Domestic Division of Labour,* Oxford University Press: Oxford.

Gershuny, J. et al (1986), 'Time Budgets: preliminary analyses of a national survey', *National Journal of Social Affairs,* Vol. 2, No. 1, pp.13-39.

Ghadially, R. et al (1988), 'Bride Burning: the psycho-social dynamics of dowry deaths', in Ghadially, R. (ed.), *Women In Indian Society,* Sage: New Delhi.

Ghuman, P. (1980), 'Punjabi Parents and English Education', *Educational Research,* Vol. 22, No. 2, pp.121-130.

Ghuman, P. (1991), 'Best or Worst of Two Worlds? A Study of Asian Adolescents', *Educational Research,* Vol. 33, No. 2, pp.121-132.

Ghuman, P. (1994), *Coping With Two Cultures,* Longdum: Bristol.

Ghuman, P. and Gallop, R. (1981), 'Educational Attitudes of Bengali Families in Cardiff', *Journal of Multilingual and Multicultural Development,* Vol. 2, No. 2, pp.127-144.

Gibson, M. (1988), *Accommodation Without Assimilation,* Cornell University Press: London.

Gillborn, D. (1990), *'Race', Ethnicity and Education,* Unwin Hyman: London.

Gillborn, D. (1992), 'Racism and Education: issues for research and practice', in Brown, S. and Riddell, S. (eds.), *Class, Race and Gender in Schools: a new agenda for policy and practice in Scottish education,* Scottish Council For Research In Education: Glasgow.

Gilroy, P. (1987), *There Ain't No Black In the Union Jack,* Hutchinson: London.

Glazer-Malbin, N. (1976), 'Housework', *Signs,* Vol. 1, No. 4, pp.905-921.

Goldlust, J. and Richmond, A. (1974), 'A Multivariate Model of Immigrant adaption', *International Migration Review,* Vol. 8, pp.193-225.

Goldstein, R. (1972), *Indian Women in Transition: a Bangalore case study,* Scarecrow Press: New Jersey.

Goody, J. (1971), 'Class and Marriage in Africa and Eurasia', *American Journal of Sociology,* Vol. 76, pp.585-603.

Goody, J. (1973), 'Bridewealth and Dowry in Africa and Eurasia', in Goody, J. and Tambiah, S. (eds.), *Bridewealth and Dowry,* Cambridge University Press: Cambridge.

Goody, J. and Tambiah, S. (eds.) (1973), *Bridewealth and Dowry,* Cambridge University Press: Cambridge.

Graham, H. (1985), *Caring for the Family: Report of a study of the Organisation of Health Resources and Responsibilities in 102 families,* Open University Press: Milton Keynes.

Gray, A. (1979), 'The Working Class Family as an Economic Unit', in Harris, C. (ed.), *The Sociology of the Family,* Sociology Review Monograph 28.

Gray, J. (1989), 'The Household in Nepal: social and experiential crucible of society', in Gray, J. and Mearns, D. (eds.), *Society From The Inside Out: anthropological perspectives on the South Asian household,* Sage: New Delhi.

Gray, J. and Mearns, D. (eds.) (1989), *Society From The Inside Out: anthropological perspectives on the South Asian household,* Sage: New Delhi.

Green, J. (1990), *Them: voices from the immigrant community in Britain,* Secker and

187

Warburg: London.

Green, P. (1985), 'Multi-Ethnic Teaching and The Pupils Self-Concept', in *The Swann Report, Education For All,* Her Majesty's Stationery Office: London.

Gubrium, J. (1988), 'The Family as Project', *Sociological Review,* Vol. 36, No. 2, pp.273-296.

Gupta, G. (1972), 'Religiosity, Economy and Patterns of Hindu Marriage in India', *International Journal of Sociology of the Family,* Vol. 2, pp.43-53.

Hakim, C. (1979), *Occupational Segregation: a comparative study of the degree and pattern of the differentiation between men and women's work in Britain, the US and other countries,* Department Of Employment Research Paper: London.

Hakim, C. (1981), 'Job Segregation Trends in the 1970's', *Employment Gazette,* December, pp. 521-529.

Hakim, C. (1991), 'Grateful Selves and Self-made Women: fact and fantasy in women's work orientations', *European Sociological Review,* Vol. 7, No. 2, pp.101-121.

Hall, S. (1978), 'Racism and Reaction', in *Five Views of Multiracial Britain,* Commission For Racial Equality: London.

Hall, S. (1992), 'New Ethnicities', in Donald, J. and Rattansi, A. (eds.), *'Race', Culture and Difference,* Sage: London.

Hall, S. and Jefferson, T. (eds.) (1976), *Resistance Through Rituals,* Hutchinson: London.

Hanjal, J. (1982), 'Two Kinds of Pre-industrial Household Formation Systems', *Population and Development Review,* Vol. 8, pp.449-494.

Hanmer, J. and Saunders, S. (1984), *Well Founded Fear: a community study of violence to women,* Hutchinson: London.

Harding, S. (1986), *The Science Question in Feminism,* Cornell University Press: Itacha, NY.

Harding, S. (1987), *Feminism and Methodology,* Bloomington: Indiana.

Harding, S. (1990), *Whose Science? Whose Knowledge?* Cornell University Press: Itacha, NY.

Harris, C. (1983), *The Family and Industrial Society,* Allen and Unwin: London.

Hartmann, H. (1974), *Capitalism and Women's Work in the Home,* unpublished PhD Thesis: Yale University.

Hartmann, H. (1979), 'Capitalism, Patriarchy and Job Segregation by Sex', in Eisenstien, Z. (ed.), *Capitalist Patriarchy,* Monthly Review Press: New York.

Hartmann, H. (1981a), 'The unhappy marriage of Marxism and feminism: towards a more progressive union', in Sargent, L. (ed.), *Women and Revolution,* Pluto Press: London.

Hartmann, H. (1981b), 'The Family as the Locus of Gender, Class and Political Struggle: the example of housework', *Signs,* Vol. 6, pp.366-394.

Hartsock, N. (1983), 'The Feminist Standpoint: developing grounds for a specifically feminist historical materialism', in Harding, S and Hintikka, M. (eds.), *Discovering Reality,* Northwestern University Press: Boston.

Hazareesingh, S. (1986), 'Racism and Cultural Identity: an Indian perspective', *Dragons Teeth,* Vol. 24.

Helweg, A. (1979), *Sikhs in England,* Oxford University Press: Delhi.

Henwood, M. (1987), *Inside the Family: changing roles of men and women,* Family Policy Studies Centre: London.

Hershman, P. (1981), *Punjabi Kinship and Marriage,* Hindustan: Delhi.

Hertz, R. (1986), *More Equal Than Others: women and men in dual career marriages,* University of California Press: California.

Hirschman, C. (1982), 'Immigrants and Minorities: old questions for direction in research', *International Migration Review,* Vol. 16, No. 1, pp.474-490.

Hochschild, A. (1983), *The Managed Heart: the commercialisation of human feelings,* University of California Press: California.

Hochschild, A. (1989), *The Second Shift: working parents and the revolution at home,* Piatkus: London.

Hooja, C. (1969), *Dowry System in India,* Asia Press: New Delhi.

hooks, B. (1982), *Ain't I A Woman?,* Pluto: London.

hooks, B. (1984), *Feminist Theory: from margin to centre,* South End Press: Boston.

hooks, B. (1991), *Yearning: race, gender and cultural politics,* Turnaround: London.

Hubbuck, J. and Carter, S. (1980), *Half A Chance: a report on job discrimination against young blacks in Nottingham,* Commission For Racial Equality: London.

Hunt, P. (1980), *Gender and Class Consciousness,* Macmillan: London.

Hutchinson, D. et al (1979), 'The Prediction Of Educational Failure', *Educational Studies,* Vol. 5, No. 1, pp.73-82.

Inden, R. (1977), *Marriage and Rank in Bengali Culture: a history of class and clan in middle period Bengal,* Vikas: New Delhi.

Independent, The (1990), '*Education Viewpoint: class inequality that only Britain accepts*', 8 March, p.21.

Ineichen, B. (1984), 'Teenage Motherhood In Bristol: the contrasting experience of Afro-Caribbean and White girls', *New Community,* Vol. 12, No. 1, pp.52-58.

Islamia (1992), *National Muslim Newsletter,* No. 19, Islamia: London.

Jackson, M. (1992), 'Towards a Historical Sociology of Housework: a material feminist analysis', *Women's Studies International Forum,* Vol. 15, No. 2, pp.155-173.

Jackson, R. (1981), 'The Shree Krishna Temple and the Gujerati Community in Coventry', in Bowen, D. (ed.), *Hinduism In England,* Bradford College Press: Bradford.

Jackson, R. and Killingley, D. (1988), *Approaches to Hinduism,* John Murray: London.

Jaggar, A. (1983), *Feminist Politics and Human Nature,* Harvester: Sussex.

James, N. (1989), 'Emotional Labour: skill and work in the social regulation of feelings', *Sociological Review,* Vol. 37, pp.15-42.

James, S. (1980), 'Introduction', in Malos, E. (ed.), *The Politics of Housework,* Allen and Busby: London.

James, S. and Busia, A. (eds.) (1993), Theorising Black Feminisms, Routledge: London.

Jayarante, T. and Stewart, A. (1990), 'Quantitative and Qualitative Methods in the Social Sciences', in Cook, J. and Fonow, M. (eds.), *Beyond Methodology: feminist scholarship as lived research,* Indiana University Press: Indiana.

Jayawandera, K. (ed.) (1986), *Feminism and Nationalism in the Third World,* Zed Press: London.

Jayaweera, H. (1993), 'Racial Disadvantage and Ethnic Identity: the experiences of Afro-Caribbean women in a British city', *New Community,* Vol. 19, No. 3, pp.383-406.

Jeffrey, P. (1976), *Migrants and Refugees: Muslim and Christian Pakistani families in Britain,* Routledge Kegan Paul: London.

Jenson, J. et al (eds.) (1988), *Feminisation of the Labour Force,* Polity Press: Cambridge.

Jephcott, P. et al (1962), *Married Women Working,* Allen and Unwin: London.

Jha, A. (1978), *Modernisation and the Hindu Socio-Culture,* BR Publishing House: Delhi.

Joly, D. (1988), *Making A Place For Islam In British Society,* Commission For Racial Equality: London.

Jones, T. (1994), *Britain's Ethnic Minorities,* Policy Studies Institute: London.

Joseph, G. (1981), 'The Incompatible Menage a Trois: Marxism, feminism and racism', in Sargent, L. (ed.), *Women and Revolution,* Pluto Press: London.

Joseph, G. and Lewis, J. (1981), *Common Differences: conflicts in black and white feminist perspectives,* Anchor Press: New York.

Jyoti, S. (1983), *Marriage Politics of the Sikhs: a study of intergenerational differences,* Deep and Deep: New Delhi.

Kalpagam, U. (1992), 'Women and the Household: what the Indian data sources have to offer', in Saradomoni, K. (ed.), *Finding the Household: conceptual and methodological issues,* New Sage: Delhi.

Kalra, S. (1980), *Daughters of Tradition,* Third World Publications: Birmingham.

Kalsi, S. (1992), *The Evolution Of A Sikh Community In Britain,* Monograph Series, Community Religions Project Collection, Department of Theology and Religious Studies: University of Leeds.

Kannan, C. (1978), *Cultural Adaption of Asian Immigrants,* Kannan: Middlesex.

Kanter, R. (1977), *Men and Women of the Corporation,* Basic Books: New York.

Kantikar, H. (1972), *The Social Organisation of Indian Students in the London Area,* unpublished PhD Thesis, School of Oriental and African Studies: University of London.

Kantikar, H. and Jackson, R. (1982), *Hindus in Britain,* Sage: London.

Karve, I. (1965), *Kinship Organisation in India,* Asia Publishing House: Bombay.

Khan, V. (1976), 'Pakistani Women in Britain', *New Community,* Vol. 5, pp.99-108.

Khan, V. (1979), *Minority Families in Britain: support and stress,* Macmillan: London.

Khan, V. (1982), 'The Role of the Culture of Dominance in Structuring the Experience of Ethnic Minorities', in Husband, C. (ed.), *Race in Britain,* Hutchinson: London.

King, D. (1988), 'Multiple Jeopardy, Multiple Consciousness: the context of a black feminist ideology', *Signs,* Vol. 14, No. 1, pp.42-72.

King, U. (1987), *Women in the World's Religions: past and present,* Pergamon House: New York.

Kirkpatrick, J. (1974), *Political Women,* Basic Books: New York.

Kishwar, M.(1986), 'Dowry: to ensure her happiness or to disinherit her?', *Manushi,* Vol. 34, pp.2-13.

Knight, G. (1988), *The Expectations and Priorities of Muslim Parents Residing in the Small Heath Area of Birmingham regarding their Children's Education,* unpublished OTTO Fellowship, Faculty of Education: University of Birmingham.

Knott, K. (1986), *My Sweet Lord: the Hare Krishna movement,* Aquarian Press: Wellinborough.

Knott, K. (1987), 'Hindu Temple Rituals In Britain: the reinterpretation of tradition', in Burghart, R. (ed.), *Hinduism In Great Britain,* Tavistock: London.

Knott, K. (1991), 'Bound To Change? The Religions Of South Asians In Britain', in Vertovec, S. (ed.), *The Modern Western Diaspora,* Oxford University Press: New Delhi.

Knott, K. and Khokher, S. (1993), 'Religious and Ethnic Identity among young Muslim women in Bradford', *New Community,* Vol. 19, No. 4, pp.593-610.

Knowles, C. and Mercer, S. (1991), 'Feminism and Antiracism', in Cambridge, R. and Feuchtwang, S. (eds.), *Anti-Racist Strategies,* Avebury: Aldershot.

Knowles, C. and Mercer, S. (1992), 'Feminism and Antiracism: an exploration of the political possibilities', in Donald, J. and Rattansi, A. (eds.), *'Race', Culture and Difference,* Sage: London.

Kolenda, P. (1968), 'Region, Caste and Family Structure', in Crane, P. (ed.), *Regions and Regionalism in South Asian Studies,* Duke University Press: Durham, NC.

Kolenda, P. (1989), 'The Joint Family Household in Rural Rajasthan: ecological, cultural and demographic conditions for its occurrence', in Gray, J. and Mearns, D. (eds.), *Society From The Inside Out: anthropological perspectives on the South Asian household,* Sage: New Delhi.

Kondo, V. (1989), 'Subjection and the Domicile: some problematic issues relating to high caste Nepalese women', in Gray, J. and Mearns, D. (eds.), *Society From The Inside Out: anthropological perspectives on the South Asian household,* Sage: New Delhi.

Kroeber, A. (1952), *The Nature Of Culture,* University of Chicago Press: Chicago.

Kroeber, A. and Kluchkohn, C. (1952), *Culture: a critical review of concepts and definitions,* papers of the Peabody Museum of American Archaeology and Ethology.

Kumari, R. (1989), *Brides Are Not For Burning: dowry victims in India,* Sangam: London.

Kumari, R. A. (1989), *Women-Headed Households in Rural India,* Radant Publishers: New Delhi.

Kysel, F. (1988), 'Ethnic Background and Examination Results', *Educational Research,* Vol. 30, No. 2, pp.83-89.

Land, H. (1979), 'Women, Supporters or Supported?' in Leonard Barker, D. and Allen, S. (eds.), *Sexual Divisions in Society: Process and Change,* Tavistock: London.

Land, H. (1980), 'The Family Wage', *Feminist Review,* Vol. 6, pp.55-77.

Lannoy, R. (1971), *The Speaking Tree: a study of Indian culture and society,* Oxford University Press: London.

Larson, H. (1988), *Culture Exchange: the religious life of children in Southall,* unpublished paper, School of Oriental and African Studies: University of London.

Laslett, P. and Carter, A. (1984), *Household and Family in Past Time,* Cambridge University Press: Cambridge.

Laurie, H. (1992), 'Multiple Methods in the study of Household Resource Allocation', in Brannen, J. (ed.), *Mixing Methods: Qualitative and Quantitative Research,* Avebury: Aldershot.

Laurie, H. and Rose, D. (1994), 'Divisions and Allocations within Households', in Buck N. et al (eds.), *Changing Households: The British Household Panel Survey,* University of Essex: Colchester.

Lawrence, E. (1982), 'Just Plain Common Sense: the 'roots' of racism', in Centre for Contemporary Cultural Studies, *The Empire Strikes Back,* Hutchinson: London.

Lee, G. and Wrench, J. (1983), *Skill Seekers,* National Youth Bureau: London.

Lees, S. (1986), 'Sex, Race and Culture: feminism and the limits of cultural pluralism', *Feminist Review,* Vol. 22, pp.92-102.

Leffler, A. (1992), 'Gender and Race Effects on Employment, Prestige, Segregation and Earnings', *Gender and Society,* Vol. 6, No. 3, pp.376-392.

Leibowitz, A. (1975), 'Women's Work in the Home', in Lloyd, C. (ed.), *Sex, Discrimination and the Division of Labour,* Colombia University Press: New York.

Leslie, J. (1988), *The Perfect Wife: the status and role of the orthodox Hindu woman,* Oxford University Press: Delhi.

Lewis, J. (ed.) (1983), *Women's Welfare, Women's Rights,* Croom Helm: London.

Liff, S. (1993), *From Equality to Diversity,* paper presented at conference, 'Organisations, Gender and Power', Industrial Relations Unit: University of Warwick.

Linton, R. (1968), *The Cultural Background of Personality,* Routledge Kegan Paul: London.

Liu, T. (1991), 'Teaching the Differences among Women from a Historical Perspective: rethinking race and gender as social categories', *Women's Studies International Forum,* Vol. 14, No. 4, pp.265-276.

Logan, P. (1988), 'The Heart Of Hinduism: Hindu women and the home', *World Religions In Education,* pp. 29-31.

Lopata, H. (1971), *Occupation Housewife,* Oxford University Press: New York.

Lorde, A. (1981), 'An Open Letter to Mary Daly', in Moraga, C. and Anzaldua, G. (eds.), *The Bridge Called My Back: writings by radical women of colour,* Persephone Press: Watertown, Mass.

Lorde, A. (1984), *Sister Outsider: essays and speeches,* Grossberg Press: New York.

Lutz, H. (1991), *Migrant Women of Islamic Background: images and self-perceptions,* Middle East Research Associates, Occasional Paper 11: Amsterdam.

Lynch, J. (1990), 'Cultural Pluralism, Structural Pluralism and the UK', in Parekh, B. (ed.), *Britain: a plural society,* Commission For Racial Equality: London.

Mac an Ghaill, M. (1988), *Young, Gifted and Black: student teacher relations in the schooling of black youth,* Open University Press: Milton Keynes.

Macdonald, M. (1987), 'Rituals Of Motherhood Among Gujerati Women in East London', in Burghart, R. (ed.), *Hindus in Great Britain,* Tavistock: London.

Macintosh, N. et al (1988), 'West Indian and Asian Children's Educational Attainment', in Verma, G. and Pumfrey, P. (eds.), *Educational Attainments: issues and outcomes in multicultural education,* Falmer Press: London.

Macintosh, N. and Mascie-Taylor, C. (1985), 'The IQ Question', *Education For All, The Swann Report,* Her Majesty's Stationery Office: London.

Mackinnon, C. (1979), *The Sexual Harassment of Working Women: a case of sex discrimination,* Yale University Press: New Haven.

Mackinnon, C. (1982), 'Feminism, Marxism, Method and The State: an agenda for change', *Signs,* Vol. 7, No. 3, pp.515-544.

Macleod, W. (1976), *The Evolution of the Sikh Community,* Clarendon Press: Oxford.

Madan, T. (1965), *Family and Kinship: a study of the Pandits of rural Kashmir,* Asia Publishing House: Bombay.

Maitland, S. (1992), *A Map of the New Country: women and Christianity,* Routledge Kegan Paul: London.

Malos, E. (ed.) (1980), *The Politics of Housework,* Allen and Busby: London.

Mama, A. (1984), 'Black women, the Economic Crisis and the British State', *Feminist Review,* Vol. 17, pp.21-35.

Mandelbaum, D. (1970), *Society In India, Volume 1,* Berkeley, University of California Press: California.

Mandelbaum, D. (1988), *Women's Seclusion and Men's Honour,* University of Arizona Press: Tuscon.

Marsh, A. (1979), *Women and Shiftwork,* Equal Opportunities Commission: London.

Martin, J. and Roberts, C. (1984), *Women and Employment: a lifetime perspective,* Her Majesty's Stationery Office: London.

Matthews, A. (1990), 'Dowry and its Various Dimensions', in Devasia, L. and Devasia, V. (eds.), *Women in India,* Indian Social Institute: New Delhi.

Maughan, B. and Dunn, G. (1988), 'Black Pupils Progress in Secondary Schools', in Verma, G. and Pumfrey, P. (eds.), *Educational Attainments: issues and outcomes in multicultural education,* Falmer Press: London.

Mayer, A. (1960), *Caste and Kinship in Central India: a village and its region,* University of California Press: Berkeley California.

McCracken, G. (1988), *The Long Interview,* Sage: Newbury Park.

McDonald, G. (1980), 'Family Power: The Assessment of a decade of theory and research 1970-1979', *Journal of Marriage and the Family,* pp.841-854.

McGilvray, D. (1989), 'Households in Akkaraipatu: dowry and domestic organisation', in Gray, J. and Mearns, D. (eds.), *Society From The Inside Out: anthropological perspectives on the South Asian household,* Sage: New Delhi.

McGuire, G. and Reskin, B. (1993), 'Authority Hierarchies at Work: the impact of race and sex', *Gender and* Society, Vol. 7, No. 4, pp.487-506.

McRobbie, A. (1994), *Post-Modernism and Popular Culture,* Routledge: London.

Mearns, D. (1989), 'Households and Social Identity: domestic groups, domestic space and ritual contexts amongst Indians in Malaysia', in Gray, J. and Mearns, D. (eds.), *Society From The Inside Out: anthropological perspectives on the South Asian household,* Sage: New Delhi.

Meggers, B. (1954), 'Environmental Limitation on the Development of Culture', *American Anthropologist,* Vol. 56, pp.801-824.

Messiner, M. et al (1975), 'No Exit For Wives: sexual division of labour and the cumulation of housework demands in Canada', *Canadian Review of Sociology and Anthropology,* Vol. 12, No. 4, pp.424-439.

Michaelson, M. (1983), *Caste, Kinship and Marriage,* Sage: New Delhi.

Mies, M. (1986), *Patriarchy and Accumulation on a World Scale: women in the international division of labour,* Zed Books: London.

Mies, M. (1991), 'Women's research or feminist research: the debate surrounding feminist science and methodology', in Fonow, M. and Cook, J. (eds.), *Beyond Methodology: feminist scholarship as lived research,* Bloomington: Indiana.

Miles, R. and Phizacklea, A. (1980), *Labour and Racism,* Routledge: London.

Miller, B. (1980), *The Endangered Sex,* Cornell University Press: Ithaca.

Miller, B. (1989), 'Changing Patterns of Juvenile Sex-ratios in Rural India', *Economic and Political Weekly,* Vol. 24, No. 22, pp.1229-1236.

Millett, K. (1977), *Sexual Politics,* Virago Press: London.

Milner, M. (1988), 'Status Relations in South Asian Marriage Alliances', *Contributions to Indian Sociology,* Vol. 22, No. 2, pp.145-169.

Mincer, J. and Polanchek, S. (1974), 'Family Investments in Human Capital: earnings of women', *Journal of Political Economy,* Vol. 82, No. 2, pp.76-108.

Mirza, K. (1989), *The Silent City: second generation Bradford Muslim Women speak,* Muslims In Europe Research Papers 42, Centre for the Study of Islam and Christian Muslim Relations: University of Birmingham.

Mitchell, J. (1971), *Women's Estate,* Penguin: Harmondsworth.

Mitter, S. (1986), *Common Fate, Common Bond: women in the global economy,* Pluto Press: London.

Mitter, S. (1990), *Dharma's Daughters,* Rutgers University Press: New Brunswick.

Modood, T. (1990), 'British Asian Muslims and the Rushdie Affair', *Political Quarterly,* Vol. 61, No. 2.

Modood, T. (1993), 'The Number of Ethnic Minorities in British Higher Education',

Oxford Review of Education, Vol. 19, No. 2, pp.167-182.

Modood, T. (1994), 'Political Blackness and British Asians', *Sociology*, Vol. 28, No. 4, pp.859-876.

Modood, T. and Shiner, M. (1994), *Ethnic Minorities and Higher Education*, Policy Studies Institute: London.

Molyneux, M. (1979), 'Beyond The Domestic Labour Debate', *New Left Review*, Vol. 16.

Moraga, C. and Anzaldua, G. (eds.) (1981), *The Bridge Called My Back: writings by radical women of colour*, Persephone Press: Watertown Mass.

Morokvasic, M. (1994), 'In and Out of the Labour Market: immigrant and minority women in Europe', *New Community*, Vol. 19, No. 3, pp.459-483.

Morris, L. (1984), 'Renegotiation of the Sexual Division of Labour: a research note', *British Journal of Sociology*, Vol. 35, No. 4, pp.606-607.

Morris, L. (1985), 'Local Social Networks and Domestic Organisation: a study of redundant steel workers and their wives', *Sociological Review*, Vol. 33, No. 2, pp.327-342.

Morris, L. (1988), 'Employment, the Household and Social Networks', in Gallie, D. (ed.), *Employment in Britain*, Blackwell: Oxford.

Morris, L. (1990), *The Workings of the Household*, Polity Press: Oxford.

Mortimore, P. and Blackstone, T. (1982), *Disadvantage and Education*, Heinemann: London.

Mortimore, P. et al (1988), *School Matters: the junior years*, Open Books: Wells.

Murdock, G. (1946), 'The Cross-Cultural Survey', *American Sociological Review*, Vol. 5, pp.361-370.

Murickan, J. (1975), 'Women in Kerala: changing socio-economic status and self image', in DeSouza, D. (ed.), *Women In Contemporary India*, Manohar: Delhi.

Mydral, A. and Klein, V. (1970), *Women's Two Roles: home and work*, Routledge: London.

Ngcobo, L. (ed.) (1988), *Let It Be Told: essays by black women in Britain*, Virago Press: London.

Nielsen, J. (1983), 'Muslims in Britain and Local Authority Responses', in Gerholm, T. and Lithman, Y. (eds.), *The New Islamic Presence in Western Europe*, Mansell Publications: London.

Nielsen, J. (1987), 'Muslims in Britain: searching for an identity', *New Community*, Vol. 13, pp.384-394.

Nielsen, J. (1988), 'Islamic Communities In Britain', in Badham, P. (ed.), *Religion, State and Society in Modern Britain*, Edwin Mellen Press: Lampeter.

Nuttall, D. (1990), *Differences in Examination Performance*, Research and Statistics Branch, Inner London Education Authority: London.

Nuttall, D. et al (1989), 'Differential School Effectiveness', *International Journal of Educational Research*, Special Issue Vol. 13, pp.769-776.

Oakley, A. (1974), *The Sociology of Housework*, Martin Robertson: Oxford.

Oakley, A. (1981), 'Interviewing women: a contradiction in terms', in Roberts, H.

(ed.), *Doing Feminist Research,* Routledge Kegan Paul: London.

O'Brien, M. (1981), *The Politics of Reproduction,* Routledge Kegan Paul: London.

Ogburn, W. (1959), *Social Change,* Viking Press: New York.

Ohri, S. and Faruqi, S. (1988), 'Racism, Employment and Unemployment', in Bhat, A. et al (eds.), *Britain's Black Population: a new perspective,* Gower: Aldershot.

Owen, D. (1994), *Ethnic Minority Women and the Labour Market: an analysis of the 1991 Census,* Equal Opportunities Commission: Manchester.

Owen, D. and Green, A. (1992), 'Labour Market Experience and Occupational Change amongst Ethnic Minority Groups in Britain', *New Community,* Vol. 19, No. 1, pp.7-29.

Pahl, J. (1983), 'The Allocation of Money and the Structuring of Inequality Within Marriage', *Sociological Review,* Vol. 13, No. 2, pp.237-262.

Pahl, J. (1989), *Money and Marriage,* Macmillan: London.

Pahl, R. (1984), *Divisions of Labour,* Basil Blackwell: Oxford.

Papanek, H. (1990), 'To Earn Less Than She Needs, For Each More Than She Can Do: allocations, entitlement and value', in Tinker, I. (ed.), *Persistent Inequalities,* Oxford University Press: New York.

Parekh, B. (1986), 'The Structure of Authority within the Indian Family', in Bath, K. (ed.), *Working With Asian Young People,* National Association For Asian Youth: London.

Parekh, B. (1988), 'The Swann Report and Ethnic Minority Attainment', in Verma, G. and Pumfrey, P. (eds.), *Educational Attainments: issues and outcomes in multicultural education,* Falmer Press: London.

Parekh, B. (1989), 'Between Sacred and Moral Void', *New Statesman and Society,* March, pp.29-33.

Parmar, P. (1982), 'Gender, Race and Class: Asian women in resistance', in Centre For Contemporary Cultural Studies, *The Empire Strikes Back,* Hutchinson: London.

Parmar, P. and Mirza, N. (1993), 'Stepping Forward: work with Asian young women', *GEN,* Vol. 1.

Parsons, T. and Bales, R. (1956), *Family Socialisation and Interaction Process,* Routledge Kegan Paul: London.

Parsons, T. and Shils, E. (eds.) (1951), *Towards A General Theory Of Action,* Harvard University Press: Cambridge.

Patterson, L. (1992), 'Social Class and Scottish Education', in Brown, S. and Riddell, S. (eds.), *Class, Race and Gender In Schools: a new agenda for policy and practice in Scottish education,* Scottish Council For Research In Education: Glasgow.

Penn, R. and Scattergood, H. (1992), 'Ethnicity and Career Aspirations in Contemporary Britain', *New Community,* Vol. 19, No. 1, pp.75-98.

Phillips, A. (ed.) (1987), *Feminism and Equality,* Basil Blackwell: Oxford.

Phillips, A. (1992), 'Classing the Self and Gendering the Class', in McDowell, L. and Pringle, R. (eds.), *Defining Women: social institutions and gender divisions,* Polity Press: Cambridge.

Phillips, A. and Taylor, B. (1980), 'Sex and Skills: notes towards a feminist economics', *Feminist Review,* Vol. 6, pp.79-83.

Phizacklea, A. (ed.) (1983), *One Way Ticket: migration and female labour,* Routledge: London.

Phizacklea, A. (1988), 'Gender, Racism and Occupational Segregation', in Walby, S. (ed.), *Gender Segregation at Work,* Open University Press: Milton Keynes.

Phizacklea, A. (1990), *Unpacking The Fashion Industry,* Routledge: London.

Phizacklea, A. and Wolkowitz, C. (1995), *Homeworking Women: gender, racism and class at work,* Sage: London.

Phoenix, A. (1987), 'Theories of Gender and Black Families', in Weiner, G. and Arnot, M. (eds.), *Gender Under Scrutiny: new enquiries in education,* Open University Press: London.

Phoenix, A. (1988), 'Narrow Definitions of Culture: the case of early motherhood', in Westwood, S. and Bhachu, P. (eds.), *Enterprising Women: ethnicity, economy and gender relations,* Routledge: London.

Phoenix, A. (1990), *Young Mothers,* Polity Press: Oxford.

Pilgrim, S. et al (1993), *The Bristol Black and Ethnic Minority Health Survey Report,* Department of Sociology and Epidemiology: University of Bristol.

Pillai, S. (1976), 'Jointness as a Way of Life', in Pillai, S. (ed.), *Aspects of Changing India,* Popular Prakashan: Bombay.

Pizzey, E. (1974), *Scream Quietly or the Neighbours will hear,* Penguin: Harmondsworth.

Pleck, J. (1977), 'Husband's Participation and Family Roles: current research issues', in Lopata, H. and Pleck, J. (eds.), *Research in the Interweave of Roles,* JAI Press: Greenwood.

Pocock, D. (1972), *Kanbi and Patidar: a study of the Patidar community of Gujerat,* Clarendon Press: Oxford.

Pomeroy, S. (1984), 'Selected Bibliography on Women in Classical Antiquity', in Peradotto, A. and Sullivan, J. (eds.), *Women in the Ancient World,* University of New York Press: Alberry.

Prabhu, P. (1963), *Hindu Social Organisation,* Popular Prakashan: Bombay.

Pratt, J., Bloomfield, J. and Seale, C. (1984), *Option Choice: a question of equal opportunity,* NFER Nelson: Windsor.

Price, C. (1982), 'The Study of Assimilation', in Jackson, J. (ed.), *Migration,* Cambridge University Press: Cambridge.

Putins, A. (1976), 'Immigrant Adjustment: a note on Kovac and Copley's model', *Australian Journal of Social Issues,* Vol. 11, pp.209-212.

Rafiq, M. (1992), 'Ethnicity and Enterprise: a comparison of Muslim and non-Muslim owned Asian businesses in Britain', *New Community,* Vol. 19, No. 1, pp.43-60.

Ram, M. (1993), 'Workplace Relations in Ethnic Minority Firms: Asians in the West Midlands clothing industry', *New Community,* Vol. 19, No. 4, pp.567-590.

Ramazanoglu, C. (1986), 'Ethnocentrism and Socialist feminist Theory', *Feminist Review,* Vol. 22, No. 2, pp.83-86.

Ramazanoglu, C. (1989), *Feminism and the Contradictions of Oppression,* Routledge:

London.

Rampton Report (1981), *West Indian Children In Our Schools,* Her Majesty's Stationery Office: London.

Rao, V. and Rao, V. (eds.) (1982), *Marriage, the Family and Women in India,* Heritage: New Delhi.

Rapoport, R. and Rapoport, R. (1971), *Dual Career Families,* Penguin: Harmondsworth.

Rapoport, R. and Rapoport, R. (1976), *Dual Career Families Re-examined,* Penguin: Harmondsworth.

Rattansi, A. (1992), 'Changing the Subject? Racism, culture and education', in Donald, J. and Rattansi, A. (eds.), *'Race', Culture and Difference,* Sage: London.

Reeves, F. and Chevannes, M. (1981), 'The Underachievement of Rampton', *Multicultural Education,* Vol. 10, No. 1, pp.35-42.

Reinharz, S. (1983), 'Experiential analysis: a contribution to feminist research', in Bowles, G. and Klein, R. (eds.), *Theories of Women's Studies,* Routledge Kegan Paul: London.

Reskin, B. and Padavic, I. (1994), *Women and Men at Work,* Fine Forge Press: Thousand Oaks, California.

Rex, J. and Tomlinson, S. (1979), *Colonial Immigrants in a British City: a class analysis,* Routledge: London.

Ribbens, J. (1989), 'Interviewing Women - an unnatural situation?', *Women's Studies International Forum,* Vol. 12, pp.579-592.

Rich, A. (1977), *Of Woman Born: motherhood as experience and institution,* Virago: London.

Rich, A. (1980), 'Compulsory heterosexuality and lesbian existence', *Signs,* Vol. 5, No. 4, pp.632-660.

Riddell, S. (1992), 'Gender and Education: progressive and conservative forces in the balance', in Brown, S. and Riddell, S. (eds.), *Class, Race and Gender in Schools: a new agenda for policy and practice in Scottish education,* Scottish Council For Research In Education: Glasgow.

Riessman, C. (1987), 'When Gender is not Enough: women interviewing women', *Gender and Society,* Vol. 1, No. 2, pp.172-208.

Ritchie, J. and Thomas, A. (1990), *Household Allocative Systems: Their Formations and Functioning,* Social and Community Planning: London.

Roberts, B. (1994), *Minority Ethnic Women: work, unemployment and education,* Commission For Racial Equality: Manchester.

Roberts, J. (1988), 'Educational Achievement of Ethnic Minorities in a Midland Town', in Verma, G. and Pumfrey, P. (eds.), *Educational Attainments: issues and outcomes in multicultural education,* Falmer Press: London.

Robinson, J. (1977), *How Americans Use Time,* Praegar Press: New York.

Robinson, V. (1981), 'The Development of South Asian settlement in Britain and the Myth of Return', in Peach, C. et al (ed.), *Ethnic Segregation in Cities,* Croom Helm: London.

Robinson, V. (1984), 'Asians in Britain: a study in encapsulation and marginality', in Clarke, G. (ed.), *Geography and Ethnic Pluralism*, Allen and Unwin: London.

Robinson, V. (1986), *Transients, Settlers and Refugees*, Clevendon: Oxford.

Rogers, B. (1980), *The Domestication of Women: discrimination in developing societies*, Anchor Press: Essex.

Rosaldo, M. (1973), 'Women, Culture and Society: a theoretical overview', in Rosaldo, M. and Lamphere, L. (eds.), *Women, Culture and Society*, Stanford University Press: Stanford.

Rothman, B. (1989), 'Women as Fathers: motherhood and childcare under a modified patriarchy', *Gender and Society*, Vol. 3, No. 1, pp.89-105.

Russell, D. (1984), *Sexual Exploitation: rape, child sexual abuse and workplace harassment*, Sage: Beverley Hills.

Rutter, M. et al (1979), *Fifteen Thousand Hours: secondary schools and their effects on children*, Open Books: Shepton Mallet.

Rutter, M. and Madge, N. (1976), *Cycles of Disadvantage: a review of research*, Heinemann: London.

Sahgal, G. and Yuval-Davis, N. (eds.) (1992), *Refusing Holy Orders: women and fundamentalism in Britain*, Virago: London.

Sammons, P. (1994), *Gender, Ethnic and Socio-Economic Differences in Attainment and Progress: a longitudinal analysis of student achievement over nine years*, paper presented at Annual Meeting of American Educational Research Association: New Orleans.

Sammons, P. et al (1983), 'Educational Priority Indices: a new perspective', *British Educational Research Journal*, Vol. 9, No. 1, pp.27-40.

Sammons, P. et al (1985), *Socio-Economic Background, Parental Involvement and Attitudes and Children's Achievements in Junior Schools*, Research and Statistics Branch, Inner London Education Authority: London.

Sanjek, R. (1982), 'The Organisation of Households in Adabraka: towards a wider comparative perspective', *Comparative Studies in Society and History*, Vol. 24, pp.54-103.

Saradamoni, K. (1992), 'Introduction', in Saradomoni, K. (ed.), *Finding the Household: conceptual and methodological issues*, Sage: New Delhi.

Sargent, L. (ed.) (1981), *Women and Revolution: a discussion of the unhappy marriage of Marxism and feminism*, South End Press: Boston.

Scanzoni, J. (1979), 'Social Processes and Power in Families', in Burr, W. et al (eds.), *Contemporary Theories about the family*, Free Press: New York.

Schlegel, A. (1991), 'Status, Property and the value on Virginity', *American Etiologist*, Vol. 18, pp.719-734.

Seecombe, W. (1974), 'The Housewife and her Labour under Capitalism', in *New Left Review*, Vol. 83, pp.3-24.

Segal, L. (1983), 'Smashing the Family? Reclaiming the 1960's', in Segal, L. (ed.), *What is to be done about the Family?*, Penguin: Harmondsworth.

Segal, L. (1987), *Is The Future Female: troubled thoughts on contemporary feminism*,

Virago Press: London.

Shaffir, W. (1980), *Fieldwork Experience: qualitative approaches to social research,* St. Martins Press: New York.

Shah, A. (1974), *The Household Dimension of the Family in India,* Berkeley, University of California Press: California.

Shaik, S. and Kelly, A. (1989), 'To Mix or Not to Mix: Pakistani girls in British schools', *Educational Research,* Vol. 31, No. 1, pp.10-19.

Shan, S. (1985), *In My Own Name,* Women's Press: London.

Sharma, U. (1981), *Women, Work and Property in North West India,* Tavistock: London.

Sharma, U. (1986), *Women's Work, Class and the Urban Household: a study of Shimla,* Tavistock: London.

Sharma, U. (1989), 'Studying the Household: individuation and values', in Gray, J. and Mearns, D. (eds.), *Society From The Inside Out: anthropological perspectives on the South Asian household,* Sage: New Delhi.

Sharma, U. (1994), 'Dowry in North India: its consequences for women', in Uberoi, P. (ed.), *Family, Kinship and Marriage in India,* Oxford University Press: Delhi.

Shaw, A. (1988), *A Pakistani Community in Britain,* Basil Blackwell: London.

Shaw, A. (1994), 'The Pakistani Community in Oxford,' in Ballard, R. (ed.), *Des Pardesh: The South Asian Presence in Britain,* Hurst: London.

Siddiqui, H. (1991), 'Winning Freedoms', *Feminist Review,* Vol. 37, pp.78-83.

Simmel, G. (1950), *The Sociology of George Simmel,* Free Press: New York.

Sims, S. (1981), 'Spatial Separation between Asian Religious Minorities: an aid to exploration or obfuscation?' in Jackson, P. and Smith, S. (eds.), *Social Interaction and Ethnic Segregation,* Academic Press: London.

Skinner, C. (1986), *Elusive Mister Right,* Carolina Press: London.

Sly, F. (1994), 'Ethnic Groups and the Labour Market', *Employment Gazette,* May, pp.147-159.

Sly, F. (1995), 'Ethnic Groups and the Labour Market: analyses from the spring 1994 Labour Force Survey', *Employment Gazette,* June, pp.251-262.

Smart, C. (1995), *Law, Crime and Sexuality,* Sage: London.

Smith, D. (1974), *Racial Disadvantage in Employment,* Political and Economic Planning: London.

Smith, D. (1980), 'Unemployment and Racial Minority Groups', *Employment Gazette,* pp.602-606.

Smith, D. (1987), *The Everyday World as Problematic: a feminist sociology,* Northwestern University Press: Boston.

Smith, D. and Tomlinson, S. (1989), *The School Effect: a study of multiracial comprehensives,* Policy Studies Institute: London.

Smith, J. et al (eds.) (1984), *Households and the Household Economy,* Sage: Beverley Hills, California.

Sorokin, P. (1947), *Society, Culture and Personality,* Harper and Row: New York.

Spellman, E. (1990), *Inessential Woman,* Women's Press: London.

Spender, D. (1985), *Man Made Language,* Routledge Kegan Paul: London.

Srinvas, M. (1976), *The Remembered Village,* University of California Press: Berkeley, California.

Srinvas, M. (1984), *Some Reflections on Dowry,* Oxford University Press: Delhi.

Standing, H. (1985), 'Women's Employment and the Household: some findings from Calcutta', *Economic and Political Weekly,* Vol. XX, pp.23-38.

Stanko, E. (1988), 'Keeping Women in and out of Line: sexual harassment and occupational segregation', in Walby, S. (ed.), *Gender Segregation At Work,* Open University Press: Milton Keynes.

Stanley, L. (1991), 'Feminist auto/biography and feminist epistemology', in Aaron, J. and Walby, S. (eds.), *Out of the Margins: women's studies in the nineties,* Falmer: London.

Stanley, L. and Wise, S. (1983), *Breaking Out: feminist consciousness and feminist research,* Routledge Kegan Paul: London.

Stanley, L. and Wise, S. (1993), *Breaking Out Again,* Routledge: London.

Stein, D. (1988), 'Burning Widows, Burning Brides: the perils of daughterhood in India', *Pacific Affairs,* Vol. 61, pp.465-485.

Stone, K. (1983), 'Motherhood and Waged Work: West Indian, Asian and White women compared', in Phizacklea, A. (ed.), *One Way Ticket: migration and female labour,* Routledge: London.

Stone, L. and James, C. (1995), 'Dowry, Bride-Burning and Female Power in India', *Women's Studies International Forum,* Vol. 18, No. 2, pp.125-134.

Stone, M. (1981), *The Education of the Black Child in Britain: the myth of multicultural education,* Fontana: London.

Stopes-Roe, M. and Cochrane, R. (1987), 'The Process of Assimilation in Asians in Britain: a study of Hindu, Moslem and Sikh immigrants and their young adult children', *International Journal of Comparative Sociology,* Vol. XXVIIII, pp.43-56.

Stopes-Roe, M. and Cochrane, R. (1988), 'Marriage in Two Cultures', *British Journal of Social Psychology,* Vol. 27, pp.159-69.

Stopes-Roe, M. and Cochrane, R. (1990), *Citizens of this Country: The Asian British,* Multilingual Matters: Clevendon.

Sumner, W. (1906), *Folkways,* Ginn and Company: Boston.

Swann Report (1985), *Education For All: final report of the committee of inquiry into education of children from ethnic minority groups,* Her Majesty's Stationery Office: London.

Tambiah, S. (1972), 'Dowry and Bridewealth and the Property Rights of Women in South Asia', in Goody, J. and Tambiah, S. (eds.), *Bridewealth and Dowry,* Cambridge University Press: Cambridge.

Tambs-Lyche, H. (1980), *London Patiders: a case in urban ethnicity,* Routledge Kegan Paul: London.

Tang Nain, G. (1991), 'Black women, Sexism and Racism: black or antiracist feminism?', *Feminist Review,* Vol. 37, pp.1-37.

Tanna, K. (1990), 'Excellence, Equality and Educational Reform: the myth of South Asian achievement levels', *New Community,* Vol. 16, No. 3, pp.349-368.

Taylor, E. (1971), *Primitive Culture,* John Murray: London.

Taylor, J. (1976), *The Half-Way Generation,* NFER Nelson: Windsor.

Taylor, M. (1981), *Caught Between: a review of research into the education of pupils of West Indian Origin,* NFER Nelson: Windsor.

Taylor, M. (1988), *Worlds Apart? A Review of research into the education of pupils of Cypriot, Indian, Ukrainian and Vietnamese Origin, Liverpool Blacks and Gypsies,* NFER Nelson: Windsor.

Taylor, P. (1993), 'Minority Ethnic Groups and Gender in Access to Higher Education', *New Community,* Vol. 19, No. 3, pp.425-440.

Taylor, M. and Hegarty, S. (1985), *The Best Of Both Worlds? A Review of Research into the Education of Pupils from South Asian origin,* NFER Nelson: Windsor.

Thomas, S. et al (1992), *The Guardian Survey of A-Level Examination results,* Guardian, Oct 22.

Thomas, S. et al (1993), *The Guardian Survey of A-Level Examination results,* Guardian, Nov 30.

Thomas, S. et al (1994), *Report On Analysis of 1992 Examination results,* Association of Metropolitan Authorities.

Thomas, T. (1992), 'Hindu Dharma In Dispersion', in Parsons, C. (ed.), *The Growth of Religious Diversity in Britain from 1945,* Open University Press: Milton Keynes.

Thompson, L. and Walker, A. (1989), 'Gender in Families: women and men in marriage, work and parenthood', *Journal of Marriage and the Family,* Vol. 51, pp.845-871.

Times Higher Educational Supplement, Editorial (1991), *'Use of Literacies',* 5 July, p.8.

Tizard, B. and Phoenix, A. (1993), *Black, White or Mixed Race?* Routledge: London.

Tomlinson, S. (1982), *A Sociology of Special Education,* Routledge Kegan Paul: London.

Tomlinson, S. (1983), 'Black Women in Higher Education: case studies of university women in Britain', in Barton, L. and Walker, S. (eds.), *Race and Class in Education,* Croom Helm: London.

Tomlinson, S. (1987), 'Curriculum Option Choices in Multi-Ethnic Schools', in Troyna, B. (ed.), *Racial Inequality in Education,* Tavistock: London.

Trautman, T. (1981), *Dravidia Kinship,* Cambridge University Press: Cambridge.

Troyna, B. (1981), *Public Awareness and the Media: a study of reporting on race,* Commission For Racial Equality: London.

Troyna, B. (1988), 'Paradigm Regained: a critique of cultural 'deficit' perspectives in contemporary educational research', *Comparative Education,* Vol. 24, No. 3, pp.273-283.

Troyna, B. and Carrington, B. (1987), 'Antisexist/Antiracist Education - a false dilemma?', *Journal of Moral Education,* Vol. 16, No. 1.

Troyna, B. and Smith, D. (1985), *Racism, School and the Labour Market,* National

Youth Bureau: London.

Uberoi, P. (ed.) (1994), *Family, Kinship and Marriage in India,* Oxford University Press: Delhi.

Ungerson, C. (1987), *Policy is Personal: sex, gender and informal care,* Tavistock: London.

Van der Veen, K. (1972), *I Give Thee My Daughter: a study of marriage and hierarchy among the Anual Brahams of South Gujerat,* Van Garcum and Company: Assen.

Vanek, J. (1980), 'Time Spent in Housework', in Amsden, A. (ed.), *The Economics of Women and Work,* Penguin: Harmondsworth.

Van Willigen, J. and Channa, V. (1991), 'Law, Custom and Crimes against Women: the problem of dowry death in India', *Human Organisation,* Vol. 50, pp.369-376.

Vatuk, S. (1972), 'Kinship and Urbanisation: white collar migrants in North India', *Southwestern Journal of Anthropology,* Vol. 16, pp.299-311.

Vatuk, S. (1975), 'Gifts and Affines in North India', *Contributions to Indian Sociology,* Vol. 9, pp.155-196.

Vatuk, S. (1989), 'Household Form and Formation: variability and social change among South Indian Muslims', in Gray, J. and Mearns, D. (eds.), *Society From The Inside Out: anthropological perspectives on the South Asian household,* Sage: New Delhi.

Vellins, S. (1982), 'South Asian Students In British Universities: a statistical note', *New Community,* Vol. 10, No. 2, pp.206-212.

Verdon, M. (1980), 'Shaking off the Domestic Yoke or the Sociological Significance of Residence', *Comparative Studies in Society and History,* Vol. 22, pp.109-132.

Verma, G. (1986), *Ethnicity and Educational Achievement in British Schools,* Macmillan: London.

Verma, G. (1987), 'The Swann Report and Ethnic Achievement: what next'? in Chivers, T. (ed.), *Race and Culture In Education: issues arising from the Swann Committee report,* NFER Nelson: Windsor.

Verma, G. (ed.) (1989), *Education For All: a landmark in pluralism,* Falmer Press: Sussex.

Verma, G. and Ashworth, B. (1981), 'Education and Occupational Aspirations of Young South Asians In Britain', in Verma, G. and Bagley, C. (eds.), *Multicultural Education,* Macmillan: London.

Vertovec, S. (1992), *Hinduism and Social Change in Village Trinidad,* unpublished DPHIL Thesis: University of Leicester.

Visram, R. (1986), *Ayahs, Lascards and Princes: the study of Indians in Britain,* Pluto Press: London.

Visvanathan, S. (1989), 'Marriage, Birth and Death: property rights and domestic relationships of the Orthodox Jacobite Christians of Kerala', *Economic and Political Weekly,* Vol. 17, pp.1341-1346.

Vogel, L. (1983), *Marxism and the Oppression of Women,* Pluto Press: London.

Vogler, C. (1994), 'Money in the Household', in Anderson, M. et al (eds.), *Social and*

203

Political Economy of the Household, Oxford University Press: Oxford.

Vogler, C. and Pahl, J. (1993), 'Social and Economic Change and the Organisation of Money in Marriage', *Work, Employment and Society,* Vol. 7, No. 1, pp.71-95.

Vogler, C. and Pahl, J. (1994), 'Money, Power and Inequality within Marriage', *Sociological Review,* Vol. 42, No. 2, pp.263-288.

Wade, B. and Souter, P. (1991), *Continuity to Think: the British Asian girl,* Multilingual Matters: Clevendon.

Wahhab, I. (1989), *Muslims in Britain: people of a community,* Runnymead Trust: London.

Walby, S. (1986), *Patriarchy at Work: patriarchy and capitalist relations at work,* Polity Press: Cambridge.

Walby, S. (1989), 'Flexibility and the Sexual Division of Labour', in Wood, S. (ed.), *The Transformation of Work?,* Unwin Hyman: London.

Walby, S. (1990), *Theorising Patriarchy,* Basil Blackwell: Oxford.

Wallace, P. (1982), *Black Women in the Labour Force,* MIT Press: Cambridge Mass.

Warde, A. and Hetherington, K. (1993), 'A Changing Domestic Division of Labour? Issues of Measurement and Interpretation', *Work, Employment and Society,* Vol. 17, No. 1, pp.23-46.

Warrier, S. (1988), 'Marriage, Maternity and Female Economic Activity: Gujerati mothers in Britain', in Westwood, S. and Bhachu, P. (eds.), *Enterprising Women: ethnicity, economy and gender relations,* Routledge: London.

Watson, J. (ed.) (1977), *Between Two Cultures: migrants and minorities in Britain,* Basil Blackwell: Oxford.

Werbner, P. (1979), 'Avoiding the Ghetto: Pakistani Migrants and Settlement Shifts in Manchester', *New Community,* Vol. 7, No. 3, pp.376-385.

Werbner, P. (1988), 'Taking and Giving: working women and female bonds in a Pakistani immigrant neighbourhood', in Westwood, S. and Bhachu, P. (eds.), *Enterprising Women: ethnicity, economy and gender relations,* Routledge: London.

West, J. (ed.) (1982), *Work, Women and the Labour Market,* Routledge Kegan Paul: London.

West, J. and Pilgrim, S. (1995), 'South Asian Women in Employment: the impact of migration, ethnic origin and the local economy', *New Community,* Vol. 21, No. 3, pp.357-378.

Westwood, S. (1984), *All Day Every Day: factory and family in the making of women's lives,* Pluto Press: London.

Westwood, S. (1988), 'Workers and Wives: continuities and discontinuities in the lives of Gujerati women', in Westwood, S. and Bhachu, P. (eds.), *Enterprising Women: ethnicity, economy and gender relations,* Routledge: London.

Westwood, S. and Bhachu, P. (eds.) (1988), *Enterprising Women: ethnicity, economy and gender relations,* Routledge: London.

White, L. (1947), *Culture versus Psychological interpretations of Human Behaviour,* Harper and Row: New York.

Wilk, R. and Netting, R. (1984), 'Introduction', in Netting, R. et al (eds.),

Households: comparative and historical studies of the domestic group, University of California Press: Beverley Hills, California.

Williams, C. (1988), *Examining the Nature of Domestic Labour,* Gower Publications: Avebury.

Williams, R. (1981), *Culture,* Fontana: London.

Williams, R. (1988), *Religions of Immigrants from India and Pakistan,* Cambridge University Press: Cambridge.

Wilson, A. (1978), *Finding a Voice: Asian women in Britain,* Virago: London.

Wilson, G. (1987), *Money in the Family: financial organisation and women's responsibility,* Avebury: Aldershot.

Witz, A. (1987), *The Spider Legislating for the Fly: patriarchy and occupational closure in the medical division of labour 1858-1940,* unpublished PhD Thesis, Department of Sociology: University of Lancaster.

Wolffe, J. (1992), 'Fragmented Universality: Islam and Muslims', in Parsons, G. (ed.), *The Growth of Religious Diversity in Britain from 1945,* Open University Press: Milton Keynes.

Woody, B. (1992), *Black Women in the Workplace: impacts of structural change in the economy,* Greenwood Press: New York.

Wright, C. (1985), 'Who Succeeds At School - and who decides?', *Multicultural Teaching,* Vol. 4, No. 1, pp.17-22.

Wright, C. (1987), 'School Processes: an ethnographic study', in Eggleston, S. et al (eds.), *Education For Some: the educational and vocational experiences of 15-18 year old members of minority ethnic groups,* Trentham Books: Stoke On Trent.

Yalman, N. (1963), *Under the Bo Tree: studies in caste, kinship and marriage,* University of California Press: Berkeley California.

Yanagisako, S. (1979), 'Family and Household: the analysis of domestic groups', *Annual Review of Anthropology,* Vol. 8, pp.162-205.

Yinger, J. (1985), 'Ethnicity', *Annual Review of Sociology,* Vol. 11, pp.151-80.

Young, I. (1981), 'Beyond the unhappy marriage: a critique of dual systems theory', in Sargent, L. (ed.), *Women and Revolution,* Pluto Press: London.

Young, M. and Willmott, P. (1973), *The Symmetrical Family: a study of work and leisure in the London region,* Routledge Kegan Paul: London.

Yuval-Davis, N. (1992), 'Jewish Fundamentalism and Women's Empowerment', in Sahgal, G. and Yuval-Davis, N. (eds.), *Refusing Holy Orders: women and fundamentalism in Britain,* Virago: London.